Joe & Vivian —

My

friends of such

long — standing —

ANATOMY
OF A
MEDIATION

All the
best

D1554694

PLI
PRACTISING LAW INSTITUTE

ANATOMY
OF A
MEDIATION

A Dealmaker's
Distinctive Approach to
Resolving Dollar Disputes
and Other Commercial
Conflicts

James C. Freund

Illustrations by Joe Azar

This work is designed to provide practical and useful information on the subject matter covered. However, it is sold with the understanding that neither the publisher nor the author is engaged in rendering legal, accounting or other professional services. If legal advice or other expert assistance is required, the services of a competent professional should be sought.

QUESTIONS ABOUT THIS BOOK?

If you have questions about billing or shipments, or would like information on our other products, please contact our **customer service department** at (800) 260-4PLI.

For library-related queries, **law librarians** may call toll free (877) 900-5291 or email: libraryrelations@pli.edu.

For any other questions or suggestions about this book, contact PLI's **editorial department** at: editorial@pli.edu.

For general information about Practising Law Institute, please visit **www.pli.edu.**

Over the years, I've dedicated each of my books
to various members of my immediate family, and that's
just what I'm going to do with this one:

To my remarkable mom,
Marcella Freund,
who in a few months will turn 105 with faculties intact;

to my terrific wife,
Barbara Fox,
whose love and support keeps me youthful and productive;

to my wonderful sons,
Erik and Tom Freund,
from their proud and loving papa;

and to my magical granddaughters,
Delilah and Paige,
who keep the old man smiling and happy.

ACKNOWLEDGMENTS

This is the fifth book I've done containing artwork by long-time collaborator Joe Azar. What a talent!—just look at the imaginative cover and the eleven interior illustrations that illuminate in vivid pictorial terms just what I'm trying to get across in words. Thanks once more, Joe, for your invaluable contribution.

I've had some useful suggestions on the book from mediator colleagues (who might be embarrassed to be named here, since they approach the process with somewhat different styles than yours truly), and help over the years from lawyer colleagues in connection with the articles that foreshadowed this book, for all of which I'm grateful. I especially appreciate the astute observations on *Anatomy* received from my first mediation colleague, Miriam Millhauser Castle (see footnote 13).

Finally, kudos to the gang at PLI; a big hug to my indefatigable secretary, Pauline Cella; and special thanks to Raymond. I, of course, take full responsibility for the opinions expressed in these pages, as well as for any excesses, errors, or omissions.

—Jim Freund, September 2012

TABLE OF CONTENTS

IN A NUTSHELL

If I were you—the reader—the question I'd be asking myself right about now is, why should I read *this* book? After all, there are plenty of tomes about mediation out there—what's different, what's compelling, about Freund's book?

I think the answer (at least to the question of what's different, if not to the compelling bit) lies in the book's subtitle: *A Dealmaker's Distinctive Approach to Resolving Dollar Disputes and Other Commercial Conflicts.*

The Distinctive Approach

Unlike most mediation professionals who hail from litigation backgrounds, I was a dealmaker for 30 years—a transactional lawyer who negotiated all sorts of business agreements but specialized in handling mergers and acquisitions at the Skadden, Arps firm that led the M&A pack. (The best-known of my seven professional books was *Anatomy of a Merger—Strategies and Techniques for Negotiating Corporate Acquisitions*[1], which has been widely used by professionals in the area.)

Although I crossed over into resolving disputes almost two decades ago, I never lost my dealmaker's attitude toward solving difficult problems and moving things to closure. As I point out in Part I, most disputes should be settled—but it's tough work indeed; and that's where mediation can work when direct negotiations fail. I bring a different mentality to dispute resolution than those whose experience has been primarily in the courts—a mentality that gives rise to the distinctive approach I'll elaborate on below and illustrate in depth throughout the book.

Now, don't get me wrong—I'm well aware that plenty of capable mediators ply their trade successfully using more traditional techniques. Some adopt a *Getting to Yes*[2] cooperative approach to resolving controversies—but that's not for me, especially in the typical dispute that is primarily over money. Other mediators utilize a facilitative mode—helpful but careful not to express their personal views on the subject matter—but that's not for me either, whether in a one-shot dollar dispute or a scenario containing issues not measurable in money. Some mediators who acknowledge the need for positional bargaining handle it in the time-worn fashion of carrying offers and counters back and forth between the parties—and that's also not for me in a straight dollar dispute (although I do a variant of this where forward-looking issues have to be resolved).

Here's what *is* for me in the kind of one-shot dollar dispute that's the grist of a commercial mediator's mill. I recognize the need to use positional bargaining, but I want to avoid the super-charged emotional interplay between adversaries that can occur, even with a mediator in between. My aim is to convert the negotiations into the kind of lower-pressure constructive bargaining that takes place between two transactional lawyers charged with making a business deal for clients keen to reach agreement.

How do I accomplish this in a dollar dispute mediation? By keeping the parties from bargaining with each other—not only directly but even indirectly. Rather, they're each bargaining separately with me, the neutral, to whom they bear none of the hostility they feel toward their adversary. The parties don't talk to each other once the bargaining starts, and I rarely transmit proposals from one side to the other. As a result, neither side knows where the other stands until the end. That's my recipe for forcing them to concentrate on their *own* situation—how much can they sensibly afford to pay (or be willing to accept) to settle the dispute—and not be distracted by the other guy's maneuvering.

 So, I engage in simultaneous confidential negotiations between myself and each party in separate private caucuses, trying with each side to locate a resolution level at which it is satisfied to settle and that hopefully will be common to both. In conducting these negotiations, I'm activist, I'm judgmental, I'm evaluative—I take issue with their unrealistic views. And at the end of the day, if this doesn't result in agreement, I conclude the mediation by giving both sides my proposed recommenda-

tion for a compromise resolution—which they can accept or reject, but can't negotiate further. (I'll have much more to say on that kind of mediator's proposal in Chapters 5 and 14.)

The Dollar Dispute

But I'm getting ahead of myself. Let me double back now to describe the kind of dollar dispute I have in mind here. I've mediated a lot, but at least 90% of the controversies I see are over money—and I bet this holds true for most commercial mediators. These are generally one-shot business disputes— the parties have no continuing relations. As a consequence, there are few other variables that can prove useful in crafting a creative resolution. Rather, it's a zero sum game—the more dollars that go to the claimant, the fewer dollars are retained by the defendant, and vice versa.

The *Getting to Yes* crowd likes to probe beneath the opposing positions of the parties to find those "shared interests" that can unlock a creative resolution. But the problem with that ap- proach in most one-shot squabbles over money is that when you look beneath the far-out dollar positions a party takes, all you find are other, somewhat more reasonable, amounts of dollars!

Actually, this isn't really so surprising. What the "cooperative" bargainers sometimes appear to ignore is that the real "inter- ests" for many business people are precisely those dollars— dollars of cash flow, of profit and loss, of net worth, or dollars to provide a suitable return on other dollars previously laid out. It may be unfortunate, but money is the principal measuring stick of success or failure in the world of commerce—it's how the players keep score.

To round out the picture, here are some other characteristics of the typical one-shot dollar dispute that comes my way:

- The parties are generally sophisticated business corporations, although sometimes well-heeled individuals are involved.
- Prior to entering the mediation, the parties have engaged

in direct negotiations, which have been downright unavailing.

- The dollars at stake are significant enough so that, if agreement isn't reached, it would make sense for the claimant to pursue the matter through litigation (notwithstanding large legal fees and other expenses).
- The substantive issues in dispute are often knotty, and plausible (if not persuasive) arguments can be made for opposing points of view on at least some of them—the facts, the law, contract interpretation, valuation, and such.
- The parties have strong feelings (or certainly give that impression) about the aggressive postures they've put forth.
- Each side is represented by competent, knowledgeable counsel, who make forceful arguments to back up their positions and seldom proffer any real concessions on their own.

Keep these characteristics in mind—particularly the first and last ones—as you traverse these pages. I have the feeling that a lot of the negative reaction some commentators have towards evaluative mediators like myself grows out of different types of cases—where unsophisticated parties aren't so vigorously rep-resented, and the mediator's views may unduly influence or even overwhelm them. Let me tell you—the guys I deal with and their combative counsel and hired experts, although will-ing to listen to my views, are unlikely to be brainwashed by anything I say. And unless I speak up forcefully, I find it's tough to generate any influence at all.

When you come right down to it, the most tantalizing as-pect of mediation is its uncertainty of outcome. I'm not talking here about what number will resolve the dispute but whether the mediation will end up with a resolution at all. In court or arbitration, you know that the process will conclude with a ver-dict—someone will prevail. But in a mediation, a successful outcome is at the mercy of the parties—or either one of them, since it takes two to tango, and they're starting out at opposite ends of the dance floor.

(I'll discuss in Chapter 5 the issue of *why* the parties are engaged in the mediation in the first place, and in Chapter 6 the significance of whether or not litigation has already begun.)

Scope of the Book

Part I of *Anatomy of a Mediation* sets forth what I see as the case for mediation—why disputes should be settled out of court, the reasons that resolving disputes is such tough work, and how mediation can work where direct negotiations fail. It also contains sections regarding the mediator and tracing the initial steps of a mediation.

Then, on the premise that it makes sense to focus on the prevalent type of dispute mediators actually tackle, the book's largest section—Part II—is devoted to my view of how to resolve one-shot dollar disputes. It explores this subject in depth by examining two disparate hypothetical situations— The Put Case and The Art Case.

In my opinion, these are the toughest of all disputes to resolve. I like to think of it as akin to the lyric of *New York, New York*—the line that goes, "If I can make it there, I'll make it anywhere." If you can successfully mediate one of these dollar brouhahas, everything else is a relative piece of cake!

In a sense, this is a "how to" book. By taking you through the mediation process as I go about it, I'm encouraging mediators and potential mediators to try it my way, since I find it works. (I apologize in advance for all the "I/my" references in these pages, but I can only speak for myself—others have to tell you how they go about it.) But the hallmark of the usual "how to" book is that if you follow the author's lead, it'll be easy—to take off weight, to win friends and influence people, to solve Japanese logic puzzles, and so on.

Well, that may be true in some other areas (except in terms of weight!), but it's not the case here. Acting as an evaluative mediator is truly hard work. Unlike an arbitrator whose decision is binding on the parties, in mediation you have to persuade people to come together. And since the two people to be persuaded are each coming at you from very different directions, getting them on the same page is no picnic. So, don't enter in here thinking there's some magic wand you can wave and compel adherence.

Other Commercial Conflicts

Notwithstanding my emphasis in Part II on mediating one-shot dollar disputes, a number of other subjects are highlighted in the book.

For a little taste of that, by changing one fact, I turn The Put Case situation into a potential continuing relationship (in Chapter 12). This presents new issues, but also opens up more creative avenues of dispute resolution for the mediator.

It's Part III, though, that fully explores a complex situation illustrating many of the possibilities mediation offers to resolve commercial conflicts that go beyond dollar disputes. I call this process "deal-dispute mediating." Here, in addition to certain issues that the parties are indeed bickering over, there are other current arrangements and forward-looking matters on which deals must be struck in order to resolve the whole shebang. For this, I use an extended hypothetical study of a business divorce (The Split-Up Case), which requires the mediator to act in a more creative fashion than when wrestling with a one-shot dollar dispute.

In Part IV, I tackle a subject that's custom-made for an energetic mediator—squabbles that involve more than two parties. As the saying goes, "Two's company, three's a crowd"—and the adversarial triangle adds layers of complexity that must be overcome to bring all concerned around to agreement. Again, I analyze this in terms of an extended hypothetical situation (The Casino Caper), by which you'll be able to see what's required to bring all parties—each with differing and conflicting interests—to a common finish line.

Up to this point in the book, the primary focus in each situation is on the mediator—it's a mediator's-eye view of the process, with less attention paid to what's going through the minds of others involved. Then, in Part V, we examine the mediation process—assess strategy and tactics—from the vantage point of the quarreling parties and their representatives. It includes a discussion of what I consider the mediation lawyer's key attribute—skill at negotiating—plus such topics as choosing a mediator, the lawyer-client relationship, and the lawyer's dealings with the mediator.

There are also four appendices: A, I'll tell you about in a bit; B, which compares commercial mediations with those involving international relations between countries and factions; C, containing a few thoughts on the role compromise should play on the national political scene: and D, my mediator's pep talk to the parties at the point things should turn from their initial adjudicative approach to a mutual search for some compromise resolution. On the other hand, here's what's *not* in this book:

- Methods of alternative dispute resolution ("ADR") other than mediation—I don't feel qualified to offer views on these.
- Material concerning mediations in areas other than commercial disputes—such as those involving personal injuries, labor negotiations, or matrimonial conflicts—as to which I have no experience.
- Mediations where the parties and their counsel are foreign nationals who utilize modes of negotiating with which I'm not familiar.
- Detailed discussion of approaches other than mine that good mediators use to resolve disputes. (No disrespect is intended by this omission, but you really should hear about those methods from their able practitioners.)

There is one aspect of mediation that I do know a lot about but will not be covered in the book. It's what might be termed "serial" mediations, involving a series of unrelated claims by a single party against multiple other parties (or, conversely, by multiple parties against a single party). I've been professionally engaged in just such an ongoing situation for the past several years. In addition to raising matters common to all dollar dispute mediations, serial mediations contain some interesting characteristics that apply only to them. I feel, however, that it would be improper for me to make any specific reference to these while I'm still actively involved in this undertaking—I wouldn't want to unwittingly offer aid and comfort (or to undercut) either side of the process.

Why Mediation?

This book is about how mediation can successfully settle a tough commercial dispute that the parties have been unable to resolve on their own, without resorting to litigation or arbitration. So, a fair threshold question to ask is—why mediation? Why should bickering parties opt for this process? To answer this, I have to go back to the basics.

The great bulk of commercial disputes, as I've said, are over money—who owes whom and how much. That's what's at stake—dollars, and not much else. But the jousting involved in such an altercation is far from simple. Either the legal issues in question, or the facts of the matter, or the interpretation of the central contract, or the amount of damages—and in many cases, two or three of these—are characterized quite differently by the parties. That's what they're arguing about—and although the merits of their arguments often tilt one way or the other, they rarely do so on a conclusive basis.

Yet, if the parties end up before a judge (or a jury, or an arbitrator), the decision rendered usually goes 100% one way or the other, as well as arriving at a fixed dollar damage outcome. That's not so bad if the merits are 90% with Party A, only 10% with Party B, and the dollar damage is pretty clear. But it's a different matter when (as is often the case) the merits are, say, in the 60-40 percentage range, and there are plausible arguments for differing amounts of damage.

Let's face it, Mr. 60 is taking a big risk in the litigation—the risk that, even though he presumably has the better case, the judge won't see it that way. Meanwhile, Ms. 40 knows she's facing an uphill battle—one that's likelier than not to end up with her stuck for the whole shooting match (as a defendant) or winding up with nothing (as a plaintiff). And, of course, the situation is further exacerbated by the fact that the two sides are seldom in agreement as to their respective odds of prevailing.

It doesn't take a genius to recognize the commercial desirability of being able to work out a settlement between the parties that roughly reflects that 60-40 split—a resolution that ends up with something for everyone. (I'll have more to say on this subject in Chapter 1 and elsewhere.) After all, that's how successful corporate executives run their companies in other respects. On each major business decision, they go through a risk-reward analysis, estimate the probabilities, and rarely make a 100% all-or-nothing bet on a course of action.

That's especially true if the decision requires putting the ultimate result in the hands of a third party they can't control. Yet, in essence, that's what people do in litigation or arbitration—they outsource the outcome to a judge or a jury or an arbitration panel.

I ought to say a few words about arbitration. Many people who are unfamiliar with the various processes of alternative dispute resolution confuse mediation with arbitration. Yet the reality is that mediation and arbitration are completely different animals, with the latter much more akin to litigation.

The key to the mediation-arbitration distinction is that the arbitrator (or arbitration panel), after reviewing all the documents, depositions, testimony, etc.—renders a verdict on the merits that binds the parties. By contrast, mediators rarely see all the documents or read depositions, do not hear testimony, and—most important—don't render a verdict (on the merits or otherwise) that binds the parties. Even if a mediator ends up (as I often do) providing the parties with a proposed resolution to the dispute (see Chapter 14), it's just a recommendation as to a feasible compromise settlement that neither party is obligated to accept. And that distinction—with its concomitant realities that the mediation might not settle the case, and that the mediator has to *persuade* the parties to accept it (rather than being able to order them to fall in line)—makes all the difference.

The other major distinction is that in mediating certain disputes, you can create flexible voluntary outcomes that are unavailable in the relatively inflexible, involuntary worlds of litigation or arbitration. You'll see vivid examples of this in Parts III and IV.

I have a confession to make. In the infrequent occasions when

24

I'm sitting as an arbitrator, listening to the absolutist rhetoric of the two counsel as they duel over matters whose merits are debatable, I feel like jumping out of my seat and getting in between the parties to guide them toward the mediated compromise settlement that I can sense is itching to occur. . . .

If you're from the transactional world (as I was) and agree with me that it makes good business sense for the parties to settle their dispute, you may be under the impression that this doesn't present much of a problem—hey, you're probably thinking, we negotiate commercial deals every day in countless different areas. But, for a variety of reasons—including the looming specter of litigation, the emotional and other baggage that frustrates the bargaining, and the combative lawyers and hardball postures that dot the landscape—you can take it from this close observer who crossed over in the mid-'90s that resolving a dispute is every bit as difficult as making a complex deal.

I'll get into these various roadblocks in more detail in Chapter 2, but here's the real nub of the problem. Even if the emotions were tamped down, and even if both sides wanted to settle, and even if the negotiations were in the hands of individuals skilled at reaching compromise resolutions, a formidable problem would still exist to thwart accommodation. Here it is in brief:

- As contrasted with the no-cost walkaway if two parties are unable to agree on a deal, the alternative backdrop against which the parties negotiate settlement of a dispute is the anticipated outcome of the lawsuit should negotiations fail;
- No one can be certain in advance what that litigation outcome will be, and the parties invariably disagree about its terms; and
- Whatever the litigation outcome may be, the negotiated settlement is almost bound to be at odds with it.

All of which means that it's hard for adversaries to know where to settle—to find the magic number or formula that will satisfy the divergent appetites of both sides; and even if this were evident, it's still a struggle to get there. When you add back in the frequent problems combatants have in communicating, their mutual distrust, and all that macho posturing, it's tough to make meaningful progress through direct negotiations.

So, what are two adversaries to do if they're stuck between the rock of all-or-nothing litigation and the hard place of unavailing negotiations? Well, they ought to try mediation— hiring a skilled neutral to help them reach the elusive settlement that each side can live with.

Mediating commercial disputes is what I now do professionally—and for the most part (but not invariably) with a good deal of success—so you won't be surprised that I favor this process. There's a lot to be said about the virtues of mediation, but for that—which is covered in Chapter 3—you should read on.

Difficulties Encountered in Mediation

I'm no Pollyanna, though, so let me outline briefly the persistent difficulties we mediators face. It starts with the fact that (unlike an arbitrator) a mediator has no power to impose a particular resolution of the dispute on the parties. Rather, the mediator has to act as a guide to the parties, steering them toward an outcome that each might be willing to settle for, and then persuading them it's in their best interests to do so.

That's a tall order—especially since, in almost all controversies that end up in mediation, the parties have previously tried to negotiate a settlement themselves and failed abjectly. So, just because the parties decide to use mediation doesn't mean the dispute is going to get settled. Some of the reasons for failure are:

- One side or the other (and sometimes both) isn't really interested in (or at best is ambivalent about) reaching a settlement—a situation discussed in Chapter 5;
- The parties want to resolve things, but one side or the other (and sometimes both) insists that it be on terms of unconditional surrender (which, in my experience, is unobtainable through mediation);
- The mediator they select may not be up to the task,

or, although able, takes a limited view of his or her responsibilities (an approach I'll have more to say about in Chapter 4);

- The representatives of the parties aren't skilled negotiators, or even if capable, are acutely uncomfortable participating in what they consider the stilted negotiating format of a mediation.

But even if none of these problems exist, the dollar-dispute mediator faces a formidable task in getting the parties to a compromise. Take, for instance, the case I mentioned above, which the mediator initially analyzes as 60-40 on the merits. Here's what typically happens.

Mr. 60 believes his chances of winning are 70-30—everyone is habitually more optimistic about his odds in court than the mediator is. When the mediator finally gets him to put an initial proposal on the table, it reflects an 85-15 split—he's giving himself some room to negotiate. Meanwhile, for similar reasons, Ms. 40 believes her chances are 50-50, and she starts out with a proposal that reflects a two-thirds piece of the pie for herself.

So, the mediator has a double hurdle to overcome. It's a real chore just to move the parties from their aggressive opening positions to the more realistic postures that reflect their actual views on the litigation outcome—for Mr. 60, coming down from 85 to 70; for Ms. 40, going up from two-thirds (her way) to a 50-50 split. But even if that's accomplished, the resulting 70 to 50 gap isn't conducive to a deal. And believe me, it's a much tougher task to move them beyond their views—he from 70 to 60, she from 50 to 40—so as to end up in the vicinity of the 60-40 deal that, with the mediator's backing, stands a chance of being acceptable to *both sides*. That "both sides" requirement doesn't always seem to register with the hard-charging combatants.

And that's just dealing with the merits, without even taking into consideration the vast gaps that frequently exist in terms of computing or valuing the dollars of damage involved.

I have a pet theory that points to one likely explanation for the unrealistic expectations so often harbored by parties to a dispute. I'm sure you've heard some people contrast mediation with litigation by noting that in litigation there's a winner and a loser, whereas mediation (if it works) produces what they like to call a "win-win" result. That sounds great, doesn't it—bestowing upon the mediation process a real "feel good" vibe. So, it comes as no surprise to encounter a party who's expecting a "win" for himself out of the mediation—and, by the way ("we must be charitable, mustn't we?"), a win for the other guy, too.

Look, there may be something to this viewpoint as regards one of those facilitated outcomes featuring an enlarging-the-pie resolution; but I regret to report that in the typical case many of us mediate—a sizeable one-shot dollar dispute between sophisticated parties, represented by clever lawyers who clash on issues lacking clear-cut determinations—a successful resolution is seldom viewed as a "win" by either side. Rather, it's considered as something I'll now dub with the acronym "SCOPOL"—a Satisfactory Compromise Outcome Preferable to Ongoing Litigation. (Some parties may even take it down a notch to "barely satisfactory" or "not unsatisfactory.") The only person who considers it a "win" is the mediator, who's feeling good, having accomplished what she set out to do. No one else is jumping up and down clicking his heels. As the parties exchange unenthusiastic handshakes, they're wondering whether they gave up too much—especially in that zone between their exaggerated views on the merits and what it took to seal the deal. And while they may thank the mediator for the effort expended, I rarely hear anyone say, "You hit it right on the nose."

Why is this the case? Because in a dollar dispute, an outcome representing a clear-cut mediation "win" for Party A requires the settlement to be at a level that Party B would undoubtedly consider a "loss," to which Party B won't agree. And the mediator has no power to make him do so.

This disconnect between a "win" and a SCOPOL is the 800-pound gorilla in the room—a prime reason, in my view, why a number of mediations that ought to result in resolving the dispute come to naught. Preaching the need to face up to

[handwritten marginalia: key P to set expectations / mediator is "dirty"]

reality doesn't come easily for a party's counsel—it's tough to tell her client he shouldn't be thinking in terms of a win but rather a SCOPOL. So the dirty work is left for the mediator to handle, with a mixed scorecard in terms of success. But I'll tell you one sure thing—if parties started out in the mediation process thinking realistically about what was likely to lie ahead, a lot more disputes would ultimately be resolved.

There's further discussion of the realistic issue in Chapter 9 and elsewhere. Then, to illustrate graphically the adverse impact of unrealistic expectations on the likelihood of achieving a successful outcome of the mediation, I've included an analysis in Appendix A (complete with a chart displaying specific odds of potential failure) that I call "The Mediation Morning Line." Don't feel the need to go there now, but later on—perhaps after you've absorbed the journey through the dollar dispute hypothetical cases in Part II—I recommend it for your perusal.

The Book Audience

Major portions of this book will feature detailed tours through several proceedings—each one, an *Anatomy of a Mediation*, if you will—from a mediator's-eye view. It's my attempt to demystify the process. While I hope these insights into how I go about settling a commercial dollar dispute will prove helpful to readers who are (or aspire to be) mediators, the book should also have value for:

- The executives or lawyers in the contesting companies (or adversarial individuals) who have to make the decision whether to litigate or mediate—and, if they decide to mediate, to determine what type of mediator to choose;
- The principals and lawyers who represent parties in mediations, to whom I'll be offering practical advice (especially in Part V);
- The transactional lawyers who should (but too often don't) get more involved in resolving disputes (see Chapter 25); and

- Those in academia who may be interested in one participant/observer's take on what's going on mediation-wise in the field.

A Dealmaker's Frame of Mind

I mentioned earlier that I bring a dealmaker's mentality to dispute resolution. I'll have a lot more to say on this subject throughout the book, illustrated by specific examples, but I want to mention a few aspects of this up front so you can get more of the general idea.

Although I wrote and lectured widely on doing deals, I was never coming from an academic or philosophical place—rather, it was the view from the trenches, where I was busy hammering out business agreements on behalf of clients who wanted the transactions to take place. And what that requires, as every business lawyer knows, is a concentrated dose of problem-solving and negotiating—a search for common ground to reach effective compromises that permit a deal to move ahead on terms reasonably satisfactory to both sides.

There was seldom any ambivalence to the instructions we received from our clients—the clear message was, "Get it done." That meant finding a way to resolve everything so the deal could proceed. We eschewed extreme positions—we knew we couldn't stick with impunity on anything less than a real deal-breaker. And most of the time, the guy on the other side of the table was operating under a similar mandate. So we yapped a lot at each other, squabbled over warranties and indemnification and such—but never lost sight of the goal to close the deal.

Here's what I had to say about the process in *Anatomy of a Merger*[3]:

> "[T]o call off a deal is no trouble at all, but it requires some real ability to hold together the pieces of a difficult acquisition and accomplish it in a way that satisfies all parties. . . . [T]he adept negotiating lawyer does not allow a seeming impasse to sabotage an otherwise viable deal, but instead devises a workable compromise (which itself can possess aspects of creativity) fulfilling the needs of both sides without subjecting either to serious adverse consequences."

The issues negotiated in a big deal like a corporate acquisition are of many kinds. Some are disagreements over money—not only purchase price but a multiplicity of other matters measurable in dollars. Others involve less tangible matters, such as covenants and escrows, or abstract concepts like "materiality" and "best efforts." Whatever the problem, the dealmaker's attitude has to be that even seemingly deadlocked issues are ultimately solvable.

To make it work, we employed various dealmaking techniques:

- Swapping among different unresolved issues and creating "package deals."
- Cutting through the rhetoric of "sacred principles" and boiling the issues down to dollars (or their practical equivalent), which could then be moved around.
- Adding in a face-saving device, to provide hard-nosed or insecure bargainers the soft cushion of backing off without embarrassment.
- Dividing up a seemingly indivisible issue, so as to satisfy the other guy's real concerns (narrower than those he expressed) while protecting your own essential interests (more limited than those you'd previously advanced).
- Structuring compromises where Uncle Sam bears part of the burden, allowing the party with the tax break to stretch further and satisfy the other side.
- Including goods or services as part of the negotiated package (in situations where the parties were going to have continuing commercial relations), the value of which to the recipient is always higher than their cost to the furnisher—creating a markup that enables the parties to bridge a troublesome gap.
- Expanding the pie, by adding some new element to the picture that permits one party, who now has more to gain, to surrender more than he was willing to previously consider.

So, we had a lot to work with in most deals. Because of that, plus knowing why we'd been hired, I always felt a sense of responsibility to deliver a favorable outcome. Here's how I expressed that thought, as part of my personal credo in *Smart Negotiating—How to Make Good Deals in the Real World*.[4]

"It goes against my grain to see deals muffed that should be made—whether because of intransigence, overtrading, miscalculation, erroneous assumptions, or whatever. I recognize that some deals simply don't make sense. But when one is itching to occur, I feel a sense of failure if I can't concoct and carry out a strategy to bring the two sides together."

Now, switching from deals to disputes, it's not easy for a lawyer representing a client to embrace all of the above in trying to resolve a controversy directly with the other side. The instructions from his client are usually more ambivalent; emotions are running high; no one is inclined to cooperate; the guy on the other side is often arrogant and condescending; in a dollar dispute, you don't have other barter ingredients to move around; all the pressure is placed on a single number, so it's tough to make progress on lesser issues (as in a deal); you don't know whether you'll have to go back to war or not; and on and on, as we'll examine more closely in Chapter 2.

But as a *mediator* of that dispute, I bring the same kind of dealmaking attitude to my work, notwithstanding the much different landscape. The parties have, after all, hired me to help them reach a settlement—that's as strong a message as any corporate client ever gave me to "make this deal happen." I know why I'm there, and it's to get this problem resolved.

To be sure, my dealmaker orientation is most evident in a deal-dispute mediation (the focus of Part III), chock full of handy moveable parts for use in promoting overall compromise. It's also invaluable in a multi-party dispute (such as on display in Part IV), which necessarily involves lots of strategy, tactics and trade-offs. But even in a one-shot dollar dispute, a dealmaking mindset is a big help in terms of:

- The awareness that compromise is the name of the game, and the disposition to embrace and nurture it—unlike some of the other participants, who register extreme wariness toward intermediate outcomes.

- The realization that the most constructive negotiations toward this goal take place between civil counterparties, not the sort of antagonistic adversaries these parties were when, prior to entering into mediation, they tried negotiating a resolution of the dispute directly with a notable lack of success.

- The recognition that for the mediator simply to carry offers back and forth between the parties—offers that the recipient will invariably find "irrational" and "insulting"—only serves to reignite the mutual antagonisms and exacerbate the tensions that are so antithetical to settlement.

- The appreciation that the most likely source of amicable negotiations here is between a party and the mediator— we're not mad at each other, we can be relatively candid (under the shield of confidentiality), the mediator's neutral critique of a party's position doesn't generate the same knee-jerk negativism as when it comes from the adversary, and the party and the mediator can join forces to develop arguments that, when delivered to the other side by the mediator, may exercise a positive influence.

- The ability to use various strategies and tactics from the dealmaker's playbook to get parties over those final humps to achieving closure.

- Finally, (if and when all of that doesn't work, then as a last resort) the mediator's recommendation to the parties on where a settlement can take place, supported by the use of rationale and other persuasive techniques honed in the dealmaking world to convince each side to accept the proposal.

Above all, I recognize the need to have a positive mindset that's not necessarily shared by the parties' representatives. No matter how entrenched the parties appear to be—no matter how vigorously they work at keeping me mired in the underbrush of their dispute—I have to remain confident that a special place exists (if only I can find it) where rational people, coming a good distance from opposite ends, will recognize it's more in their interests to settle on those terms than to litigate.

In all the cases I handle, prior attempts at direct negotiations between the parties have been utterly unsuccessful. As a result, I know that the parties aren't going to find that special settlement place by themselves—and even if they could locate it, they won't be able to get there on their own. So I see it as my responsibility both to find it and to get them there—that's what I was hired to do. Assuming both sides would like to settle and are ultimately rational, then if I can't find that special place and persuade them to join me there, the onus should be on me, not on them. In such a case, I feel as a mediator the same sense of responsibility for a successful outcome of the dispute as I did representing a party to make the deal happen.

Putting in a Good Word for Compromise

That "special place" I've referred to, of course, has to be a compromise. It's the only way hotly contested points of view can be resolved—whether in a deal or a dispute. There's no unconditional surrender in mediation.

This book is about forging compromises. I'm a great believer in them and an active practitioner of the craft. I would have thought that put me on the side of the angels—but when you read the copious stream of fire-breathing vituperation in the daily press, and watch those extremists who hijack opinion shows on television, any receptivity to compromise appears to be in short supply nowadays.

I'll get back to the world of commerce in a minute, but first permit me a brief disgression to the "other world" out there.

The most intractable world conflicts in recent years have been between nations or factions within nations, in such venues as the Middle East, Northern Ireland and the Balkans. At times, the United States offers its good offices to help mediate such disputes.

Compared to what I (and other commercial mediators) go through in our trade, this kind of mediation is really tough on the mediators. They take a lot of heat from both sides, while prodding the parties to face reality and adjust their behavior to what's required for a deal. It's a task for which you not only need large doses of determination and perseverance but also a very thick skin.

Dennis Ross, one of the mediators for the United States in the Middle East, wrote a fine book a few years ago called *State-craft*[5], in which he set forth his "Eleven Rules for Mediation" in this arena. I was intrigued by the comparison it offered with my own precepts for conducting a commercial mediation, so I wrote an article on the subject, which (in slightly altered form) is contained in Appendix B.

In the deeply-rooted grievances that Ross and his colleagues deal with (described by one participant as "your grand-pappy did it to my grand-pappy"), each side sees itself as a victim of the other side. Self-proclaimed sacred principles drive each side to its most rigid position, and no one wants to be perceived as conceding on them. Ross puts it this way: "One side's principle is the other side's impossibility." Then too, there's always the threat of external events—acts of terrorism, for example—triggering crises that must be dealt with to keep the mediation process from unraveling.

So, although in some instances the Ross guidelines coincide with my own, the differences are such that I closed the article with this thought:

"Whenever we commercial mediators feel a little frustrated in our work, we ought to pause for a moment and envision Dennis Ross, in a room permeated by ancient myths, dealing with a couple of Arafat wannabees, plus some terrorists in the wings—and be thankful for the dollars-and-cents 'problems' in front of us."

As for the national scene, I find myself appalled at the partisan state of American politics today. What's especially troubling is that so few effective people are stepping up to the plate to broker honorable compromise on the polarizing issues of the day. It wasn't always so, and in Appendix C, I've set down a few thoughts on that—with particular reference to the memorable Compromise of 1850, featuring the man known to his contemporaries as "The Great Compromiser," Henry Clay.

Getting back to the world of commerce, I'm a tireless advocate of compromise—especially in trying to resolve business disputes. Any negative connotation (from those whose pretentious mantra is "standing on principle") is undeserved. In my book, a compromise—however messy or inelegant—that satisfies both parties sufficiently to do a business deal or resolve a commercial dispute, is one hell of an accomplishment.

Now when I talk about compromise, I'm not talking about splitting things 50-50. Just where the compromise takes place will depend on a lot of factors that can tilt toward or away from one side or the other; but it's still a compromise—defined in the dictionary (as I remind the parties frequently) as "a settlement of differences in which each side makes concessions."

Every compromise has two key elements. The first is finding the precise number or formulation that does the trick for both sides. The second is how and when it should be introduced, so that it's viewed as a resolution to the problem and not just another position that becomes the subject of further negotiating. I'll have a lot more to say on this in future chapters, as well as about how to negotiate to that end—keeping the pressure on and the momentum building within a compressed time frame.

All this is not only hard work for the mediator, but also a lonely experience. Lacking a support system—no one to bounce ideas off, to ease the pressure—you're all on your own.

So, that's how I approach mediation, as you'll see in these pages—especially the tough chore of resolving a commercial dispute, in which what really counts to the parties is where the dollars (or things translatable into dollars) end up going. You're unlikely to hear much in these pages about seeking out hidden shared interests or enlarging the pie or transformative elements, admirable as such concepts are in an ideal world—one that this mediator of commercial disputes rarely sees.

The truly difficult task that mediators need to become adept at—as to which they have no real power except that of persuasion—is how to bring one side way down and the other way up to reach a point (not reachable on their own) where they can shake hands on a deal. I'm going to show you how I go about it.

PART

THE CASE FOR MEDIATION

The underlying premise of this book is that a well-handled mediation is the most effective way to resolve a thorny business dispute. The main alternatives are, on the one hand, litigation (or arbitration), and on the other, direct (unmediated) negotiations. Chapter 1 is a brief statement of why, in my view, the great bulk of commercial conflicts should be settled rather than litigated (or arbitrated). In Chapter 2, I discuss the reasons why it's so tough to settle cases through direct negotiations. Chapter 3 contains some rationale as to why mediation can succeed in cases where direct bargaining has failed.

WHY DISPUTES
SHOULD BE SETTLED

There are many reasons why, in the great bulk of commercial cases, it makes sense to settle rather than go to trial (or even to arbitration). Litigation is expensive; it takes a long time to get a final judgment; lawsuits are a great source of aggravation and negative energy; lawsuits can disrupt business operations; there is a potential for negative publicity; an unsettled publicized case can arouse the interest of the regulators—to name just a few obvious factors.

But to my mind, assuming that a goodly sum of money or other meaningful consideration is at stake in the dispute, one reason trumps all the others—especially (but not exclusively) when viewed from the perspective of the defendant. The way I look at this, it's simply too great a risk for companies and individuals to entrust their fate to the inscrutability of a judge or the vagaries of a jury or the uncertainty of an arbitrator.

For business people, litigation is not a logical way to resolve a dispute. That model isn't the way smart executives run their companies in other respects. They try to make rational risk-reward decisions, basing their business judgments on an assessment of the probabilities. By contrast, a judge or jury—although occasionally donning a Solomonesque hat—generally goes all the way for one side or the other, even when the probabilities are more nearly balanced.

When I was representing clients in these matters, my usual advice to defendants was to calculate what they could rationally afford to pay to eliminate the problem, and to plaintiffs, to assess what they considered reasonable balm for their wounds. Then I attempted to devise a negotiating strategy to make that deal. I freely conceded that this didn't represent a perfect solution—but I reminded them that messy situations don't lend themselves to ideal outcomes.

With a client who relished his adversary's unconditional surrender—unattainable through negotiations but possible in court—I empathized with the passion but then refocused the client on settlement as a way of controlling his own fate, rather than the client rolling the dice and facing the possibility of a devastating judicial decision. Operating in today's world, I would borrow the apt phrase of a younger colleague and tell the client, "The outcome of this dispute is just too important to your company to outsource."

I realize that other bolder advisors—particularly those representing plaintiffs—may commonly counsel the client to go for broke, and some less risk-averse executives may well be amenable to such advice. But the great bulk of the business people I encountered in my years of practice impressed me as more concerned with the possibility of a serious adverse result than enthralled with the prospect of a complete victory.

Incidentally, the six pior paragraphs are what defendants (and sometimes plaintiffs) are likely to hear from me at the time I present my mediator's proposed resolution, as I try to persuade them that settling at my recommended number or formula is in their best interests.

2

WHY RESOLVING DISPUTES IS SUCH TOUGH WORK

Beginning in the '60s, I spent most of my professional life negotiating mergers and other business deals. Toward the end of my active practice in the '90s, I got involved in trying to resolve a few commercial disputes, both before and after litigation had begun.

Going in, I thought this wouldn't be too difficult. Cutting up a finite pie seemed a lot easier to me than pulling together all the pieces of a complicated business transaction. But I was so wrong. Resolving disputes is strenuous work—just as tough as making a complex deal. Still, I found that my experience in putting deals together provided me with a fresh perspective on the litigator-dominated settlement process.

Obstacles to Settling

There are many reasons why resolving disputes is so difficult. Here's a rundown of problems that litter the landscape.

In part, it's emotional. Each side is typically enraged at the other, creating an irate atmosphere that isn't conducive to compromise. And the resulting distrust that each side feels toward its adversary in a messy dispute hinders the ability of the parties and their lawyers to negotiate.

Coming from the world of voluntary deals, I wasn't prepared for the depth of negative feelings on this score. Yet, in retrospect, it's perfectly natural; how else could the parties have reached this hostile impasse? The plaintiff feels terribly aggrieved by the defendant who (in the plaintiff's view) has committed a serious tort or breach of contract; the defendant, who is convinced he hasn't transgressed, harbors a sense of betrayal at being accused of wrong doing and hauled into court. What basis is there for trust between the parties?

Yet trust is basic to successful negotiating. Issues of trust abound: Has each party received accurate information from the other about the subject matter of the dispute? Will a party use what he learns in the negotiations to his adversary's disadvantage? Will the other side renege tomorrow on what he agreed to today? If the settlement involves future conduct—as it sometimes must to bring the full range of settlement options into play—can the other party be trusted to live up to his end of the bargain? Without trust, it's tough to make a deal.

In corporate transactions, lawyers and businessmen usually start by assuming they can trust their opposite numbers. In litigation, trust is hard to win and harder to maintain. A pair of opposing lawyers who are able to create an atmosphere of mutual trust (and who have some influence with their clients) can be instrumental in closing what seems like an irreconcilable gap between the parties' positions. But for two litigators who have been at each other's throats right up to the point that the discussion shifts to settlement, this isn't easy to do.

Here's another aspect that struck me when I "crossed over." In contrast to a deal where everyone is working hard to make it happen, there's a noticeable ambivalence of attitude in many disputes—one day, it's "let's settle"; the next, it's "see you in court."

In a business deal such as an acquisition, the prevailing mood is, "Let's get it done." All the pressure is driving the parties to arrive at an agreement, to consummate the closing. The businessmen want the deal done yesterday, the investment bankers sweat over their contingent fees, and the lawyers get caught up in the frenzy. The emphasis is on being "constructive"—finding ways to resolve whatever impasse arises and get on with the transaction. A lawyer whose heart isn't in it—who tries to delay (or even worse, sabotage) agreement—is anathema. The *bete noir* of all concerned is a "busted deal."

Where the parties are at loggerheads in a dispute, however, the mood is entirely different. Sometimes one of the parties (or his lawyer) prefers that the conflict remain unresolved—and he invariably turns out to be the guy on the *other* side! Perhaps he has something to gain in another sphere from continuance of the litigation, such as imposing pressure on a business competitor.

But even the party who has *more* to gain from a negotiated settlement often appears ambivalent about settlement—alternating between working things out and resuming the conflict. Settling differences is tough enough if your heart's really in it. When lawyers reflect their clients' hot-and-cold moods, the task becomes monumental.

In dealmaking, most good lawyers start with the attitude that everything is ultimately solvable. Sure, you have to reduce what sound like sacred principles to mundane dollars, then throw in a face-saver or two—but eventually, you expect to get all the way home. Part of this attitude is the realization that the other guy's problems are *your* problems, too. If your counterpart can't solve a particular tax issue, for instance, there may be no deal at all. So you have to help those on the other side develop a structure that works for them.

This attitude of ultimate solvability is conspicuously absent in litigation. The parties' positions always seem irreconcilable—just read the briefs! There is no disposition to solve the other side's problems; everyone's having a hard enough job untangling his own.

Still, the crux of accommodation is often to figure out what your adversary's *real* problem is (since in a dispute he may have been less than forthcoming on this score) and then to come up with an inventive solution. But my sense is that the lawyers handling these cases, influenced by their clients' huffing and puffing, often neglect this particular avenue.

In the typical one-shot dollar dispute that sprouts in the aftermath of a sale or other completed deal, the parties generally have little or no post-closing relationship and thus lack shared interests that might facilitate resolution of the conflict. In short, there's no incentive to give an adversary the time of day. And when the dispute arises after one party has paid the other in full (as in a sale), possession of the money is a powerful leverage factor contributing to the recipient's hardball posture.

In a deal, there are dozens of issues to resolve, and no single issue (other than price) takes on disproportionate importance. You can make progress on resolving issues as you go—agree on A, swap B for C, or even sponsor a "package deal" that resolves all the open points in one fell swoop. But in a dispute, where everything often depends on ultimately agreeing to a single number, it's tough to make progress. One party's gain is the other's loss and vice versa—there's little to trade off. Much more pressure is placed on the final breakthrough.

In most one-shot dollar disputes I'm involved in, the final compromise relates solely to resolving past events, and its terms are fixed at the time the settlement agreement is signed. There are seldom any forward-looking portions that might be fodder for cutting deals—where, for example, it's unknown how something will work out, so you can use the resultant uncertainty to bridge pesky gaps. In the stuff that comes my way, what you see is what you've got to work with. (In Chapter 12, however, I explore the possibilities raised by a continuing relationship; and in Part III we'll be examining deal-dispute mediations, which open up plenty of opportunities.)

Another problem in settling commercial litigation, as compared with negotiating a deal, is the scarcity of good models on which to rely. In an acquisition, opposing counsel argue over a number of points, but we have a plethora of precedents for how most issues are usually resolved, and these precedents provide a built-in standard of reasonableness. I know what can be yielded—others have done so before me, so my client won't feel too exposed—and, conversely, where I should stand firm. In contrast, many commercial litigation situations have their own unique facts and dynamics. While analogies may be available and damages measurable within a range, litigators often lack useful benchmarks.

The Biggest Difficulty

But looming above all these problems is the biggest difficulty in dispute resolution—assessing the litigation alternative against which any proposed settlement has to be measured.

In dealmaking, if negotiations prove unsuccessful, either party can just walk away. This continuous possibility keeps a negotiator from taking positions that are manifestly unreasonable, unless his leverage is overwhelming. So, when a business lawyer decides whether to stick or yield on certain major points without bluffing, the key question is whether the issue is a "deal-breaker." If it is, then the alternative to compromise is clear—no deal. Someone has to budge if the transaction is worth doing; otherwise, both sides just go home.

In the realm of disputes, by contrast, there is no neutral walkway. The alternative to settling is to try the case—to let the judge (or jury or arbitrator) decide the outcome. The consequences of not settling will be determined by a third party— someone whom the parties can hope to influence, but over whom they have no control. And at the moment they're trying to settle, no one knows for certain how the trier of fact would come out. Yet, in order to evaluate the proposed settlement, a disputant needs to assess both the likelihood of prevailing in court and how much he's likely to win or lose if the case is taken to judgment.

Actually, it's even more devilish than that. In order to estimate the range of potential settlements, you not only have to evaluate how well you will do in the case, but also how well your adversary *believes he* will make out (which may be different from what he says during the negotiations). Since that's true for both sides, each of you will be trying to influence what's in the adversary's mind so as to lower his expectations; but unfortunately the predicates for this exercise move each party away (rather than toward) mutual accommodation.

The central problem in valuing the litigation alternative is that a judge cannot just whack up the pile of dollars at issue somewhere in the broad middle, which is where the parties are heading when they try to settle. If the judge finds for the plaintiff, he will probably award him much of what he reasonably claims; if he finds for the defendant, the plaintiff gets little or nothing. So today's negotiated settlement is almost bound to be at odds with tomorrow's litigation outcome.

As a result, even if the two sides could agree on the likely outcome (which they're almost never able to do), it wouldn't be usable as a settlement figure. The potential loser would then say, "I'd rather take my chances; I can't do worse."

As for the potential winner, the compromise that's necessary to resolve the dispute is hard to accept. And this "not-getting-your-due" factor fosters the ambivalence that disputants feel over whether to settle or take their chances at total vindication in the courthouse.

Deciding the likely outcome and how likely it is to occur, in order to discount back to a fair settlement—that's a tough call. And if a jury is involved, the prospects are even more inscrutable. It's definitely not the hothouse in which negotiated solutions bloom.

Well, say some litigators, it's not all that difficult; just try the winners, and settle the losers! This reminds me of Will Rogers' advice on the stock market: "Don't gamble; take all your savings and buy some good stock and hold it till it goes up, then sell it. If it don't go up, don't buy it."

Some Thoughts About Litigators

It pains me to say this, but I think the fact that the primary lawyers for each side are litigators may often be a significant problem in settling some disputes.

I've worked with a number of fine trial lawyers during my career and have great respect for them, individually and as a vital breed of attorneys. Their special skill lies in trying cases and handling all the steps leading up to their day in court. The good ones are masterful at coming up with powerful justifications for their strong points and plausible arguments to support what might otherwise seem dubious premises. They're expert at fashioning effective rebuttals to the positions their adversaries take. Most deal lawyers pale beside top litigators in the latter's ability to put everything—facts, law, contract interpretation, valuations—in the best light to burnish their clients' case.

Moreover, a well-rounded litigator also knows how to go about settling a case. As one of them put it to me, "A good litigator's skill set includes the ability to be both aggressive and conciliatory. These are traits that coexist in any litigator worth his salt."

In my view, however, it's more of a mixed bag. I've observed a number of litigators over the years—skilled professionals in their primary area—whose disposition toward settling disputes

and proficiency at negotiating their resolution have been only so-so. I believe that, as a result, many cases—disputes that might have been resolved a lot earlier and with better results—get settled on barely satisfactory terms on the eve of trial.

I attribute litigator shortcomings in this regard to certain underlying problems that exist in the typical contested situation and also to some attitudes and predilections that aren't conducive to settlement.

My sense is (although some litigators wouldn't agree) that it's tough for a trial lawyer to switch from the bristling contacts with the other side in the courtroom or at depositions to a rational discussion of a settlement that satisfies both sides. For some of them (although not the really savvy ones), even placing the first call to suggest that negotiations take place can be a wrenching experience, fraught with concern over portraying weakness.

For a litigator to promote settlement, there needs to be a moderation of those extreme demands and utter denials—the making of conciliatory gestures that don't come naturally to many trial lawyers. And each settlement foray is made more difficult by the litigator's knowledge that he may have to go back to court, which can lead to a rigidity that's anathema to effective compromise.

I also believe (although some litigators don't) that it's difficult for a trial lawyer—who's been hired as a gladiator to go to battle for the client's interests—to sheathe his or her sword and prod the client in what so often is the wise direction of settlement. This is especially true with a client who, like so many of them, takes the lawsuit personally. The litigator can almost hear the client saying, *sotto voce*, "What's the matter, tiger—are you scared to try our case? If you are, we can always get someone else." Yet this lawyerly prodding is often what's needed to tame the client's machismo and encourage negotiating toward a constructive resolution.

Forgive the pop analysis, but I think there's also an underlying psychological factor at work here. For a deal lawyer, the goal is to close the deal, and all efforts are directed to that task. When it happens—and that black binder of documents goes up on your shelf—you feel fulfilled, knowing you accomplished what you set out to do in pursuit of the client's interest.

If you're a litigator, the goal is to win the case. That's what you're hired to do, and the great bulk of your efforts are aimed in that direction. To short-circuit that result by a settlement on terms that, from your client's viewpoint, are inferior to what he would have achieved if you'd been able to carry things to a successful judicial conclusion, is not nearly as satisfying. And since you'll never know how things would have worked out in court (although you've convinced yourself you had the better of the case), there's always the nagging suspicion that you shouldn't have settled for second best.

In short, the predilection to vindication in court and the attitude of reluctance to abandon that effort doesn't foster the concerted effort to forge a settlement that's needed to overcome the obstacles that stand in the way.

In a deal, we're used to having investment bankers and similar specialists provide expert opinions on key elements like price, valuation, and fairness. In a dispute, the expert advice on the probable outcome of the lawsuit usually comes from the litigator who is handling it.

In dealings with the other side, we expect litigators to exaggerate their favorable chances in court. How about in a lawyer-client caucus? In conversations I've had with seasoned litigators, they've rejected my hypothesis that some trial counsel embellish the anticipated results in advising their clients. My theory was that when a litigator has a client who's convinced of his company's rectitude and anxious for the gladiator to share that sense of outrage, it's hard for the litigator not to go with the flow. Besides, the litigator has been hard at work embellishing the client's case—that can lead to some self-deception in terms of both its strengths and weaknesses. Their rejoinder was that, if anything, good litigators tend to undervalue their positions, consciously or unconsciously, which permits them to be heroes if they win or, conversely, to be able to justify a less-than-ideal outcome.

Whatever the merits of that disagreement—and I suspect it varies from litigator to litigator, client to client, and case to case—this much I do know. Even when a litigator provides a balanced account—"there's good news and there's bad news"—the clients hear what they want to hear, which is the good news. This is especially true when the executive in charge of the case is the same individual whose conduct has been called into question in the dispute.

As a result of this, and except in those cases in which a savvy litigator has managed client expectations so as to avoid disappointment, each side ends up with exalted aspirations that run in diametrically opposed directions. To make this worse, when settlement talks finally begin, the parties and their litigators pick aggressive starting points—opening proposals that are much further from their expectations than in the situation where two contracting parties, trying to reach a deal, give themselves a little negotiating room. So the gap going in can be enormous, which tends to discourage each side from making the effort to bridge it.

But here's the most daunting part. Even if, in the rare case, both sides (in the privacy of their own caucuses) were in basic agreement as to the range of outcomes at which a settlement could take place, the journey to get to an agreed outcome from their overheated starting points dwarfs everything else in difficulty.

This is precisely why, in my view (although litigators may well disagree), a smart deal lawyer—who has some experience in settling disputes and who approaches this kind of negotiating challenge with a sense of solvability that's conspicuously absent in the usual litigation context—can play a useful role in seeking an out-of-court resolution. (I discuss this subject in detail in Chapter 25.) But, sad to say, experienced deal lawyers who got involved in dispute resolution are, in my experience, few and far between; and, more over, not all who do so are up to the task.

What About *Getting to Yes* and *Smart Negotiating*?

Even for those who are disciples of the conflict resolution methodology articulated in *Getting to Yes*,[6] dollar disputes such as the ones we're primarily considering here can cause plenty of problems. The authors (Messrs. Roger Fisher and William Ury) of that widely read book advocate cooperative negotiating in order to reach wise and efficient agreements. They emphasize four basic points: separate the people from the problem; focus on interests, not positions; invent options for mutual gain; and insist on using objective criteria.

But one-shot dollar disputes often don't lend themselves to the cooperative approach, to wit:

- The adversarial nature of the dispute, and the bruising litigation that often accompanies it, make it difficult to adopt the attitude of partners-in-a-side-by-side-search-for-a-fair-agreement that's the hallmark of a *Getting to Yes* negotiation.
- Against the backdrop of the irreconcilable positions frequently taken by the parties in a bitter dollar dispute, it's hard to find the kind of shared and compatible interests to be reconciled that *Getting to Yes* thrives on—to say nothing about the difficulty of having a reasoned discussion of those interests between two implacable adversaries.
- Brainstorming about options with the other side, refraining from criticizing an adversary's proposed solutions, trying to help them solve their problems— these techniques are laudable indeed, but unlikely to be utilized in the heat of a commercial dollar dispute.
- And while the joint search for mutually agreeable objective criteria, fair standards and impartial procedures isn't out of the question, it's no piece of cake in a bitter dispute—just watch as each side brandishes its own standard of "objectivity," insisting that it be used as the basis for resolution.

In my *Smart Negotiating*[7] book, I advocated a four-point "game plan" approach to negotiating a deal, designed to answer the negotiator's most pressing questions: What do I want? Where do I start? When do I move? And how do I close? The *Smart Negotiating* technique works quite well in the context of a deal, but it too encounters some real problems where a dispute is involved. For instance:

- Assessing your realistic expectation for the negotiations (*What do I want?*) runs smack into the difficulty of predicting what's likely to happen in the litigation. It also faces the added hurdle that your adversary—whose presumed views must be factored into the assessment, in order to make your expectation realistic—is likely to have a different slant on the probable judicial outcome than your own.

- Determining an appropriate opening proposal (*Where do I start?*)—one that neither appears to overreach nor manages to underachieve—is a crucial step toward launching the parties on the right path to a deal. In most disputes, however, each side is so determined to put its best foot forward that the initial bid-and-asked disparity can be enormous. As a result, the negotiators are often discouraged from taking what seem like futile steps to try to close the gap.

- Engaging in a constructive concession pattern (*When do I move?*), designed to deliver both parties into the vicinity of their realistic expectations, is difficult enough in a deal context, but in a dispute—where there's no premium on momentum and reciprocity can be viewed as a sign of weakness—it's very tough indeed.

- And arranging the ultimate compromise (*How do I close?*), where all the focus is on a single finite number with few opportunities to be creative or expand the pie, is no picnic—especially when the settlement calls for more "give" from one of the parties than he had previously anticipated.

As a consequence of these and other factors, many disputes remain deeply enmeshed in litigation, with only half-hearted forays in the direction of a negotiated settlement. And these forays often fail, at least until that moment, on the steps of the courthouse (and after a lot of time, energy and expense), when the parties finally face up to reality.

So, if you're caught between the rock of litigation and the hard place of unsuccessful negotiations, is there some better way?

CHAPTER
3

WHY MEDIATION CAN WORK WHERE DIRECT NEGOTIATIONS FAIL

Mediation—featuring a neutral third party helping the disputants to reach a mutually acceptable settlement—may just be that better way. Introducing an impartial mediator into the picture can help alleviate many of the problems that bedevil negotiators when they try to resolve disputes on their own.

For example, in the *Getting to Yes*[8] formulation previously alluded to:

- The very presence of a mediator frequently serves to help "separate" the people and the problem—to say nothing of the physical partitioning of the parties so often associated with mediation. A properly handled mediation lessens antagonisms and reduces the opportunities for further misunderstandings.
- In the course of private dealings with each of the parties, a mediator may be able to uncover shared interests suitable for reconciliation, thus opening up fresh settlement possibilities.
- The mediator can engage each party privately in the exercise of inventing options, without the party fearing that what he suggests will be held against her (since the mediator is pledged to maintain the confidentiality of their discussions).
- A mediator can inject her own impartiality into the search for mutually satisfactory objective criteria; and her independent imprimatur placed on any such reference point will carry great weight with the parties.

Similarly, in terms of my four-part *Smart Negotiating*[9] game plan:

- A mediator can help the parties assess their realistic expectations, functioning as an "agent of reality" with regard to how the various issues are likely to play out in the litigation.
- The mediator, dealing separately with the parties, can discourage them from digging into (and posturing about) their far-out "winning" positions—encouraging more reasonable starting points that provide the negotiations with a better chance of success.
- One of the mediator's principal functions is to help the concession pattern along by his private prodding of the parties to move constructively in the direction of each other.
- A mediator can be invaluable in bridging that final gap—proposing the terms of a possible compromise, initiating a "split," being creative, suggesting novel business relationships that "enlarge the pie," and otherwise taking the initiative in ways that the parties and their attorneys often find so difficult to do themselves.

In addition to all that, the mediator can overcome the parties' reluctance to institute talks, help them surmount feelings of ambivalence, mitigate their distrust, introduce a sense of solvability, maintain momentum, and ease the litigator's special burdens (the problems alluded to earlier).

Mediation represents a very inexpensive alternative to litigation. The cost of the mediator is modest in comparison to the other expenses incurred. And, in the eyes of clients, the fees of the lawyers who prepare for and participate in the mediation may seem more justifiable, since they're spending their time trying to resolve the problem peaceably.

If the mediation works, the participants should feel better about the result—which they have voluntarily determined— than they would after a bruising court battle and judicially-imposed resolution, especially when a continuing relationship is involved. And when the successful mediation is over, it's really over—there's no counterpart to the appeal from the trial court's verdict that typically occurs in the judicial system.

Let me note that, in focusing on mediation, I don't mean to slight the other forms of alternative dispute resolution that have been developed in recent years to achieve similar ends. Although the other techniques do present some additional wrinkles, many of the same principles enunciated here are equally applicable. Nevertheless, I'm going to stick to mediation, the most straightforward of the procedures, the one I'm most familiar with, and usually the easiest to get the other side to try.

4

ABOUT THE MEDIATOR

If mediation is to succeed where direct negotiations have failed, the mediator has to play a critical role. This chapter explores both the professional and personal qualities a mediator should possess in order to be effective, and also the type of approach different mediators bring to the task.

The Qualities of a Good Mediator

Obviously, there are a number of desirable qualities for a mediator to possess. I saw one compilation[10] that suggested an effective mediator should have as many of the following attributes as possible: absolute impartiality, trustworthiness and ability to motivate people to disclose confidential information, mediation experience, good listening skills, ability to understand the law and facts, good people skills, leadership qualities, problem-solving skills, flexibility, strong negotiating skills, patience, good management skills, a sense of humor, and good business sense.

There's a natural tendency to consider someone with experience as a judge or arbitrator as a classic mediator. Clearly, such individuals possess many virtues, including their stature and fair-mindedness, the ability to inspire trust, and an informed view on how particular issues are likely to play out if litigated.

Still, I believe that the prime skill called for in a mediator is his or her negotiating ability. Make no mistake about it, a mediation is definitely a negotiation—a negotiation in which a prime negotiator is the neutral mediator.

Unlike a judge or arbitrator, the mediator does not rule by

fiat. Rather, he or she operates by persuasion, by conciliation, by adopting many of the techniques associated with negotiating a deal. Judges and arbitrators aren't necessarily skilled in that regard (although they may well be).

In addition to litigators—the lawyers most often tapped to serve as mediators—I think some astute business lawyers who negotiate for a living have a lot to offer as mediators. Their skill set should include a sense of what's feasible; a positive problem-solving mentality (and this dispute, after all, is a big problem!); an understanding of complex business-type issues, as well as tax and accounting considerations; and a feel for developing and proposing an acceptable compromise.

How about expertise in the subject matter of the dispute—is that requisite? Of course, it can be helpful, especially if the brouhaha involves highly technical matters. The mediator who has previous expertise doesn't need to be educated as to the basics, has a better sense of whether a party's argument that sounds okay is actually preposterous, and can opine on matters with a surer hand.

Still, I don't feel that subject-matter expertise is a prerequisite, and, in fact, isn't as important as negotiating ability. I've mediated plenty of disputes that lie outside my particular comfort zone. I find that the written submissions of the parties and their responses to the questions I pose educate me quite well—sufficiently so that I'm able to grasp what are the prime levers to operate in order to bring the parties together. Also, many commercial disputes—however esoteric a field they're played out on—turn on the meaning and interpretation of contractual language, something that isn't at all foreign to us business lawyers.

There's another quality that's quite important for a mediator. That's the capacity to be a good listener—to hear the disputants out. The parties need to feel they've had a full hearing before they'll be willing to listen to advice from the mediator on a possible settlement.

For the mediator, this isn't just a passive exercise—not simply a matter of being patient and knowing when to keep one's mouth shut (although that's not unimportant). There's listening and then there's hearing—not just what is said, but what's left unsaid, what's hovering between the lines. Signals and clues abound in a negotiation. For instance, parties will sometimes throw out a number by way of using an example; that choice of number may be significant. A good mediator stays alert.

How About the Use of Humor?

Although mediating disputes is serious business, I find that injecting a little humor into the situation can sometimes be helpful to ease the tension that inevitably builds up. But it's not just a matter of cracking an out-of-context joke every so often—humor is much more effective when it relates to, and at best sheds light on, what's happening in the mediation. Let me give you a few examples.

Let's say the plaintiff is attempting to enforce a liquidated damages clause in a contract. The defendant has argued that the clause is really a penalty and therefore isn't valid. But the defendant then goes on to say that if any damages are assessed (without reference to the clause), the dollar figure in the clause should be the upper limit of his liability.

Clearly, the defendant is arguing two inconsistent positions, and I could of course just make a statement to that effect. But I prefer to relate the Woody Allen gag from the opening moments of *Annie Hall*—the one about the two elderly ladies, discussing a resort they had recently visited. "The food was so terrible," says the first lady, to which the second replies, "Yes, and such small portions, too. . . ." This not only draws a laugh but gets across the inconsistency point in spades.

Not long ago, I came back into a plaintiff's room to announce, with some pride, that—after a major effort—I'd succeeded in persuading the defendant to yield on a major point. But instead of the warm reception I'd expected for my triumph, the response of the plaintiff's lawyer's focused on a minor adjunct to the main point that I'd neglected to bring up with the defendant. The letdown bothered me, and I decided not to let it pass.

"Your reaction reminds me of the grandmother who took her young grandson to the beach. The kid was swimming in the ocean, when suddenly he became caught in a riptide and was being carried out to sea. Three lifeguards jumped into the water, braved the fierce currents at peril to their own lives, reached the struggling youngster, brought him back to the beach, performed CPR, and restored him to life. The grandmother, surveying the scene, said, 'He had a cap. . . .' "

Sometimes, I'll have to admit, my humor does turn a bit pointed. For instance, when one party's own wrongful action has created the situation as to which it's seeking recompense from the other party, my standard retort is, "That's like the boy who killed his parents and then threw himself on the mercy of the court as an orphan."

Every once in a while, I employ some literary whimsy. Here's one of my favorites that I keep around for appropriate use. It's usable in a case where one party's argument lacks a solid foundation. Each flimsy conclusion is dependent on some equally debatable premise. A quote from Lewis Carroll's *Through the Looking Glass*[11] points up the party's feet of clay:

> [The White Knight to Alice:] "I [invented] a new way of getting over a gate—would you like to hear it?"
> "Very much indeed," Alice said politely.
> "I'll tell you how I came to think of it," said the Knight. "You see, I said to myself 'the only difficulty is with the feet; the head is high enough already.' Now, first I put my head on the top of the gate—then the head's high enough—then I stand on my head—then the feet are high enough, you see—then I'm over, you see."

To which I then add: "And you, my friend, have vaulted the gate, traversed the garden, and are now trying to break into the mansion. . . ."

The Mediator's Approach

I'm convinced that a key to the process is not just the quality of the individual selected as mediator, but the approach he or she takes toward the mediator's role. And on this subject there is some difference of opinion.

Let me illustrate this with a simple but pretty typical example in a dollar dispute. Imagine a situation where the plaintiff (Mr. A) is seeking $10 million in damages in court. His lawyer has advised him that they have a strong case, so Mr. A is looking for a settlement in the $7.5 million-plus area. To give himself some bargaining room, he starts out settlement discussions asking for $9 million.

The defendant's lawyer, however, believes the case could go either way. So the defendant (Ms. B) is aiming at a settlement in the neighborhood of $5 million. She begins by offering $3 million.

As a result, there's a $6 million spread in their positions (between $9 million and $3 million), which both sides realize will be hard to bridge. So they decide to try mediation.

Now, some mediators restrict their role to acting primarily as a facilitator. They see themselves as providing important services, including fostering a constructive environment for the parties, helping each party understand its legal position, assisting them in their evaluations of what the other side proposes, trying to find out their underlying interests with a view to reconciliation, and possibly helping them to create additional values by "enlarging the pie"—but they're reluctant to voice their own views on the merits or on where the dispute can be settled.

Let's say the parties use such a mediator, and he or she is successful in getting behind those opening positions and gaining access to the actual expectations of the parties—perhaps (on a good day) even persuading them to communicate those to each other.

Does that mean there's a deal? Not by a long shot—because once the plaintiff (Mr. A) comes down from $9 million to $7.5 million, and the defendant (Ms. B) comes up from $3 million to $5 million, there's still a big gap of $2.5 million. As for reconciling interests, the typical one-shot dollar dispute offers far fewer opportunities for this than situations involving continuing relationships. And in my experience, creating value and enlarging the pie work best when the parties are close to a deal and just need something to get them over the hump—not, as here, where they have very different ideas as to the value of a case.

If the parties, underneath their posturing, were in basic agreement as to the value of the case but just wanted to engage their adversary to see how much better they might be able to do, a facilitative mode of mediation may be worthwhile—and I might even try it. But in the mediations I handle, this is almost never the case.

What I see in the complex commercial disputes I mediate is that when you get underneath the posturing to what is hopefully fertile ground for agreement, you discover that one (or often both) of the parties is unrealistic in terms of overestimating the strength of his case or anticipating the other side's giving in, or is misreading the situation in some other respect.

In my view, these parties need a different kind of mediator—not just a facilitator, but one who is activist and judgmental ("evaluative" appears to be the adjective of choice). Those exaggerated aspirations need a splash of reality in the face—and the mediator has to function as the agent of that reality. Both sides have to undergo the ordeal of seeing the dispute and their "winning" positions through a pair of impartial eyes, in order to justify the sizeable movement needed to bridge a big gap.

And so, when I'm the mediator in one of these dollar disputes—and assuming the parties have indicated their receptivity to this approach—I give my views on the merits of the issues involved, help the parties arrive at a basis for settlement, and try to play an instrumental part in actually negotiating it. I realize that many fine mediators may disagree with me, but in my view, nothing short of this has a decent chance of success in the kind of cases I handle.

I'm telling it like it is. Being an effective mediator in a dollar dispute is one of the toughest jobs a lawyer can undertake. These two sparring parties are mad as hell at each other. They've tried to settle the dispute, but haven't even made a dent in it. The litigators representing them would probably rather try the case than settle it. Even if everyone were disposed to settle, they're not sure how to go about it.

Do you think you can get everyone to sit around a round table and make nice? Forget it!

Sure, I've heard mediation referred to as "facilitated negotiation," which it certainly is—but the real issue is, what's meant by "facilitated"? And the place where the facilitative-evaluative distinction is most acute is the one-shot dollar dispute.

The main thing to keep in mind about mediation is that you can't *make* the parties settle. Even if you give both sides a feasible number, you have to *persuade* them to buy into a result they don't like very much (because it's a long distance away from where they started). You have to convince them that although the number may seem unpalatable, the litigation alternative (which is inherently unknowable) is worse. You also have to assure them that the other side is suffering at least as much as they are.

So, I ask you—with parties who feel strongly about the merits of their case and are unafraid of litigation, represented by litigators who would just as soon try the case as resolve it, and with both parties and litigators knowing they're under no compulsion to settle since the mediator can't force them to do so—what's going to get them to move?

I'll tell you what *won't* get Party A to move—anything that Party B says about the case. Each side has a negative knee-jerk reaction to anything his adversary puts forth, discounting it to zero in the most unflattering terms—not only directly to the other side, but also to the mediator in private.

In my view, the only thing that will get them to move is to receive a realistic evaluation of the situation from a neutral they respect and trust. What happens from that point on depends a lot on the mediator's style.[12] My style is to do everything I can to generate real movement from a standing start and to persuade them that a feasible outcome they're not crazy about is preferable to the litigation alternative. Contrast this with the approach of a friend of mine, a superb mediator, who tries to give the parties as much control as he can and as much ability to work their way through their own negotiations. Good mediators, he says, need to play to their own strengths.

The fact is that almost no one gives in easily here. The main reason for this is because they don't like the idea of leaving money on the table—money that they'd get as plaintiffs if they were to win in court, or wouldn't have to pay as a prevailing defendant. And, unfortunately, no one can know for sure about the judicial outcome when the mediator is trying to get them to compromise at a level they're not so happy about.

I've seen some criticism of evaluation as undercutting the mediator's neutrality, with one side (or possibly both) feeling aggrieved toward the mediator for expressing views that don't help their case. It's certainly possible—sometimes I can feel the air go out of the room, when I come down hard on a party's position. But as far as I'm concerned, this just goes with the territory; and individuals who are apprehensive about voicing their honest views because one of the parties won't like where those views come out should probably find some less stressful line of work. A good evaluative mediator knows very well that he or she doesn't have a horse in this race, other than the goal of ultimately resolving the dispute. Hey, we're just calling it as we see it, trying to bring a badly needed dose of reality into the proceedings, whatever the reaction of the party whose ox may be gored.

As for my mediator's proposed resolution, that's just the final shot at resolving the case (the mediator's last clear chance) if the mediation proper hasn't resulted in a settlement. It's not different in kind from what came before—just different in degree of specificity and in the accept-or-reject, no-more-negotiating dictum that accompanies it. It's still totally voluntary on the part of the disputants as to whether to go along. (This is in contrast, for instance, with the ADR process called "Med-Arb," where the parties agree in advance that issues unresolved during the mediation will then be subject to binding arbitration by the neutral—a process I have real problems with, for reasons I won't go into here.)

What can I tell you—this is the real world. And that's what this book is about.

Let me be clear on one point, though. I hope I haven't given the impression that a mediator ought to try to impose on the parties (albeit, voluntarily) his or her *own* preferred solution. No, no—that's for an arbitrator. What the mediating parties want is the neutral's help in finding *their* own solution—one that they consider mutually acceptable.

While the mediator's reaction to the merits of the issues involved certainly plays a role in this, so does his appraisal of the parties themselves, their relative leverage, where they started out, the history of their prior negotiations, and so on. A successful dollar dispute mediator has to come to grips with *feasibility*—taking dead aim at a number (or narrow range) that he suspects would suit *both* parties if they could locate it and mutually arrive there in one piece.

I recommend that, at the outset of the process, the mediator do one of two things. She can ask the parties whether they have any preconceived ideas as to what role she should play. In the absence of a strong mutual indication otherwise, the mediator can then indicate her own preference to be, say, an activist, or to be a facilitator—to be judgmental or to be more reserved—or to conduct herself in some manner in between the two.

Or, she can do as I do and just tell the parties what her style is. If they don't object, that's the way it'll be, and they can't complain later.

It's important for the mediator to make sure she's tuned in to the same wavelength on which the parties are transmitting. I may prefer, in one-shot dollar disputes, to be an activist and judgmental mediator; but I don't want to be perceived as uppity if that's not what the parties have in mind—and it's definitely their call. I have to say, though, that I've never been tested in this regard by the parties saying, "No, Jim, we just want you to play a facilitative role." Frankly, if that were to happen, I'm not sure whether I'd take on the assignment.

CHAPTER
5

THE INITIAL STEPS
OF A MEDIATION

When I'm first contacted to act as a mediator—usually by a lawyer for one of the parties, although sometimes by both—I try to get a general idea of what's involved, without probing into the facts of the dispute or the parties' positions. I want to know, in a general way, where things stand between the parties. Have they engaged in unfruitful negotiations? Has litigation begun? How did they decide to try mediation?

How the Parties Have Come to be Mediating

I'm especially interested in *how* the parties got to the table and *why* they're engaged in the mediation. To oversimplify, there are three basic ways this occurs:

- They arrive totally voluntarily, having attempted to negotiate a settlement and failed. They may or may not have already initiated litigation, but would like a shot at resolving things voluntarily before pressing ahead in court.
- They're in mediation because the court (or arbitration panel) before which their case is being heard has directed them to attempt to reach a mediated settlement before trial and judgment.
- They've come to mediation because there's a provision in the contract over which they're fighting that says they have to try mediating before suing each other.[13]

As a mediator—and I think most of my colleagues would agree with me here—I much prefer mediating where there has been a totally voluntary submission to the process by the parties (which is the basic model I'm using in this book unless noted otherwise). Both combatants want the dispute settled short of litigation, if it can be accomplished on satisfactory terms. That's the best you can hope for as a mediator—that the parties at least have constructive intentions. It doesn't ensure success by any means—there will still be hard slogging ahead—but I've been consistently more successful in this category than in the others.

At the other extreme—at least potentially—is the mediation featuring parties who are there because a judge told them to be. My fear here is that whatever propelled them (or at least the claimant) to go into court first—before trying to work things out with neutral help—continues to motivate them in directions antithetical to a compromise settlement. The time in court may have further reinforced the mindset of one of them that the position he's espousing before the judge is a sure winner—so he's unwilling to accept (or pay) a lot less (or more) than that amount, regardless of the mediator's entreaty. Or there may be business reasons why one of the adversaries prefers the litigation to be continuing—to put pressure on the other party or to influence a competitive situation. I've had some of these doomed cases; and although I tried my best to suggest fertile ground for a rational settlement, I ultimately got nowhere with one (or sometimes both) of the parties.

The in-between situation occurs when the parties are in mediation pursuant to a contractual provision obligating them to mediate before suing. With these adversaries, I take some comfort in the fact that, at least back on the day they inked their business agreement, both sides concurred on the desirability of trying mediation before going to war. But their appearance in the mediation today is not on a strictly voluntary basis, since failing to mediate would constitute a breach of their agreement. So I don't know whether their prior receptivity to the process has been undermined by what has taken place between the time of signing the contract and now—not least of which may be the fractious circumstances of the dispute itself. The relative good will that existed at inception and nurtured the commitment to mediate before suing may well have evaporated in the heated emotions accompanying the current fuss—so I'm never sure what lies in store.

Conflicts, Fees, Scheduling and Lineup

I have to make sure I don't have any conflicts. Operating strictly on my own with no firm affiliation (as I do now), there rarely is one. At times, I may have previously served as a mediator in a different dispute involving one of the law firms in this case—in fact, that may be why they've recommended using my services now. I don't consider that disabling in and of itself, since both then and now my service was and will be in a neutral capacity—but I do want the other side to be aware of this, in case it bothers them for any reason.

When I was still affiliated with a law firm, there was obviously more chance of a conflict existing—where the firm was currently representing one of the parties on an unrelated matter. I also disclosed any prior representation by the firm, but in a number of cases, the other party was willing to waive that—especially after my ties with the firm (as an inactive Of Counsel with no financial interest) became more attenuated.

In an initial call with both sides' lawyers, I talk to them about my fee arrangement, making sure we're all on the same page. I charge by the hour, so they have to be satisfied with my hourly rate. They should also understand that I bill for all the time I spend in preparing for, as well as in conducting, the mediation. I ask the parties (who are usually splitting my fee) to pay me a non-refundable retainer in advance (at the time they sign the mediation agreement referred to below), against which I'll bill my initial hours; and I let them know I'll be submitting regular invoices as we proceed. Once, early in my mediating career, I didn't do this and got stiffed for my fee—I'm not about to let that happen again.

I also discuss in general terms my technique for conducting both the initial stages of the process and the mediation itself (matters that I'll be spelling out here as we proceed). I want to make sure that they're comfortable with my evaluative style and to acquaint them with my idiosyncrasies (such as not transmitting interim proposals, discussed in Chapter 10), so that none of this comes as a complete surprise to them later on.

We select a date and place for the mediation session to occur. In terms of the date, unless there is a pressing need for speed, we schedule it sufficiently far down the road so we can accomplish the pre-session activity described below.

My preference (except for the infrequent simple case) is to reserve two consecutive days for the mediation session. In the kind of complex dispute I tend to get, even though we accomplish a lot before the session takes place, it's still difficult to discuss the merits and then negotiate the numbers to a conclusion in a single day. I like to have that second day as a fallback without losing momentum. But sometimes the parties or their lawyers are too busy and can only allot one day—and if that's the case, I reluctantly go along with it.

As for the place, it's generally held at the office of one of the law firms involved—I don't consider this a significant factor. We also schedule due dates and ground rules for the pre-mediation activity that I'll talk about in a moment, and I outline briefly what will be in the mediation agreement I'll be sending to the parties that week (including the special provision referred to below).

Just a word on the lineup. I emphasize to them the importance of having at least one business person present on each side who has authority to make the deal. I would stress this, even if the lawyers themselves possessed the requisite authority. In addition to their obvious interest in putting the dispute behind them, business people know (or at least *should* know) how to make a deal. And the more this dispute can be turned into a deal, the better I think are the chances of resolving it.

Two caveats here. The advantage achieved through the active participation of business people can turn into a disadvantage if the specific person attending has been actively involved in the events that gave rise to the dispute (which is often the case) and, in addition, feels such a need to defend his past actions that he lacks the flexibility required for a successful mediation (which needn't be the case, but sometimes is). Similarly, if there's a lot of bad feeling between the responsible individuals on the two sides, this can stand in the way of meaningful movement, dooming the mediation before it even starts.

I usually close this conversation with the parties' lawyers by making a statement along the following lines.

"Over the years, I've enjoyed a lot of success in resolving disputes through mediation when both sides genuinely wanted to settle but were having trouble finding the right number or formula to do so. I've been less successful where one of the parties wasn't really so interested in settling, but was sitting there in the mediation because of a contractual requirement or having been ordered to mediate by a judge. I hope this is a case where both of you would genuinely like to put the dispute behind you. If you both enter the mediation with that goal and a willingness to negotiate, we should be able to resolve this."

Then I ask each side to express its views on that point. To this, I invariably receive statements indicating their desire to resolve the dispute. I can't always tell if these are heartfelt, but at least it lays the groundwork for what I'm going to be doing later. And if they prove to be obstreperous, it's something I'll remind them of—"You're not living up to what you told me on our first call."

The Mediation Agreement

Shortly after the initial conversation, I send out a draft mediation agreement to the parties—a three-sided letter agreement to be signed by each of them and by me as the mediator. Here's what is included:

- Dates and times for the mediation and submissions (discussed below), and place for the session.
- A brief statement of how I intend to conduct the mediation.
- The special "mediator's proposed resolution" provision referred to below.

- An affirmation of the non-binding nature of the mediation.
- Assurances as to the confidentiality of the whole process.
- The responsibility of the parties to hold me harmless from liabilities and expenses (other than as a result of my own willful misconduct).
- A reference to my total separation from my prior law firm, so no conflicts will later be raised.
- My fee and details regarding payment.
- Contact information for me.

I like to get this signed by the parties and my retainer paid prior to receiving their initial submissions (and thus before I spend any appreciable time on the matter).

I mention in the phone call, and then include in the mediation agreement, one particular aspect of the process that has become very important for me.

Sometimes, notwithstanding my attempts to narrow the gap at one or more mediation sessions, the parties are so far apart—and their bargaining arteries so hardened—that I realize we're not going to reach a resolution in the course of the mediation. When that happens, I tell the parties that there's no sense prolonging the agony—we should proceed to the final step.

That step is set forth in a special provision I incorporate into my mediation agreement with the parties—provided the parties want it, and they almost always do. It says, in effect, that if the mediation doesn't result in a mutual agreement (which I would much prefer happening), I will then recommend a specific overall resolution to the parties.

How I go about this in a dollar dispute—my method of arriving at the determination, the way I present it to the parties, and so on—is spelled out in Chapter 14, along with an illustration of its use in The Art Case. I look on this recommendation as a last resort—available only after all other attempts at helping the parties agree on their own number have come to naught—but for me it has become a critical factor in resolving these thorny dollar disputes that so often come my way.

I've even decided now to give this final step an appropriate acronym. I call it a Mediator's PROD—the letters standing for Proposed Resolution Of Dispute. As a noun, a prod is a stimulus, something that "rouses to action"; as a verb, prod means to incite, a word that evokes such synonyms as spur, coax, influence, motivate, urge on, arouse and stimulate. And that's exactly what I see myself doing with my PROD—attempting, to give compromise one last chance when all else has failed.

You may ask why I put this provision in the agreement—as contrasted with merely asking the parties, at the end of a process that hasn't produced a resolution, whether they want me to do it (as is the situation in The Put Case in Chapter 11). The reason is my concern that, after the rigors of the mediation, one of the parties may feel I'm leaning the other way and accordingly doesn't want to hear what I have to say. Well, I think he should hear it, especially if I consider his position to be unrealistic—that's a big part of what he's paying me for. When the PROD recommendation is spelled out in the agreement, then he can't decline to have me propose it—although, of course, he retains the ability to reject my resolution.

Each party is free to accept or reject my recommendation—and I give them a decent interval to respond—but it's not subject to further negotiation in the mediation and only becomes effective if both parties consent. If a party rejects it, I won't reveal to the rejecting party what decision the other party made (so that an acceptor won't be at a disadvantage should new talks ensue after the litigation is commenced). My recommendation and their reaction to it are not admissible in any subsequent court proceeding.

Having seen my PROD work in a number of cases where the parties were far apart at the end of the mediation, I believe in its efficacy. Moreover, I think its looming presence provides some extra incentive for the parties to come to final terms on their own—although I'm aware of the counter-argument that it could act as a deterrent to meaningful moves on their part in the endgame. (I'll discuss these matters also in Chapter 14.)

It also points up one practical reason why mediation works well in a corporate setting. In two-party dispute resolution without a mediator, it's difficult for the responsible executive to agree to a settlement figure that's much worse than what he's been advising his superior or the board to expect. But the mediator's judgment on the merits provides neutral cover for the executive, making it less likely for higher-ups to question his decision to settle. You could almost call it a "negotiated settlement insurance policy." And the responsible executive isn't going to want to see his decision to reject my PROD second-guessed, if and when the court's verdict turns out to be much more negative to his cause than what I've recommended.

Most of the time (but not always), the compromise number I propose, together with the accompanying rationale, bears fruit, and the parties accept what I recommend. Not with any noticeable enthusiasm, though—the typical reaction of each side is, "I'm going further than what's reasonable in agreeing to this number, but it's just barely better than the alternative of continuing the battle in court." (It's basically the SCOPOL formulation I proffered in *In a Nutshell* at the beginning of this book.) That's okay, though—I don't need plaudits or huzzahs. The fact that it works and the compromise is accepted is satisfaction enough.

Pre-Mediation Submissions and Responses

Undoubtedly, some mediators try to downplay the differences between the parties right from the start—moving briskly into the search for common ground, along the lines of a *Getting to Yes*-mode negotiation.[14] That's not my style, and I think the contrast derives from a different approach I take to negotiation.

Getting to Yes disciples pride themselves on aiming at intrinsic fairness, an admirable goal. The problem here, however, is that the two sides to a one-shot dollar dispute often have widely divergent views of what's fair under the circumstances. And while the use of objective criteria is a sensible focal point for agreement, there's seldom a single objective test that compels mutual acquiescence.

So, instead of aiming at the elusive goal of fairness, I preach the gospel of satisfaction. The parties have to feel satisfied with the ultimate result. When they are satisfied, then they're likely to consider the result *not unfair*, which is close enough for me.

In my view, the key to any negotiation (including the bargaining that takes place in a mediation), and the surest means of generating mutual satisfaction, is the *process* the parties participate in—the movement away from opening positions, the familiar maneuvers along the road, the sense of having engaged in a strenuous undertaking—all of which allows each disputant to arrive at the finish line reassured that he got the best deal possible and didn't leave too much on the table.

In this spirit, I think it's important for the aggrieved parties to feel that the mediator has heard their strongest arguments on the major points involved in the dispute before they talk meaningfully with him about settling. Then they can say, "Hey, at least we tried."

It's especially significant for the litigators—who, after all, are preparing to go at each other in court, and have been giving a lot of thought to their winning positions. They should have this opportunity to put forth the essence of their case in its best light at the outset of the mediation—particularly if there's not going to be a trial. Understand, this isn't just for its impact on the other side or even on the mediator—they want their clients to see they're not pussycats. And for a mediation to work, the litigators need to be a constructive part of the process, rather than influencing their clients in ways that preserve the impasse.

Another reason I encourage these "best case" presentations is that they may have some influence on the other side's executive—especially when the argument being made is a telling one. This may be the first time one side's executive has been directly exposed to the other side's version of the facts or legal issues—well-presented by competent litigators. It may include elements negative to his cause that he hasn't previously grasped; and even if something was raised earlier in the aborted settlement negotiations, the mediation's less adversarial nature might make him more willing to listen to a point he'd rather not hear.

But allowing those "winning" positions to be uncorked isn't just for the benefit of the parties. The mediator needs to get a real feel for the strength of each party's case. And there's no better way to initiate that process than through the interplay of arguments between the parties, who clearly know more about the case than the mediator does at this point. Often it's less a matter of the mediator being persuaded by what one party says and more a means for the mediator to confirm the lack of persuasiveness of an uncompelling argument—particularly after the other side has taken its best shot at the vulnerable proposition.

So, although we'll have an all hands session at the outset of the mediation in which oral presentations will be made (see Chapter 7), I ask the parties to furnish me in advance of the mediation with separate written statements setting forth their views on the principal issues. It's helpful for a mediator to be able to review these respective "winning" positions—as well as to examine the key documents involved in the controversy itself—before the actual session begins.

I don't impose any page limits or such on these submissions— the lawyers are urged to use their good judgment. They should also furnish me with any pertinent documents in issue; and if they cite any cases, rulings or writings that are of importance to their case, I ought to receive copies. If the subject matter isn't in my special discipline (which is M&A), I tell them not to assume I'm an expert in the area; "You'd be better off," I say, "adopting an explanatory tone than a dazzling one."

To the extent these submissions contain arguments for each side's position (as they invariably do), I tell each side to simultaneously send a copy of its submission to the other side. Each party should be aware of what the adversary is claiming, the facts it is presenting, and the legal arguments they are relying on.

I also tell them that if they want to communicate to me other non-argumentative matters of a more confidential nature, they can do so without sending the other side a copy, and I will keep it confidential (unless they tell me otherwise). You might not be surprised to learn that I rarely get any takers on this score— no one's giving an inch at the outset. But in declining to take me up on this, they pass up a golden opportunity (discussed in Chapter 14).

From the submissions I do receive, you'd never dream the parties have come together with me to reach a compromise settlement. Every argument is no holds barred, all or nothing, with much of the fervor of actual litigation. Any direct negotiations they've engaged in before the mediation began have usually gotten nowhere, and this has only served to raise the temperature of the conflict.

I don't invite the parties to send reply submissions, but rather do something different that I consider more valuable in sharpening the terms of the debate. As I peruse the submissions, I jot down the questions they raise in my mind. Sometimes it's a question to Party A relating to something it said in its submission that isn't clear or seems counter-intuitive or begs for a follow-up question. Other times, the question to Party A relates to something that Party B has included in its submission, raising an issue or citing an authority that Party A hasn't mentioned— and I want to hear what Party A's response is. And sometimes I've had a thought neither has addressed, on which I'd like to hear one or both of their views.

I then send Party A an email containing my questions to it (usually under a dozen), but without sending a copy to Party B, and vice versa. My reason for this is that I want to be free-wheeling (or even impliedly critical) in my questions—in a way, it's like firing a first shot of reality across their bow—but I don't want the other side to derive any comfort from that before the mediation even begins. I tell the parties that their written response need not be shared with the other party, so they can respond to me on a confidential (and hopefully constructive) basis.

The great bulk of the time, a party's response is akin in spirit to the initial submission—all-out combat. Still, I often learn something from the strength or flabbiness of the response. Sometimes it contains arguments or facts that I think the other side ought to know (if we're going to get anywhere at the session), and then I ask the responding party for permission to forward the extract to the other side (which is usually granted, since the extract rarely gives an inch).

On the basis of the parties' submissions, my detailed study of them and posing of pertinent questions, the parties' replies to my questions, and the private outline I prepare of avenues to pursue at the session, I feel I'm ready to hit the ground running when the mediation gets underway. I want to be well-prepared to make something happen within the limited time constraints, without having to go over a lot of ground that has now been fully covered.

PART

MEDIATING
THE DOLLAR DISPUTE

The principal focus of this book is on resolving one-shot dollar disputes. In this Part II, comprising Chapters 6 through 14, I take the reader through the process—the *Anatomy of a Mediation*, so to speak. I do this using two hypothetical situations, to illustrate what I consider an important differential in the type of cases I mediate.

In the first and principal one that I call "The Put Case," the parties would really like to resolve their dispute, they're relatively realistic about the merits, and they display a sense of receptivity to what I have to say. Even in that constructive atmosphere, however, it's no cinch to end up with a deal—but at least everyone's trying.

The various facets of The Put Case are described in Chapter 6. (You need to review the specifics to grasp my approach to resolving this.) The mediation begins in Chapter 7 with a joint session at which the parties present their "winning" views. The action then shifts in Chapter 8 to separate party caucuses, for private discussions of the merits with the mediator. In Chapter 9, the mediator goes off by himself to develop his negotiating strategy. Dollar discussions between the mediator and each party take place in Chapter 10, while Chapter 11 explores various aspects of the end game. Chapter 12 adds a new element—the possibility of a continuing relationship—and then explores its ramifications.

The second shorter hypothetical, which I call "The Art Case," deals with a mediation in which it's not so clear that the parties intend to resolve matters, one of them is quite unrealistic, and they're less responsive to my mediator's urgings—as a result of which, things appear to end up in an impasse. The facts, the arguments and the course the mediation takes are presented in Chapter 13. The ultimate weapon I have in this kind of case—the mediator's proposed resolution—is the focus of Chapter 14.

6

THE PUT CASE

For this exercise, we need to have a specific hypothetical situation in mind. The first one I'm using (which I'll refer to as "The Put Case") is based on a favorable experience I had as a mediator a good while ago, but the names and many of the facts have been changed to preserve anonymity and simplify the issues.[15]

The Facts

Parent Corporation owns 80 percent of Company's shares; the other 20 percent is owned by Executive, the Company CEO. Their stockholders' agreement provides that, at certain times, Executive can "put" all his Company shares to Parent (i.e., at Executive's option, he can require Parent to purchase his 20 percent interest) at a formula price.

The price is calculated by multiplying Company's net income for the most recent twelve months by an industry-wide price-earnings multiple (determined at the time of the put) derived from external sources (but without naming a specific single source), and dividing the result by five (to reflect Executive's 20 percent interest). At the time the contract was signed, the external sources for obtaining industry-wide multiples (including the best-known and most widely consulted source) all produced multiples in the low teens.

During a certain year (the "Year"), Executive gives notice he is putting his shares to Parent, accompanying the notice with his calculation of the formula price. The net income figure he uses, based on the unaudited books of Company prepared under his direction, is $2 million. And now, lo and behold, the price-earnings multiple emanating from that best-known outside source is 30! He multiplies the $2 million by 30, and, after dividing the resulting $60 million by five, arrives at a $12 million price for his shares.

Parent disagrees sharply with Executive's calculation. In the first place, Parent believes that Company's net income should be substantially reduced by a variety of audit adjustments (such as an increased reserve for accounts receivable) and also to account for various inter-company items between Company and Parent (such as the need for Company to reimburse Parent for services performed for Company's benefit by certain Parent employees). The aggregate effect of such adjustments, in Parent's view, reduces Company's net income from Executive's $2 million figure to $1 million.

In addition, Parent disagrees with Executive on what the proper price-earnings multiple should be. Parent argues that the multiple produced by using Executive's best-known outside source is aberrationally high due to unforeseen developments (big losses reported by several component companies, which greatly skew the overall results). Parent points instead to a less widely used alternative source, which has eliminated the effect of such skewing and produces a more normalized multiple of 15. Multiplying $1 million by 15 and dividing the resulting $15 million by five, Parent takes the position that, instead of the $12 million Executive seeks, the correct price for the put shares is $3 million.

The parties try to reach a compromise price, but direct negotiations fail—at which point there's a race to the courthouse in order to obtain the most hospitable jurisdiction. The resulting lawsuit and counterclaim transcend mere money—alleging fraud, dereliction of duty, and much else.

Still, certain factors are present in The Put Case that suggest the matter should be settled. The litigation is likely to be expensive and time-consuming, since no quick-fix motion will carry the day and the accounting and contract interpretation issues are complicated. Executive is still running Company with a few months to go on his contract, which makes for an uncomfortable situation. Surprisingly, though, his brief continued employment turns out to be of little importance to either side, which is why this case falls into the one-shot category. Both sides have made it very clear to me that they have zero interest in any further dealings down the road. (By changing this one fact in Chapter 12, to contemplate an extended term, the situation turns into a continuing relationship, with some interesting opportunities for the mediator.) Of more significance, at least from Executive's viewpoint, is the fact that it makes a lot of sense to do the deal by Year-end, due to the likelihood of higher tax rates the next year with a new administration in Washington.

Accordingly, shortly before the end of the Year, the parties decide to see if mediation can help resolve this dispute. I'm selected as the mediator. I have a feeling that the reason the parties don't reach out instead for an impartial CPA is their implicit recognition that, notwithstanding the number of issues which appear to turn on accounting practice, a mutually satisfactory outcome is more likely to emerge from productive negotiations than the application of abstract auditing principles.

So now, return with me to the final days of December in the Year, and let me escort you through The Put Case mediation. We'll be viewing this strictly from the mediator's perspective. I won't take you inside the private minds of the parties, because in this case I'm not privy to that information—although it's the object of a good deal of surmise on my part. Still, I think that readers who are more likely to participate in mediations as a party representative than as a neutral can profit by observing how a mediator—who also has represented parties on other occasions—views the process needed to bring the disputants together. (We'll be looking at mediations from the viewpoint of party representatives in Part V.)

Some Mediator Musings

Let's assume we've gone through the initial steps discussed in Chapter 5. Executive, Parent and I have signed a mediation agreement along the lines there described, with one exception. It does *not* contain the special provision for a proposed resolution—the Mediator's PROD, as elaborated on in Chapters 5 and 14. (I want to save discussion of this for the second hypothetical, The Art Case, in Chapters 13 and 14.) And let's further assume I've received the initial submissions of the parties (referred to in Chapter 5), containing the facts and arguments I laid out in the last section.

One of the first things I look for in these submissions is whether there are any considerations other than money that might be of use in resolving the dispute. That's my dealmaker's attitude coming to the fore—I want to have trading material to find creative ways around impasse. Although I won't know its possible utility, I mark in my mind at the outset anything I find of that nature, putting it aside for possible later use.

Most of the time, though (and The Put Case is in this camp), I don't find anything of substance meeting that description. There are no continuing relations between the parties; Executive wants out of the Company as soon as this dispute is resolved, and Parent feels the same way. The parties don't wish to do future business with each other, and the lack of trust evident in the submissions precludes possible resolutions that depend on future conduct. So I realize that I'm mediating the most difficult of all disputes—where there's nothing but money involved, and each party has a quite different idea of how much should be paid.

However, the need for the parties to agree upon a single dollar figure to resolve the dispute doesn't mean there's only a single issue involved—in fact, that's the rare case. More often, as in The Put Case, we have a number of different issues— some factual, some legal, some contract interpretation, some in terms of valuation. The common thread is that they're all ultimately measurable in money. Some may be important enough to swing the whole result in a courtroom (although not necessarily in the mediation); others affect the availability of certain auxiliary claims or defenses; still others might just go to the issue of how much a valid claim should be valued at.

Legal issues are right up a lawyer-mediator's alley—and even more so when the mediator is a retired judge. I find it more comfortable to deal with these (and my views carry more weight with the parties) when the issue involves an area I consider myself to have expertise in (such as M&A). But even when you're out of your comfort zone, you can form a view—based on the authorities and arguments presented by the parties—just as a sitting judge would do.

The issues in The Put Case (other than valuation) are more of an accounting nature than legal. In an area such as this (and tax issues also fall into this category), a mediator like myself is obviously not an expert. Still, I need to deal with the concepts and numbers, formulate a viewpoint, and when the time comes, express it—but always with a caveat, such as, "Well, I'm no CPA [or "no tax lawyer"], but it seems to me. . . ."

In my role as a mediator of business disputes, the number one area of conflict I see is over contract interpretation. I used to negotiate the terms of complex agreements, especially in the M&A area, so I feel at home here, even when the subject matter is new to me. In my drafting, I would always strive for clarity—what I didn't want was ambiguity. But the fact is that when you draft the terms of an agreement, you're not always able to foresee all the possible fact situations to which the contractual language will apply. When the language doesn't explicitly cover the situation that arises, arguments can often be made for diverse readings, creating a big difference in terms of the dispute's outcome.

These issues are right up an evaluative mediator's alley; and although it's easier to be definitive when passing on matters that lie within your area of expertise, a good lawyer doesn't feel constrained from parsing language that's less familiar. Just remember to also broaden your focus from the contract section in question to other sections that might affect the interpretation. Also, if you consider the language ambiguous (and think a judge would conclude similarly), then you have to look at the extrinsic evidence that bears on the negotiated contractual provision—although here you're on less firm ground, to the extent that this depends on fact-finding and individual recollections. (This latter point is discussed in The Art Case.)

Factual issues are more difficult for the mediator. We can't assess credibility and don't have the advantage of testimony or full-scale discovery, so I'm leery of making factual judgments. But in situations where a party wants to put a construction on a document that it won't bear, or refuses to recognize that a sequence of events gives rise to real issues about whether he'll have problems selling his story, the mediator can play a useful role in pointing this out. So I'm not above saying things like, "I don't think the judge will buy that illogical testimony," or "Your version of this isn't too compelling." (We'll see later how I handle some of the factual issues in The Put Case.)

Competing valuations often play a large role in the matters I mediate, and this is clearly the situation in The Put Case. Experts are frequently brought in, and I'm always amazed at how far apart their assessments are. Since the mediator is rarely an expert in such matters, he can't take as strong a position as on a legal or contract interpretation matter (but perhaps stronger than on a factual question). I usually look for a mediated outcome on these that's somewhere between the extremes, although more often closer to the side whose views I consider sounder than just splitting it down the middle.

We'll see how various of these issues play out in The Put Case, and I'll have further commentary at that time. This hypothetical also contains an example of something else regarding issues in dispute that mediators should pick up on, which I want to comment on more generally here.

Oversimplified, I see two kinds of issues arising in a dollar dispute—those that are straight money issues and those where, at least for one party, there's a seemingly sacred principle lurking underneath the dollars involved.

In a multiple issue dollar dispute—where the amount of money attached to each issue differs widely—you might think that the parties would be most adverse on the ones carrying the largest price tags. But what I've observed is that a party often has less to say about some of the quantitatively significant issues and rather focuses his attention on several "underlying principle" issues—even though the dollars involved are relatively small—because he's so convinced as to what the "right" outcome of these should be.

For the mediator, the negative here is that it will be hard to influence a party's posture on an issue of principle to him. But viewed positively—and assuming that what's sacred for him may not be so for the other side—down the road he may be willing, in exchange for my acquiescence to his position on one of these principled-but-smallish issues, to "swap" his concession on a larger straight dollar issue that doesn't move him so deeply. Let's see if that happens in The Put Case.

Some of the mediations I handle are occurring before the parties have entered into litigation (although it's usually threatened) and some (like The Put Case) are after. As a mediator, you rarely get to choose which way it is. In terms of whether mediating before or after litigation is more conducive to resolving the conflict, there are a variety of arguments pro and con.

If it's before, neither party has yet made a big litigation investment of time, effort or fees. This can be beneficial to the mediation, since the momentum and passions of the contest are yet to come, they haven't had to incur heavy litigation costs—so perhaps less animosity stands in the way.

But an early mediation occurs before there's been discovery—a process that can give the parties a keener sense of the strengths and weaknesses of their cases. In an early mediation, the parties can get locked in to their own version of events. Such prematurity may cause indecision in the minds of those trying to agree upon a compromise number, without all the evidence that might bear on it. And I often hear the plaintiff's lawyers speculating about the "smoking gun" they expect to find in the emails of the defendant once they bring the suit. Litigation can also work off some of the parties' venom—as they see their legal bills mounting with no trial in sight, they may be more receptive to working things out.

I've always taken the position that, all things being equal, I think parties are better off trying to settle the dispute *before* suing—provided they can grasp enough about the relative merits to decide on a settlement amount. And sometimes, when both the parties and I need more information to evaluate the case, I've worked out informal exchanges of documents and other material between the parties in the mediation itself.

Plaintiff and Defendant Variances

Most of the points I've been making have been equally applicable to the mediator's dealings with the plaintiff (actual or potential) and with the defendant. Let's look now at some aspects that can differ.

If the plaintiff is claiming he's due a large amount that would be difficult for the defendant to swallow, a failure to resolve the dispute will present the defendant with a real risk of incurring a hefty adverse court verdict. (As for the plaintiff, I usually think about his claim more in terms of an opportunity—such that failure to settle simply means the plaintiff will have to pursue it in court, where he can win more or lose all.) I never let the defendant forget this risk—up to and including the final speech that accompanies my mediator's proposed resolution or PROD (referred to in Chapters 1, 5 and 14). Even when I think the defendant has the better of the merits—and tell him so—I stress the risk, since an inferior case still has a chance of prevailing and causing the damage the defendant should be worried about. And, by the way, just because defendants respond by pooh-poohing the risk involved (as they often do), I don't assume that they're not worried about it. They should be (and may well be) concerned—they just don't want the mediator to know they are.

Sometimes, I have a case where the mediation is occurring before any litigation, and I'm not getting anywhere with the defendant recognizing his risk. Then it dawns on me—the defendant may be thinking that if the mediation doesn't work, the plaintiff may well choose not to sue. "And if that's the case," reasons the defendant, "why should I offer anything in the mediation?"

If and when I sense this—and assuming I've gotten strong indications that the plaintiff will pursue his remedies in court following a failed mediation—I bring the matter up directly with the defendant, along these lines:

> "Don't assume that you won't be sued here, if we're unable to settle this—my sense is that you will be. Your risk analysis should be to compare what the case can be settled for in the mediation with the very real risks you have in litigation—not with the non-risk of you getting a free ride."

Sometimes I see the flip side of this, with a tight-fisted plaintiff who's passing up a pretty good settlement that's available for him. I realize he may be thinking that if the mediation doesn't work, he'll sue the defendant; then, at some point down the line, the defendant will initiate talks to settle at a number that's at least as good for the plaintiff (and maybe better) than the number he could likely settle for today.

When I suspect that's the case, I've been known to share my supposition with the defendant. His inevitable response is that this is the one chance plaintiff will have to receive dollars in settlement—if the mediation fails and the case goes to litigation, the defendant is prepared to go all the way to trial without any resumption of settlement talks. Of course, I pass this along to plaintiffs ("...so that, just in case you're thinking about second opportunities, forget it.").

I illustrate this next point in The Art Case, but it's worth mentioning here. Oversimplified, when a plaintiff has two separate claims, each of which (if prevailing in court) would gain him victory, the defendant needs to realize that she must win twice to get off scot-free (which may make settlement now look more desirable to her). Conversely, if the defendant has two separate defenses, either of which (if prevailing in court) would dismiss the plaintiff's single claim, the plaintiff should be made to recognize that he has to overcome both of these to claim victory (so perhaps the compromise number I can sell the defendant on might be more appealing to the plaintiff than before).

When the plaintiff's suit involves an issue on which other persons (not involved in the mediation) could bring similar claims against the defendant (but haven't so far), I certainly stress this to the defendant as a powerful reason for settling and not running the risk of creating an adverse judicial precedent. If the defendant is worried about setting a harmful precedent by settling, I remind her that the terms of the settlement are confidential, so she retains flexibility in dealing with other prospective plaintiffs. Even if word of the settlement amount leaks out, the defendant can respond to a putative plaintiff by citing "special factors" present in the settled case "that aren't in yours."

Pre-Mediation Settlement Negotiations

If you share my views of negotiating as a process and the mediator as a neutral negotiator who joins the proceedings along the way, you'll agree that the history of the negotiations that preceded the mediation is of real significance.

In my early days as a mediator, I would ask the parties—while they're still together in the same room—to describe the course the negotiations have taken, both before and after filing of the lawsuit (if they're already in court). It's possible, in some cases, that the parties have agreed to keep this information confidential, but I've never encountered that problem. This exercise can be ticklish, with the potential for reviving some unpleasant memories; but the mediator needs this background in order to determine what's feasible to accomplish.

My rationale for doing it while they were still together was that their recollections of events may well differ in significant detail, and this needs to be thrashed out. When this did happen—and then, after some jockeying back and forth, they finally agreed on a composite version—I used to consider this modest accord to be significant. After all, the parties are unlikely to agree on a resolution of the dispute if they can't even concur on an historical account of the path the negotiations have taken thus far.

Of late, however, I've more often been discussing this subject with each side separately. My thinking is that I'm likely to learn more from their respective initial versions—spurred on by questions from me that I might be reluctant to pose in a joint session. As for any conflict that occurs over pertinent details (and assuming a party hasn't designated the details as confidential), I just go back to the other side and report what its adversary said, which can lead to some revealing reactions.

One aspect I'm particularly interested in is what their initial negotiating positions were—and how these might differ from both their litigation postures and the positions with which they're beginning the mediation. It's not telling any tales out of school to say that if parties to a mediation started out closer the first time they talked, then—unless they've learned significant new information through discovery or otherwise—whatever stronger stand they've cooked up for the mediation doesn't carry much weight. I'm also interested in any concession pattern that may have developed earlier—who made the bigger moves and in what order, what rationale (if any) was attached to particular shifts, who "went last," who broke off the negotiations, and so on.

Most significant to any mediator, of course, is identifying the levels at which the parties arrived before negotiations halted. Usually, this reflects a closer spread than the "winning" positions paraded at the outset of the mediation (which more closely resemble their "unconditional surrender" litigation postures). Unless something notable has occurred in the interim, however, the bid-and-asked range that emerged from their prior negotiations forms the practical ballpark in which the mediation settlement is going to play out—and at the appropriate time, I let the parties know I see it this way.

In The Put Case, I'm surprised to learn that in their initial negotiations the parties progressed from the $3 million–$12 million range of their extreme positions—the same ones to which they reverted for the mediation—to a more reasonable $5 million–$9.5 million range. (That's actually a lot more bargaining progress than I'm used to seeing in the mediations I handle, and it tells me that these parties do want to settle their dispute, although they're having trouble doing so.) At that point, however, both sides appear to have become exhausted by the effort, since each stiffened noticeably, and the race to the courthouse ensued.

CHAPTER 7

The Beginning Joint Session

Now The Put Case proceedings begin, with all the participants together in one room. In addition to outside counsel for each side, Executive is present in person; and the chief executive officer, the chief financial officer, and the inside general counsel of Parent are appearing on its behalf. There's a noticeable coolness on each side toward the other—I notice that no hands are shaken.

Presentations by the Parties

Following my brief discussion of the ground rules and other preliminary remarks designed to demystify the process, I allow each side to make a short (generally about 30 minutes) oral statement of its views on the important issues in dispute. If one side is clearly the claimant, that side should probably go first; otherwise, as in The Put Case, the order of presentation isn't that important—particularly since each side has a pretty good idea of what's going to be said, based on the pre-session submissions they've exchanged.

This first step is usually handled by the outside lawyers (who are likely to be the respective litigators), although the principals can certainly address particular issues if they care to. I caution each side not to interrupt its adversary's presentation, and I try not to break up the flow myself unless some significant reference is unclear. After each side has spoken its piece, I give the first side an opportunity for a brief rebuttal, and the second side a chance to reply to anything new that comes up in the rebuttal. I discourage one side from posing questions to the other.

The arguments I hear today are just about what I expect, based on the written presentations submitted earlier. I listen in vain for signs of a conciliatory nature. On the other hand, neither side digs itself into a hole from which it will be unable to emerge.

In addition to the strength or weakness of the respective arguments, I often find significant the choice of issues that each party decides to emphasize. As a mediator, you can tell a lot by a party's selection of issues. Obviously, each side in The Put Case has to address the determination of the appropriate price-earnings multiple, since that looms so large in the outcome. But I do pick up some useful information by noticing which of the accounting and inter-company issues contained in their written statements each side chooses to include in its oral presentation.

So, for instance, I take note of the fact that Executive's lawyer keeps his distance from the conclusory argument in his submission that certain inter-company adjustments (which have the effect of increasing net income) should be treated on a pre-tax basis, while everything else is being calculated on an after-tax basis. I didn't think much of that point when I read it, and I think even less of it now.

I may be disappointed not to observe any signs of conciliation, but by now, of course, I'm not surprised. What I don't want to have happen in this opening joint session is to see the adverse feelings become exacerbated.

I've come to realize that this is a critical juncture in a dollar dispute mediation—the point at which the parties should (but often don't) shift from "selling" their version of the case to joining in a search for a compromise outcome that can resolve the dispute short of litigation. Lately, while they're still together before heading off to separate rooms, I've been giving them what I call a "pep talk," to urge the needed change in attitude and approach. A verbatim version of my pep talk is contained in Appendix D, which I recommend you read before moving ahead.

The Mediator's Warning Admonition

On occasion, the pre-session submissions I receive are so nasty toward the other side that I fear this opening session—as well as the private caucuses that come later—will be dominated by non-constructive invective. I want to head that off, and can usually do so with a few admonitions along the way, either privately or in the joint session itself. Sometimes, though, a preemptive strike might be in order.

I recall one such mediation where, fearing the worst was about to erupt, I laid down the law to the parties as follows (practically verbatim) at the beginning of the initial joint session:

"I want everyone to understand at the outset that the purpose of this mediation proceeding we're having today is to resolve the dispute.

"The accusations and personal invectives in the papers I received from both sides—going way beyond the requisites of causes of action and defenses—are, in my view, antithetical to this purpose.

"If we fail to achieve a resolution in this mediation, and if one or both of you subsequently reject my mediator's proposed resolution, then you can go to court—a step that I consider very foolish for both sides, for reasons I'll go into with each of you separately. And in court, you can resume —or, for all I care, increase—the belligerence.

"But for today, in my bailiwick, I'm going to frown on those tactics. I don't want to hear how outrageous each side thinks the other is or has been. I don't want you to ascribe evil motives to each other—this is neither a criminal proceeding nor a psychotherapy session. I'd like the adjectives and adverbs used to describe even the darkest deeds kept to a minimum. That heavy artillery only makes it more difficult to bring the two of you together for a settlement.

"In my prior life, I was an M&A lawyer. I come from a background of making deals, of solving problems. The principals here are, first and foremost, dealmakers also.

"The matters at issue involve a business deal gone awry.

No one assaulted anyone or burned down his house.

"I'm here to help resolve this dispute the only way I know how—by making a deal.

"Because it takes two to tango, there's no unconditional surrender in mediation—and neither of you will be ecstatic over any ultimate resolution we reach—but you'll be putting something behind you that should have been resolved a long time ago.

"So, to mix a metaphor, at least for today, muzzle your machine guns and put on your dealmaking hats—and instead of making my task more difficult, help me get this thing settled."

I think this had a beneficial effect in tamping down the emotions and the rhetoric. Not completely, of course, but every time some accusation was hurled, I was able to state in a very stern tone, "I told you, I'm not listening to any of that stuff" – and we moved on to more constructive ground. It took until midnight, but the matter was finally settled. I wish I could tell you there were handshakes all around . . . .

Questions in Joint Session

In my early days as a mediator, while everyone was still together in one room, I would direct questions to both sides concerning the facts of the matter, the legal and accounting principles involved, the positions each had taken on the issues, and certain points raised that had thus far gone unanswered. If, after one side had replied on a particular matter, the other side wanted to comment, I permitted them to. I felt the questioning and the interplay brought out certain nuances of the issues that could prove helpful to me later on.

I handled this in open forum for two reasons. First, if one side fudged an answer—which might slip by me as the unfamiliar mediator—the other side could spot the fudge and speak up. Second, the interplay may have provided enlightenment to each business person—particularly if he heard a pet theory of his side shot down by the adversary. To be sure, there was a risk of some sparks flying during this step; but I felt that, as the

mediator, I should be able to keep things under control, and I was hopeful that the results would be worth the risk.

As time has gone by, though, I've gotten away from doing this in open forum. The reason is not so much that I think I'll find out more information privately (I may even learn less), but that I don't want to squander my credibility.

In joint session, even if I pose my substantive questions to one of the parties in as neutral a voice as possible (and certainly never in a disparaging tone), I run a risk of being perceived as favoring the other party. A mediator's most precious commodity is the presumption of neutrality with which he starts out. If the mediator loses that, he can no longer be effective. Yet even the most fair-minded mediator can't take this for granted; rather, he has to work hard to keep the presumption operative—especially if he favors (as I do) an evaluative approach. Certainly, at this early stage of the proceedings, the mediator should not appear to be concentrating his fire on either party's weak points for the benefit of the other side. Thus, I now handle this in private session.

CHAPTER
8

THE CAUCUS DISCUSSION OF THE MERITS

After each side has completed its presentation in the joint sessions, I escort them into separate conference rooms for the remainder of the mediation. In most cases, they never talk to each other directly for the balance of the time. I shuttle back and forth between the two rooms, spending anywhere from ten minutes to an hour in each place, depending on what I'm trying to achieve at the moment.

Why Private Caucuses?

I'm aware that some mediators bring the parties together for substantive discussions, but for a number of reasons I'm a strong advocate of the private caucus. The reasons hinge on the activist role I play with each side and my attempt to shift the negotiations from party-to-party to party-with-mediator.

Under my approach, I have to be able to tell a party which of his arguments are strong and which aren't—going right to the merits. The party won't like the negative judgments that emanate from the mediator, but it would be much more painful (and make the dispute harder to settle) if this were done with the other side present.

The technique I favor for resolving a one-shot dollar dispute through mediation gets away from traditional positional bargaining. I don't coax Side A to improve its offer, convey A's improved offer to Side B, urge B to improve its offer, convey that to A, and so on. Rather, I work separately with each side to reach a common satisfactory level at which the dispute can feasibly be settled—without either side knowing, until the end, just where its adversary stands. (More on this in Chapter 10.)

To bring the parties to this level of comfort, I need to discuss with each of them independently the merits of the issues underlying the dispute, after I've gotten all the information I need. The contrary dogmatic positions each has espoused, if left intact, will produce a stalemate that defies resolution of the dispute. Neither side is listening to what its adversary has to say. It's my job to get their attention—to introduce a sense of reality into the picture.

So, where appropriate, I tell a party that, viewing a particular issue as a neutral—as the judge will be looking at it, if you don't settle here—I think your position is a loser. Or perhaps, on an issue a party thinks is heavily in his favor, I see it as a toss-up.

But if all the mediator does is denigrate a party's arguments, he or she runs a real risk of undermining the mediator's apparent neutrality. Parties to a dispute will listen to, and may well be influenced to move by, the mediator's negative judgments on certain issues, but only if they're convinced the mediator is speaking from the heart—not from any kind of bias against them or favoritism toward the other side. And believe me, in the emotional context of a bitter dispute, this kind of commercial paranoia (the friend of my enemy is my enemy) can find fertile ground.

So I make a real attempt to combat this problem. I hear both parties out and engage in protracted discussions with them. I try to balance the negativity I display by speaking approvingly about some other aspect of the party's case that I think is deserving. Often I go further and seek that party's help on how best for me to communicate its strongest issues to the other side—in effect, becoming the party's agent to do a little "selling."

None of this can be accomplished with the other party in the room. And, at a later point in the proceedings, I have to be able to suggest outcomes and dollar levels and such—places where a deal might find fruitful ground—and this can only be handled in private and in confidence.

Gathering Information

I usually begin with each party by asking some questions that have occurred to me since I sent them my written inquiries or because of what I've heard in the joint session.

So, in The Put Case, I may have questions as to the legal and accounting principles involved, the positions each side has taken on the issues, and certain points raised which have thus far gone unanswered. I don't want to start out by going right to my views on the merits of these items—it would be premature. I have to work my way through the thicket first before coming out on the other side.

During these early sessions, I stay away from any possible compromise numbers and just stick to the merits of the issues. In a one-day mediation, after the first joint hour, I often tell the parties that we'll spend the next two or three hours before lunch dealing with the merits, and then in the afternoon we'll work on the dollars.

So for example, one issue here is the appropriate reserve for accounts receivable in the financial statements, since it affects net income. I probe the recent history of collections at the Company, trying to determine the extent to which the parties have factored this into their disparate positions. In the course of my inquiry, I learn that on one large doubtful account—representing a significant portion of the sizeable reserve Parent has applied—the situation has markedly changed in the past month, so that it now appears Company may well receive over several years close to 100 percent of what it's owed. I don't attempt to quantify this in terms of price at this time, but I'll definitely use the information in dealing with the merits of the reserve—and then, later on, I'll attach some numbers to it.

We mediators all have different personal styles in terms of dealing privately with a party in caucus. I always start out on an affable note and try to keep things that way as much as possible—treating it more like a deal negotiation than a dispute squabble. We may disagree, but there's no reason we can't be civil about it.

I must confess, though, that it doesn't always stay that way. When one of the disputants or his lawyer makes an assertion that not only defies common sense but has the potential to undercut the search for accommodation, I feel the need to speak up and let them know I'm not buying it.

Take, for instance, the situation of a corporate party, confronted with a damning act that occurred (or an inconsistent statement made) in some other part of the organization, who reacts with this kind of refrain: "Oh, we don't know anything about that," or "Well, that was never officially authorized." I don't let such nonsense pass. "Hogwash!" I say (although admittedly my verbiage may often be a bit more Anglo-Saxon). "It's all one company, and you're responsible for everything that goes on there. I don't want to hear any more abandonment of responsibility today."

Likewise, when a party or a lawyer is trying to elevate what's just a straight dollar issue into something approaching holy writ, I've been known to snap, "I won't have it! No verbal alchemy is going to convert into principle (with an 'l' and an 'e') an issue that's strictly principal (with an 'a' and an 'l'). . . ."

The Merits Discussion

In attempting to assess where the parties stand on the merits, I'm sure many mediators would initiate this process by asking each side in private for its "real" feelings about the issues—to get at the differences between their public and private positions. More often than not, however, I prefer another method, which I use in The Put Case. I tell each side how I feel about the various issues.

I have two reasons for this. First, I place a high value on the parties staying flexible—it's often the key to making a deal. If I press a party as to her "real" posture on every issue, I run the risk of her digging in to private positions that turn out to be pretty close to her public positions. What a party tells the mediator at this point (if asked) is unlikely to represent a realistic appraisal by the party, but rather something closer to the absolute best she could possibly hope to achieve through the mediation. The parties are very much aware they're in a negotiation (albeit one cloaked in the robes of mediation), and the mediator has to recognize this as well.

In the second place, I hope that my telling the parties how I feel about the issues may have a moderating influence on the private attitudes they ultimately express. This is partly because a neutral opinion generally carries weight with reasonable people, who implicitly recognize that they themselves aren't approaching the merits on a disinterested basis. And partly it's because there's a natural tendency on a disputant's part to want to appear reasonable to the mediator.

So, I tell Executive and his lawyer how I come out on each issue, but in very general terms, without attempting to put any dollar values on my evaluation at this time. I ask them to hold their comments until I've gone through all the issues. My presentation is in the nature of, "Well, issue #1 could go either way" [and then explaining why]; "#2 should come out your way as a matter of equity, but Parent's technical argument can't be ignored" [with discussion]; "#3 is strong for you, but not conclusive" [and here's why]; "#4 is hands down for Parent" [with reasoning]—and so on. I phrase some of my judgments in terms of how I think the issue would play out in court, and others in terms of what I see as an appropriate mediated resolution of that issue based on other factors.

Take, for instance, the issue involving reimbursement of Parent for services performed by certain Parent employees for the Company's benefit, the amount of which will diminish Company earnings. I give a lot of weight (in Executive's favor) to the fact that although these services were performed over several years, Parent never saw fit to charge Company for them, or even to raise the issue of reimbursement, until this controversy began. I'm also influenced, although to a lesser degree, by the knowledge that the work produced some collateral benefits for Parent not shared by the Company. But I don't ignore a factor pointing the other way—that to the extent these services were necessary, Company would have had to incur additional costs to obtain them had they not been furnished by Parent employees.

The big issue, of course, is the appropriate price-earnings multiple. I've listened carefully to the opening arguments on this and questioned both sides closely on a number of matters I consider pertinent to the outcome. The result obtained through Executive's approach appears to represent a quantum leap from what the parties originally envisaged when they contracted (although Executive does make some arguments to the contrary, which are unconvincing). By contrast, Parent's approach provides a more equitable (if somewhat conservative) outcome; yet it clearly constitutes a less straightforward reading of the pertinent provision of the agreement. Difficult questions of contractual interpretation abound—most notably, is the language of the contract provision clear as a matter of law, or sufficiently ambiguous that the court will look beyond the words to try to derive the real intentions of the parties? And, if so, what were those intentions? (There's more on this issue of contractual ambiguity in Chapter 13.)

I won't take you through the entire exercise, but bottom line, I can see plausible rationale for a court to go either way (or even stop at points in between) on the proper multiple. For settlement purposes, however, I believe the greater merits lie with Executive, because of the legal hurdles Parent would have to overcome on this issue in court. And that's about what I tell each party, although I don't attempt to quantify the extent of Executive's advantage. It's important to stay loose on this key issue for the time being, because this is where movement will have to occur if any resolution is to be reached.

Since my background isn't in litigation, my main thrust is toward how to accomplish a deal; but I do realize that failure to reach an agreement means there will be litigation, and that's very much on the minds of the lawyers and others I'm dealing with. So, some of the comments I make on the merits go directly to how a certain issue is likely to play out in litigation. I might not bring to this exercise the same level of authority as a former judge sitting as a mediator, but I don't apologize for my efforts either.

So, for instance, I might say about a certain issue that I think the court is "unlikely to be sympathetic to your line of reasoning." Or I'll say that proving a certain point will depend on the testimony of a certain witness "who, from what I can see, isn't likely to be too dependable"—this to the party sponsoring that witness, never to the other!

If the case will be before a judge who has shown a tendency

in other cases (cited to me by one of the parties) to come down hard on certain issues analogous to ones in the mediation, I might say to the other side, "In my view, you've got a credible argument on this point; but it's a loser in Judge X's court—you would have to count on getting it reversed on appeal. But he may couch his opinion in such factual terms that it'll be hard for an appellate court to overrule him." And so on.

I complete my rundown of the issues for Executive and his lawyer. At this point, some mediators might ask for the party's comments on each issue, in order to ascertain whether the party concurs with or dissents from the mediator's individual judgments. I don't usually proceed that way. I feel this just encourages the party to take issue with me on a number of points, resulting in more to overcome down the road. My preference is to limit the areas of overt disagreement to what's significant, which has the added benefit of providing me with some real insights into the party's state of mind.

So, after I finish my survey of the issues, I say to Executive and his lawyer, "Now, I'm not asking you to agree with all my evaluations—in fact, I assume you probably have a number of reservations—but what I want to know is whether there are any particular issues on which you feel I'm way off base?" Those are the ones I want focus on, and I'm content to let the residue sit unexplored for the moment.

Executive and his lawyer do disagree with me on several key issues, and let me know about it, but they don't feel obliged to run down the entire list. It's interesting, though, to observe the issues on which they choose to file a dissent—which serves to illustrate a theory of mine about two kinds of issues arising in dollar dispute negotiations (that I spoke about earlier in Chapter 6). There are straight dollar issues and others where, for at least one party, a seemingly sacred principle lurks underneath the dollars involved. This dichotomy occurs in The Put Case.

Parent is attempting to adjust the income downward by increasing Company's warranty reserve. To the extent the increase is predicated on a higher-than-historical level of sales (and thus based on more products in service as to which something could go wrong), it's a straight dollar issue—particularly where the resolution has no precedent value for potential future disputes. But to the extent the increase is predicated on a purported decrease in the quality of Company's products, it quickly becomes an issue of principle for Executive—"What are you talking about? My products are better than ever!"

Executive does choose to dissent on some issues carrying big price tags—for instance, he clearly takes issue with the slightness of my tilt in his favor on the price-earnings multiple, which has such a major impact on the total outcome. But still, Executive passes by a number of the other quantitatively significant issues and focuses instead on the warranty reserve and several other "underlying principle" issues—even though the dollars involved are relatively small—because he's so convinced as to what the "right" outcome of these should be. As I said before, this may be useful to me in putting together a compromise later on, especially if the same kind of possibility exists with Parent.

At any rate, I hear out Executive and his lawyer on the issues they do raise. In at least one case where their argument makes excellent sense (which, as you might anticipate, happens to be on a mid-sized "principled" issue), my view on that issue changes in their favor; and I promptly tell them so. Such give and take is an essential feature of mediation. The parties and their lawyers need to know that they're having a positive impact on the proceedings—that their presence isn't superfluous. A mediator who isn't flexible enough to admit being persuaded by a party's reasoned argument will be less able, at a later time, to convince that party his best interests lie in a particular direction.

After completing this process with Executive—and making sure not to stay away so long as to make Parent anxious—I then proceed to the other conference room and go through a similar exercise with Parent's team. My views on the merits are roughly the same as those conveyed to Executive, although not always expressed in the same words or with the same degree of emphasis. The response I receive is comparable to what I heard from Executive. Here too, I find myself changing my views on one "hot button" issue in response to the persuasive comments of Parent's officers.

At some point, though, a mediator has to stop talking about the merits—although the parties, and especially their lawyers, could go on for hours reiterating their view of things. (They always seem much more comfortable on this than discussing the dollars.) In effect, we agree to disagree on a variety of points, but now it's time to move on.

CHAPTER 9

DEVELOPING
THE MEDIATOR'S STRATEGY

T his is a good moment to send the parties out to lunch. The time has come, I tell them, for me to go off by myself and do some thinking. What I have to do now is prepare myself for the serious negotiations that are about to begin. Since the success of those negotiations is going to depend in large measure on my ability to persuade the parties to move from seemingly irreconcilable positions to a mutually acceptable compromise, I have to work out a strategy to accomplish this difficult task. I don't believe in just winging it.

Forming a Realistic Expectation

At the core of the mediator's strategy is the formulation of a realistic expectation as to where a settlement might be feasible. This is not something I share with the parties—at least, not yet—but is rather for my own guidance. What figure is most likely to resolve this dollar dispute? What number can I envision each side ultimately accepting? It won't be near the best price that either party might achieve if his adversary caves in, but rather it's a hardheaded look at what's feasible to achieve— the price that both parties (and I stress *both*) would rather shake on than return to court.

Once formulated, the mediator's realistic expectation should become the centerpiece of his negotiating strategy, dictating his subsequent actions. But the exercise isn't static. I find I have to continually reassess my expectation as the mediation progresses through the subsequent steps, and the number may

change as new factors or information enter into the equation. Still, I need to start somewhere; and, based on the information culled in the previous sessions, I should now be able to take a first cut at the task.

How does the mediator go about setting his realistic expectation? There's no single right way, and each mediator should develop his or her own technique. (This subject is explored, in terms of direct negotiating without mediation, in Chapter 7 of *Smart Negotiating*.[16]) Let me tell you how I do it in a mediation.

I start down two roads simultaneously. The first road represents an attempt to attach dollar values to my views on the various issues. This is, to be sure, more of a practical than a scientific exercise. In some cases, there may be compelling logic to the use of a particular figure; at other times a rough percentage approximation of the comparative merits will have to do.

For example, in The Put Case, there's a dispute about the appropriate accrual for vacation pay in the Company income statement. Executive has no accrual at all in his computation; at the other extreme, Parent accrues into the current income statement not only amounts from the Year but also amounts relating to prior years (since these were never previously accrued). Based on generally accepted accounting principles, the merits lay more with Parent here; but for purposes of settlement, a good outcome is obtainable through accruing the larger component for the Year and forgetting about the lesser amounts from prior years (the inclusion of which would have the effect of unduly penalizing Executive for past omissions).

On the other hand, take a different accounting issue with no such logical dividing point, and which, if decided in Parent's favor, would reduce Executive's net income computation by $100,000. If I believe the issue could go either way, I'm inclined to use a $50,000 income reduction figure. If the merits clearly favor Executive, my reduction might be $25,000, or, if Executive's case is truly compelling, even $10,000.

The second road I go down consists of asking myself what I think is the most feasible dollar amount at which settlement of this dispute can occur. To a large extent, this is a matter of feel, utilizing my negotiating experience in other deals and disputes and then trying to apply good judgment to the determination. It reflects my overall view of the merits, but also depends on the answers to a number of other questions.

Some of these questions are: What do I believe are the realistic expectations of the parties themselves regarding the mediation (assuming their expectations are realistic, as to which I'll have more to say in Chapter 13)? How well does each of them expect to make out in the lawsuit? What leverage factors are operative? How badly does the claimant need the money? How strapped is the party who will have to pay? Which side is more anxious to see the case settled? Is time an important factor? Where have the parties come from—both at the beginning and end of the initial round of negotiations and at the outset of the mediation? How strong is their attachment to particular issues, as measured by their statements and reactions to my expression of views? And finally—less scientific but perhaps most important of all—what settlement number has the right "feel"?

I end up with two rough numbers to compare—the one resulting from my evaluation of the merits and the other resulting from this amalgamation of other factors. If the numbers differ by a lot, then I have to reconfirm my views on the merits. If these views stand up, then I need to adjust the second figure to get a lot closer to the actual merits. I'm not going to be able to persuade the parties to adopt a settlement that's at real variance from my own views on the issues.

But if the two results are in the same ballpark, and I have a strong sense that my feasibility number is a good one, then I think you can guess what I end up doing! Remember, a mediator is *not* a judge whose dictate the parties must accept, nor should he press upon the parties his own view of the "right" place to settle. A mediator has to locate the spot that he considers feasible for both parties to accept (which might *not* be the mediator's idea of where a settlement *should* take place), and then be able to persuade the parties to get to that spot.

I touch on various applicable leverage factors at many points in this book, but there's one I want to focus on now. "Possession is nine-tenths of the law" is a venerable concept; and while I might quarrel with the fraction, there's no doubt it's an element of leverage that a mediator should take into account in aiming the parties at a resolution that's feasible for both sides.

To illustrate this, take a simple situation where S agrees to sell something to P for $1 million. The contract provides for S to pay P $100,000 of liquidated damages if S fails to deliver it at the closing. Now compare these three possible situations: (A), where S advances $100,000 to P upon signing the agreement as a downpayment on the purchase price; (B), where no money changes hands upon signing; and (C), where S delivers the $100,000 into escrow, to be held by a disinterested third party. Under all three situations, S defaults at the closing.

In situation (A), it's clear that P is sitting pretty, holding the liquidated damages. If S wants part of the money back—on the grounds that it was really a penalty—S is going to have to sue and convince the court to rule out of bounds a contractual provision that he was willing to live with. It's a tough scenario for S.

In situation (B), by contrast, P will have to sue S for the $100,000 to which she considers herself entitled. S is unlikely to fork over this amount in full, since he's got the use of the funds, it's the most he'd be liable for in court in any event, and he knows P will incur legal expenses. But S has real risk in court—so this one is tough for each of them.

In situation (C), upon default P will make a claim against the escrow; the escrow agent will alert S, who will dispute the claim; and the agent will hold the funds pending resolution of the dispute. For P it's like situation (B), except that here neither of them has the use of the money—so S has more incentive to settle, and the leverage tilts more toward P (although not as much as in situation (A)).

I played around with the various negotiating ramifications of these three situations in my book *Lawyering*.[17] I won't go into the details here, except to relate what I concluded as to the probable value of settlements: In situation (A), P would end up with $85,000–$90,000; in situation (B), P will receive maybe $50,000; and in situation (C), P is likely to end up at around $70,000. So, as you can see, possession of the loot ain't hay.

Just a word on the presentation of numbers. I invariably round numbers to the nearest number containing a lot of zeroes. So, if the case I'm mediating involves a sum of $10 million, I would round to the nearest $100,000. If only $1 million were at stake, I might use $50,000 intervals. If it were a $100 million, I'd do away with thousands altogether. In any event, don't get hung up on decimal points.

Having said that, though, I don't like to propose a number that's too pat—such as "$5 million"—which looks like I just pulled it out of the air to use for compromise. If I think that's about where the number should be, I would generally use $4.9 or $5.1 million, and adjust the logic of the rationale to come out there.

Relatively Realistic Parties

The dynamics of a mediation can be affected greatly by the degree of reality or unreality the parties exhibit. Unfortunately for the mediator, this isn't always apparent at the outset, although there may be signs the mediator should pick up on.

The best a mediator can hope for is that when she finally gets underneath their posturing, it turns out that neither party is too far away from a plausible outcome. To put it in positive terms, each is roughly as realistic as the other in terms of reacting to possible settlement scenarios that lie somewhere in the broad middle between their respective positions; there's a sense of movement that the mediator can generate and feed off; and her major chore is to prod each side into moving toward such a feasible compromise.

These are the mediations that generally result in a settlement, although the journey to that special place can still be rocky. Even though neither party is delighted over the outcome (because it's a good distance away from what they each hoped), it's sufficiently satisfactory that, compared with the risks, uncertainties and expenses of litigation, they're both willing to accept it and move on with their lives.

Of course, even in a dispute falling into this relative reality category, each side generally believes that the other side is unrealistic. It's no wonder, considering the outrageous "unconditional surrender" demands that are often made at the outset. But since (underneath the posturing) that's not really the case, this mistaken belief itself constitutes a form of unreality for the party believing it—namely, an unrealistic assessment of where the other side will be willing to settle. So, in cases falling into this category, the mediator may have to privately persuade an otherwise realistic and flexible party that his adversary isn't unrealistic.

This is easier to do, however, than acting as an agent of reality in the unreality cases we'll be discussing in Chapter 13. The mediator's independent assurance to the skeptical party— "Don't worry, your adversary isn't as unrealistic in private as the positions he's been taking might imply"—provides the needed credence for the adversary. Bottom line, it's easier to persuade a guy that the other side *isn't* unrealistic than it is to persuade him that *he's* being unrealistic.

I would like to think that when you get beneath the posturing, more dollar disputes that go to voluntary mediation fall into this relative reality category; and that's the type I'm focusing on in The Put Case. Admittedly, mediation works best on these disputes, where the resolution is likely to be somewhere in the broad middle between the parties' positions.

In many dollar disputes, both the merits *and* the apparent feasibility point to a figure significantly closer to the opening position (or final position in the prior negotiations) of one side than the other. For settlement to occur, that *other* party—who isn't at all realistic—will have to move a much greater distance than his adversary. The problems created by this situation are discussed in Chapter 13.

Put Case Strategy

Getting back to The Put Case, I manage, through a combination of the merits and assessing feasibility, to work out a realistic expectation for settling this case at $6.8 million. My analysis, oversimplified, is that the merits on the various accounting and intercompany adjustments tend to favor Parent, but this is partly balanced by Executive's better case on the price-earnings multiple. The net effect of the non-dollar factors points somewhat in Parent's direction. In particular, and even though Executive has been careful not to concede that it has any effect on the outcome, I sense that Executive feels some pressure to reach a settlement in the Year.

The number I've selected ($6.8 million) is closer, in absolute dollar terms, to the highest number Parent offered in the aborted negotiations ($5 million) than it is to the lowest number Executive indicated he was prepared to take ($9.5 million). This might make it seem like persuading Executive to move sufficiently will take more work than is required for Parent, but in this regard I'm comforted to know that I have an ace up my sleeve.

As I pointed out in my book *Smart Negotiating*,[18] there's one fact of bargaining life that's often overlooked, even by astute negotiators. It can be expressed by the following axiom: *equivalent dollar concessions always represent a greater percentage shift for the buyer or defendant than for the seller or plaintiff.* The reason, of course, is that the buyer or defendant is working off a lower base.

So, for instance, in The Put Case, the dollar move that I'll be looking for from Parent (as buyer) is $1.8 million, as compared to a $2.7 million move from Executive (as seller). But Parent's move represents a 36 percent increase, while Executive's reduction is only 28 percent. I expect to be able to make use of this disparity, either affirmatively or in countering any suggestions on Executive's part that he's being asked to do more for the deal than Parent.

Now, a mediator has to realize that neither side is likely to embrace with open arms any proposal the mediator puts on the table regarding the place at which a settlement might occur. No matter how logical the mediator's number or how persuasive his arguments on the merits, nothing is going to be accepted without a struggle. (I know this firsthand, having sat in other mediations in the chair of counsel to a party!) So, the mediator has to think like a negotiator. And just as I always advise negotiators to give themselves some room to maneuver, I tell myself as mediator to do the same thing.

Still, whatever I propose has to be rooted in reason—clearly related to the merits of the various issues—and capable of being a plausible (if not persuasive) final outcome. In The Put Case, having determined that $6.8 million is the optimum place to expect a settlement, I decide to aim Executive at the $6.5 million level (i.e., to be satisfied receiving that amount) and point Parent toward the vicinity of $7 million (i.e., to be satisfied paying that amount).

In planning to deal with Executive, I turn my primary attention to the price-earnings multiple. For him, this is clearly the key item—he feels he outsmarted Parent on this point in the contract and doesn't want the fruits of his victory snatched away. You'll recall that, in Executive's computation, he used a multiple of 30, while Parent countered with 15. The mid-point of these two numbers is 22.5. So, in order for Executive to feel he's won a clear victory here, I reckon he has to end up with a multiple of at least 25.

Now I work backwards to derive the net earnings. At the $6.8 million level of my realistic expectation for Executive's 20 percent of Company's shares, this translates to a total Company value of $34 million. Using the 25 multiple, earnings would have to be around $1,360,000—considerably less than halfway between Parent's $1 million and Executive's $2 million initial computations. Then I have to make minor modifications to both earnings and multiple to arrive at my starting point, which for Executive is $6.5 million.

In reflecting on how to deal with Parent (and especially its sharp-eyed CFO), I realize that the key lies in the income statement adjustments, many of which seem to rise to the level of sacred principles in the CFO's mind. Because of this, I feel the need to end up with earnings no greater than $1.3 million (much closer to Parent's $1 million number than to Executive's $2 million figure). To get from there to my $6.8 million realistic expectation requires a multiple of around 26¼, which clears the 25 hurdle for what Executive needs to get. But how would I explain such an odd number to the parties?

Then it hits me—a quite logical (and serendipitous) computation, indeed. Since I'm letting Parent know that (in my view) it has the worst of the argument on the multiple, I tell him that the multiple I'm using represents the midpoint between Executive's initial position (30) and the midpoint of their two positions (22½)—which just happens to work out to 26¼.

In fact, I like this rationale so much that I decide to go in with the 26¼ figure and stick with it all the way. To get to the $7 million level that I'm aiming Parent, using the 26¼ multiple, I need earnings of about $1,330,000—giving me $30,000 leeway to move down to $1.3 million.

As you can see, there's no question in my mind that for the dollar dispute mediator, a pocket calculator is a more important tool than the rules of evidence!

Now, I go back and work on the dollar figures for the various earnings issues. I have to be able to show how I arrived at the aggregate earnings computations for each side, although the components can differ. I'm also interested in identifying which numbers are the best candidates for modification in order to end up at the necessary levels for the deal to get done.

I should note that another way for a mediator to do this exercise is to come up with a separate range of "on the merits" outcomes for each party, where the appropriate midpoint of the range is the "bargaining" number the mediator wants to convey to that party, and the most favorable end of the range from that party's viewpoint (which is the same number for each side) is the mediator's realistic expectation. (So, for Executive the range might be $6.2 to $6.8 million, while for Parent it could be $6.8 million to $7.2 million.)

The problem with a range, though, is that each party often ignores the end of the range that's most negative to him, convinces himself that the mediator is really suggesting the number at his favorable end of the range, and then starts negotiating with the mediator from there! For that reason, any range a mediator uses should never have an extremity that's more favorable to a party than the mediator's realistic expectation— and probably shouldn't even go that far. Keep in mind also that a range detracts from the definitiveness with which the mediator may want to present his proposal, and it may undercut any finely tuned rationale developed to support it.

10

DEALING WITH THE
PARTIES ON THE DOLLARS

Up to this point, the way I've conducted the pre-mediation and mediation obviously differs from a *Getting to Yes*[19] or facilitative approach, but perhaps not so much from how other evaluative mediators operate. What I do at this point, however, does diverge from most of them. That's because of my effort— first described in *In a Nutshell*—to turn the negotiations over this dollar dispute into something approaching the way dealmaking negotiations are carried out.

My Non-Transmittal-of-Offers Technique

As I said earlier, my favored technique is to get away from traditional bargaining—carrying offers and counters back and forth from room to room—and engage in simultaneous private negotiations between myself and each of the parties in separate caucus. I try with each side to find a common resolution level at which both of them are satisfied to settle—but without either side knowing, until the end, just where its adversary stands.

My technique here sometimes makes the parties and their counsel uncomfortable—they're not used to this kind of mediation format. But I stick with it for several reasons.

First and foremost, my negotiations with each side are conducted in a non-adversarial way—more in the nature of two parties, who aren't at each other's throats, bargaining over a business deal. We may disagree on issues, and both of us tell it like it is, but there's no animosity. Each side to the dispute may be hopping mad at the other, but they respect my neutrality and understand I'm just searching for whether there's any common ground—as dealmakers do. I feel I can accomplish more this way than by carrying provocative proposals back and forth.

Second, it's clear to me that if each side heard the chintzy offers I'm getting from the other side, they'd be indignant and self-righteous—attitudes that induce them to reciprocate in kind. After all, that was a major contributor to what went wrong when they negotiated directly before the mediation began. I want to get them away from such non-constructive activities as trying to read the other guy's mind, or making erroneous inferences from the proposals the other side has made, or feeling they "have to send those idiots a message."

If, as sometimes happens, a party or its counsel expresses discomfort at not knowing where the adversary stands, I tell them that they shouldn't be fussing about the other side's foibles, but rather ought to concentrate on what makes sense for themselves. When I suspect they're trying to discern what's going on in the other room, so as to figure out how far they ought to move, I say, "Forget about those birds—just look at where you're at."

If it suits my purpose at the time, I may pass along some general information, such as, "The guys in the other room made a constructive first offer," or, "Believe me; the two of you are still far apart." But I don't offer up specific numbers or proposals.

Another reason for my approach is that I'm convinced many of the problems arising in direct negotiations can be attributed to foolish excessive actions by one side or the other that throw a monkey wrench into the works. Examples include premature "final" offers, dangerous bluffs, unwarranted threats that lead to counterthreats, and the like. A real advantage of mediation is that by keeping the parties apart and limiting the information the mediator conveys back and forth, such ill-advised exchanges are prevented from happening. I just go further than most mediators in trying to eliminate this problem.

Finally, I'm hopeful they'll be more forthcoming about the dollars this way than otherwise, because they know their number won't be shared with the other side. It makes good sense to presume that confidentiality is a positive factor in getting parties to level with me. But, to be perfectly candid here, this aspect doesn't always work with some of the tight-fisted adversaries I encounter.

Sometimes I find myself daydreaming about whether, if I were to receive a really constructive proposal from Party A (such a rarity), I would change my practice and (with A's permission, of course) pass it on to Party B? I can see a possible advantage to this—that when Party B sees how constructive Party A has been, Party B may be influenced to respond in kind.

But to my mind, even in this situation, the negatives outweigh the positives. Since Party A's proposal doesn't go all the way to Party B's position, Party B might not consider it as forthcoming as I do, and may not be influenced to reciprocate constructively. On the other hand, if Party B recognizes it as a good proposal, Party B may read the situation as Party A starting to cave in—not confident of his case—which might just cause Party B to hang tough. So I probably wouldn't deliver it—although, if it seemed appropriate, I'd comment to Party B that my talks with Party A were "going very well," adding that "I hope ours will improve to the point I can tell Party A the same thing about us."

How about a real pipe dream—that I've received worthy proposals from *both* sides (fat chance!)—would I deliver each side's offer to the other side (assuming the proposers were amenable to my doing so)? The advantage would be that when each side saw how constructive the other has been, they'd be encouraged to take it from there on their own—or perhaps with me serving as a messenger between them—to make the ultimate deal. I'm sure many commentators would say that kind of behavior should be encouraged. But to my mind, there's a countervailing disadvantage—that I lose control of the proceedings, each side starts focusing on the other guy's subsequent foibles, and who knows where that may lead. . . . Well, if this ever happened to me, at least I'd think about it—but in over two decades of mediating, it never has!

Dollar Discussions in The Put Case

Now let's return to The Put Case. I share my dollar analysis of the dispute with each side separately. I go first to the

Executive and take him through the issues, attaching dollars and numbers to the views on the merits I expressed at our last meeting. (In at least one case, though, where my view has been changed by Parent's arguments, I tell Executive of my conversion —reminding him, however, that on a different issue, *his* arguments had a similar effect on me.)

After taking Executive through my dollar calculations on each issue and applying my multiplier, I end up at around $6.5 million. I concede the imprecision of my approach, but say that what it tells me is, "If you can sell your stock for $6.5 million or more, you'll be doing quite well here." Later, I perform a similar exercise for Parent, arriving at a $7 million result; and I tell the officers that, in my view, "If you're able to buy Executive's stock for $7 million, you'd be in business."

I present my suggestions to the parties without explicit reference to their prior negotiations—it's strictly "on the merits." But when I finish, I say something to each of them to this effect: "Hey, you got yourself into the right bid-and-asked ballpark on your own—you just didn't go far enough to resolve matters." I believe this is worth saying where (as here) it's merited, because it confirms for the parties and their counsel that they knew what they were doing—they were on the right track—and just needed some help to finish things off.

After going through my analysis with each side (which I ask them to let me complete without interruption), I invite them to point out any places where they take strong issue with my calculations. I don't discourage them, if they're so inclined (and they probably will be), from putting their own numbers on certain of the issues (and, of course, on the multiplier), and then performing their own calculation to see where it comes out— even though it will undoubtedly come out a good ways from mine. A mediator can't expect the parties to subscribe totally to his findings. And the issues that each party picks to revise my numbers, as well as the arguments advanced to support their case, can be very significant. I take careful note of them, realizing I may have to use this information later on in helping to fashion the final compromise.

If the resulting gap between a party's thinking and mine isn't too wide (which is the case with both sides here), then I don't attempt to persuade or push the party at this point. It's better to let this lie for the moment; there will be plenty of time to come back to the merits later on.

If, on the other hand, a party's thinking is far removed from mine, then I have to face up to our very different views of the merits. This is good ground for the mediator, because the views of the party—who has a clear interest in the outcome of the dispute—are, to say the least, suspect. I like to think that the parties implicitly realize this, although they never admit it. By contrast, the mediator's neutral stance gives his judgment on the merits added stature. "Let's examine where we differ more closely," I might say, "because without some common ground, there's little I'm going to be able to do about resolving this matter." Some progress then has to occur before moving on to the next step.

For the first time in the whole process, this is now the right moment for me to quiz the parties separately on where they might be willing to settle the dollar dispute. Having postponed "popping the question" until now—and after extensive discussions of the issues, and following their exposure to my views on the merits translated into dollars—my hope is that what I'll hear from them will be a lot closer to my realistic expectation than if I had posed the same question at an earlier point in the proceedings.

I make it clear to each participant that I'll hold his answer in confidence and not reveal it to the other side. Its sole use is to help me assess the situation and determine whether a resolution is in the cards. This assurance of confidentiality is essential if I hope to extract a "real" number, as contrasted with purely a "positional" one. Moreover, since even the real numbers I get are unlikely to overlap or even mesh, this keeps what are hopefully "interim" numbers from hardening into non-negotiable bottom lines. Here, I might add, is where the parties' trust in their mediator can be crucial. If Executive and Parent's officers aren't convinced of my discretion, they're unlikely to level with me.

Even with trust, though, I think the best I can hope to get from each party at this point is a number lying somewhere between the "valuation" number I gave that party earlier and a number reflecting that party's differing view of the merits. This is precisely Executive's response, to wit: "Well, even though my calculations suggest that I should be getting at least $7.5 million for my stock, in the interests of settling this today, I would take $7.1 million." It's a good ways from the $6.5 million I suggested he consider, but less distant from the $6.8 million at which I'm aiming.

No matter what number a party provides in reply to my question—or what unyielding language (verbal and body) accompanies it—I figure there's some more give there. When they say, "This is as far as we can go"—and they almost always say it— most of them can go further, so I don't credit it. I'm especially unimpressed when the bluff pertains to a number that has no obvious significance and isn't based on solid rationale. So, when a party says he's tapped out, I just keep plowing ahead. Let's face it, the parties are going to negotiate with the mediator.

If someone wants to make me believe he really means to stick, he should give me a decent rationale that persuades me it's not a bluff. Here's an example in another context: "Look, Jim, we paid $10 million for this property. If we settle below that amount, we'll have to recognize a loss. That's going to cause us problems with shareholders," etc. Of course, I'm skeptical here as to what may be "creative motivation," but at least it gives me pause to consider its veracity.

If the number a party puts on the table is fairly reasonable, I don't attempt to negotiate at this point. That's the case with the figure Parent proffers in response to my question—$6.6 million ("But that's about it, Jim."). (You'll recall I had aimed Parent at $7 million, with $6.8 as my silent target.) I'm not all the way home yet, but I think I've made some real progress (from Parent's previous best offer of $5 million). I'd rather not push just yet, and I don't want to solidify the $6.6 million figure with a struggle or make Parent's officers feel they have to defend it.

If, however, the number a party provides at this point is excessive—for example, if instead of $7.1 million, Executive were to tell me that his real number is $7.75 million—then I have to confront the situation more directly or the mediation may be doomed. I'd have to make Executive understand that his number poses two real obstacles to eventual agreement. First, based on what I've learned in the other room, there's no chance of Parent accepting it. Second, since it ignores my neutral evaluation of the merits, I can't put my weight behind pushing for a deal at that level.

And so, in The Put Case, although the parties' settlement numbers don't overlap, the resulting range (which only I am privy to)—$7.1 million for Executive and $6.6 million for Parent— is encouraging. Still, a mediator should never get prematurely cocky about the end result in a one-shot dollar dispute. Too many things can happen—people can turn obstreperous, litigation can seem more of an acceptable alternative, issues "of principle" can gum up the works. And those final five yards against a goal line defense are always the toughest to overcome. So, although we've made real progress, in my mind the outcome is still very much in doubt.

CHAPTER 11

THE ENDGAME

Now we're in what I call the endgame. The movement needed at the end of a dollar dispute negotiation like this, in order to go from the place the parties are stuck at to arrive at a resolution, may not be large in terms of absolute amounts; but these final steps are often the most difficult psychologically, and some mediator-choreography is definitely in order.

A Break in the Proceedings

It's now 7:00 p.m., so the question I have to address is whether to send out for pizza and keep pressing ahead, or take a break in the proceedings. If I sense real momentum on both sides to wrap this up, the decision is easy—"One plain, one with pepperoni." Any lull in the action results in loss of momentum, and I've got no other plans for the evening.

Sometimes, however, I sense that the parties need some breathing room. They can only be pushed so far; by applying too much pressure, a mediator can risk jeopardizing the process. And in such a situation, there's usually little perceptible momentum to lose. So a short break in the mediation at this point—I'm thinking of an overnight or other brief interval—may work to the deal's advantage.

With a lengthy interruption, however, the risk goes beyond loss of momentum to the specter of reversion to extreme positions, which may prove impossible to overcome. So, if scheduling difficulties are such that the parties can't resume the mediation the next day, then the mediator is probably better advised to press ahead while everyone is still in the same building.

Conversely, if (unlike The Put Case) the mediation has thus far produced little in the way of encouraging signs, a longer break may actually be the best course of action at this point. The hope here would be that, after some time for reflection on the alternatives to peaceful resolution of their quarrel, the parties may eventually come back to the mediation with more realistic attitudes and the requisite flexibility to do a deal.

In The Put Case, I'm aware that the parties will be able to return the next day to resume negotiations. Right now, they're showing some signs of irritability and a perceptible hardening of positions. So I decide to adjourn the mediation until 9 a.m. tomorrow. Here's how I go about doing that, in order to enhance the chances of success when the parties come back.

Before meeting with each of the parties, I reassess my realistic expectation in terms of recent developments. It might be, in some cases, that one side is showing such resistance—in terms of either the merits or its willingness to advance a realistic settlement number—that I realize I won't be able to achieve my expectation, and it may be time to aim at a different, more feasible goal and a new strategy.

This, however, is not what has occurred in The Put Case. It turns out that I estimated pretty well; and depending on how the endgame plays out, my $6.8 million expectation (or something slightly higher) should produce a deal—if the parties can just get there.

Now I go back to each of the parties separately. I tell each that progress has occurred, although not enough to do a deal. Each side knows, of course, how far it has moved, but I don't reveal what the other side has done—citing the pledge of confidentiality that I gave each of them. When they express their frustration over this, I remind them: "But they don't know about you either."

What I want to convey is that movement will be needed from both sides if something constructive is to happen here. Still, I take off any immediate pressure by announcing at the outset that, after a short discussion, we're going to break for the night before resuming tomorrow. This tells them that I'm not looking for an additional move at this point, which allows them to be less defensive during this segment.

Now, I return briefly to the merits, making two types of arguments. The first is that I—the impartial mediator—don't agree with your position on such-and-such a point. The second is that the other side feels strongly about another point and is unlikely to back off. Of course, I'm most effective where both arguments coalesce on a particular point—where, in effect, the mediator's impartial view of the merits serves to sanction the other side's refusal to budge.

I emphasize different issues in dealing with each of the parties, and also focus on different facets of the same issue. In talking to Parent about the appropriate multiple, for example, I emphasize how adamant Executive is about the correctness of using the well-known outside source, since in his view that's the plain import of the contract. On the other hand, in talking to Executive about this issue, I characterize such a court outcome of that view as a "windfall" to him; and I stress the line of cases holding that courts should attempt to interpret a contract so as to give effect to the parties' reasonable expectations. Without ever quite saying it, I imply that this is what I would do if I were sitting as a judge on the case.

I have three principal aims here. First, I want to make my own determination of whether there's enough ultimate flexibility to get a deal done, and whether that flexibility is roughly equivalent between the parties or greater on one side. Second, I'm trying to soften the parties up for what lies ahead. And finally, I'm looking for insights that might help me develop a more imaginative approach to the endgame—of which, more later.

I try to strike a balance here between, on the one hand, keeping the parties upbeat about the prospect for an ultimate resolution of their dispute through the mediation, and on the other hand, alerting them that there's a real possibility of failure if they're not a little more flexible. Deep down, though, I'm pleased that they've both agreed to come back the next day and resume efforts to reach a deal.

This is a good place to break off the mediation for the night. I close with each side by saying that I hope things will loosen up some more tomorrow, and that they should reflect overnight on further movement they might be willing to make. I also ask them to think about whether there may be some more imaginative way to resolve the dispute than has emerged thus far—adding that I'll also be thinking along those lines.

Resumption of the Proceedings

When the mediation resumes the next day, I begin by asking each side in separate caucus what constructive movement they've come up with overnight. The replies don't surprise me. Instead of some new proposal that helps to bridge the gap, each side has a newly minted additional justification for a harder-nosed position than the "more generous" figure it proffered privately a dozen hours earlier.

A mediator has to be prepared for this. The constructive mood of yesterday's mediation doesn't easily survive the cold shock of a night off! What's more, each side wants me to convey this fresh justification to the other side—just to show they mean business and to send a clear message as to who ought to be thinking about the need to make a move at this juncture.

When this happens in my caucus with Executive, I react by telling him and his lawyer that I don't consider this to be a constructive step; but I'm willing to pass his views along to Parent, if that's what he wants me to do. He does, and so I comply. This isn't a very encouraging development, but frankly, it doesn't worry me too much. Even though things seem to be going in the wrong direction, I see this as a final gesture of defiance—a last salute to the ambivalence about settling that most adversaries feel—before the endgame begins in earnest.

What do you think happens when I communicate Executive's message to Parent? You guessed it—Parent responds with its own argument on a different issue pointing in the opposite direction, which (as instructed) I dutifully communicate to Executive.

So, this certainly hasn't advanced the ball, although hope

springs eternal—and maybe one day I'll find myself surprised to receive a constructive proposal emerging from a good night's sleep.

Adding a Creative Element

Now, with things at a standstill, the time is ripe for me to offer up a creative compromise that I worked on overnight. It's a new twist that gets away from the rigidity of the inexorable numbers in a one-shot dollar disputes—albeit still dealing only in dollars, since there's no other commodity to work with.

In general terms (not necessarily applicable to The Put Case), a creative compromise can serve to enlarge the pie in some way, or make something contingent on a future event, or utilize the transfer or pricing of goods and services—all in the interests of adding a new element to the equation. I find, however, that it only works when the parties are already close, as a means of getting them over the last hump—it's not helpful in the early going.

The imaginative solution shouldn't be too complex; it ought to flow from the situation without introducing an entirely foreign element; and above all, given the tense personal relations, it can't be premised on the good faith of one or the other party down the road. So, for instance, anything based on a future computation of earnings is definitely off limits in The Put Case.

First, I ask each of the parties separately if they have any thoughts as to a creative compromise. If either does, then I would explore it with the proponent. But if they don't (which is the case here), then I ask them if they would like me to present a possibility I've thought of. Each of them is curious, and since it's something new that's not on the table, neither feels threatened by it. So they give me the green light to proceed.

In presenting my proposal, the technique I prefer is to first approach the party I think will be more receptive to the notion and try to sell him on it, before taking on the other side. I realize, though, that the first party will undoubtedly want to tinker with it—and I want him to feel he's part of the creative process—so I leave myself a little room to maneuver.

Here, I try my solution out on Executive first, because I see

131

him as someone who's more inclined to roll the dice than Parent. My pitch might go something like this.

"Look, you've heard Parent say that the best-known source for deriving the price-earnings multiple produces an aberrational result at the present time. You've been arguing that this isn't really the case. So, here's a way for each of you to put a little of your money where your mouth is.

"You complete the stock purchase with a fixed payment of $6.2 million, plus an escrowed contingency payment of up to $1 million, payable a year from now, based on the multiple taken from the best-known source *at that time*—when any aberrational items should, by all rights, have been expunged.

"If the multiple is at or higher than the current level of 30, you get the whole $1 million. If it's under the current level of 15 that Parent considers normalized, you get nothing. In between these two extremes, you get $66,666 for each point it exceeds 15."

Executive, after a skeptical initial reaction, becomes intrigued with the possibilities and starts negotiating with me about the relative size of the fixed and contingent payments, the date of determination for the contingency, the levels I've picked for the outside numbers, and so on.

As a mediator, I have a real advantage in this negotiation. After all, it's supposed to be my creative solution that I'll be proffering to both sides. Thus, it has to be even-handed—a solution I can stand behind. So, when Executive presses too hard on a point, I tell him that I can't make that particular change because then I won't be able to put my imprimatur on the compromise—which it clearly must have in order to gain Parent's acquiescence.

Still, I've left myself a little room, which I end up ceding to Executive in return for his agreement to the compromise. I assure him that I won't pass along the fact of his acquiescence to Parent—I'll merely say that Executive is "considering my proposal"—unless and until Parent signifies its own willingness to go along with the compromise.

Well, the creative compromise works with the first side, but it doesn't get me all the way home. Parent balks at it—the CEO claiming that his conservative board of directors would be unhappy with the uncertain "crapshoot" element it embodies. This may, in fact, be the case; but the rejection might also reflect Parent's concern that a big chunk of that "aberration" is likely to stick around for another year!

Still, the creative proposal has served an important role, in at least three respects. One, as my attempt at a solution, it lays the groundwork for me to make a more mundane proposal later on if the impasse persists. Two, it keeps things rolling at a crucial point when the parties appear to be backsliding. And three, it sets them up for the final—not particularly creative—dollar compromise.

Reflections on the Endgame

Let's leave The Put Case for a few minutes and discuss the endgame more generally. Assume for these purposes that the parties are within a range where reaching an agreement is feasible, but there's still a tough hurdle to surmount.

What often happens at this point in the process is that both parties feel they've given their all—walked the final mile. For two decades now, I've been observing this phenomenon—where a sense of entitlement akin to "I gave at the office," mixed in with a muscular machismo and a reluctance to be seen as a patsy, join forces to clog the bargaining arteries.

Needless to say, there's lots of bold talk and bluffing. To listen to these guys, they've gone as far as they can possibly go (when they haven't); they lack authority to move further (which, even if technically accurate, may only require a phone call to fix); and they're just itching to litigate this case (though I doubt most of them want to). I try my best to disregard all this[20]—but coming from these warriors, you can never be certain that what seems like a bluff may just turn out to be real.

Above all, no one wants to leave anything on the table. This is a key fact of bargaining life that I never let myself forget—and one way to keep it in mind is to recall the negotiating scene from that memorable movie, *Pretty Woman*.

The wealthy businessman (Richard Gere) tells the stunning hooker (Julia Roberts) that he has a business proposition for her—he'll be in town until Sunday and would like her to spend the week with him. Roberts looks up from her bubble bath and says, "You're talkin' twenty-four hours a day—it's gonna cost you." Well, Gere urges, give me a ballpark figure. She does a quick mental calculation and replies with four thousand dollars. "Out of the question," he responds, and offers two thousand dollars. "Make it three thousand dollars," she says. Gere doesn't hesitate: "Done!" Roberts, blurting out an ecstatic expletive, dunks her head underwater.

Later, as Gere is going out of the door of the hotel suite, Roberts confesses: "I would have stayed for two thousand." He turns around slowly, pauses a beat, and replies: "I would have paid four."

This simply *cannot* be allowed to happen in the mediations I conduct! One confession like that, and the deal would unravel in an instant. So the mediator has to ensure that no defendant feels he could have gotten away cheaper, and no plaintiff suspects that the defendant would have paid him more. The holy grail you aim for as a mediator is to have each side believe the other went the total distance.

Anyway, I'm aware of the various techniques (noted in *In a Nutshell*) that experienced negotiators employ to get over this final hurdle; and in my deal negotiations of yore, I used (and wrote about) many of them:

- Dividing up seemingly indivisible issues, so that you can satisfy Party A's real concerns (which are generally narrower than those he has expressed) while at the same time protecting Party B's essential interests (which are usually more limited than those he has previously advanced).
- Boiling down what are expressed as sacred principles into dollars (or their practical equivalent), which can be moved around—perhaps with a face-saving device to provide a hard-nosed or insecure bargainer the ability to back off without embarrassment.
- Expanding the pie, by adding some new element to the

picture that permits Party A, who now has more to gain
from making a deal, to surrender more to Party B than
Party A was willing to consider previously.

• Swapping among separate issues—especially where the
principle involved in one issue is of more concern to
Party A, and the larger dollars at stake in the other issue
are more important to Party B—and sometimes coming
up with a "package deal" that wraps everything together
into a single compromise.

• Appreciating the significance of payments spread out
over a period of time—so the recipient can say, "I
settled for five million dollars" (the face amount of the
payments), and the payor can say, "I got rid of the case
for four million dollars" (the net present value of the
future installments).

I'm also sure that disciples of the *Getting to Yes*[21] school of negotiating would be searching for those "shared interests" of the
parties underneath all the posturing.

But in most one-shot dollar disputes I've mediated, those
techniques haven't been readily available when crunch time arrives. (I make an exception to this for deferred payments, which
can be useful in certain situations.) As for shared interests, let
me repeat here what I said in *In a Nutshell*: I find that in most
dollar disputes, when you look beneath the monetary positions
a party takes, all you find are other, somewhat more reasonable,
amounts of dollars. What the *Getting to Yes* people sometimes
seem to ignore is that these dollars are the real interests for
most business people. Money forms the principal measuring
stick of success or failure in the world of commerce—it's how
the players keep score.

So, what the endgame often comes down to is some variant
on "splitting the difference." And what I've found is that
accomplishing this is easier in a mediation than when two dis-
puting parties attempt to do it directly.

In any dispute—mediated or not—splitting the difference
only works in the endgame, and premature attempts at this are
usually unavailing. But in two-party bargaining, even when the
gap has narrowed, there's still a problem—the tactical decision

of who will suggest the split. If you wait for the other side to make the move, it might never happen. If you do it yourself, you run a risk.

Take a case where the plaintiff has come down to asking $10.8 million to settle, the defendant has come up to $10.4 million, and each side has dug in tight. The $400,000 difference is less than five percent of what's at stake, which is a suitable gap for splitting. But if the defendant offers to split it at $10.6 million, then—regardless of the caveats she attaches to her proposal—that $10.6 million number becomes, in effect, her new position. Meanwhile, the plaintiff is still at $10.8 million, so the likely resolution is going to be somewhere around $10.7 million. And make no mistake, that resulting $100,000 differential is meaningful to the parties—even if not monetarily, then for more subjective reasons.

I included a bunch of suggestions in *Smart Negotiating*[22] on handling the split so as to avoid this problem happening in two-party bargaining. Here's how I might approach it in mediation. (Keep in mind that, under my method, neither side knows where the other is at this point.)

Basically, I say to the plaintiff in the above case, "If I can get the defendant up to $10.6 million—I really don't think I can get her any higher—would you be willing to do a deal at that number? And don't worry, I won't tell her of your willingness to do so, unless she's also willing." If I get a "Yes" from the plaintiff, then I go to the defendant and say, "If I can get the plaintiff down to $10.6 million—I really don't think I can get him any lower—would you be willing to do a deal at that number? And don't worry, I won't tell him of your willingness to do so, unless he's also willing."

If both of them are willing, I go drink coffee for a while and then return to announce to both—with a big smile—that they've got themselves a deal.

Let's say the parties aren't that close—the plaintiff has moved a ways but is still asking $11 million, while the defendant is offering $9 million. I'm not having much luck getting any more voluntary moves from either of them. Here's a technique I might try.

I say to the plaintiff: "If you can come down from $11 million to $10 million, I can get behind that and try to get the defendant (who hasn't gone that high yet) to buy into it." I couple this, of course, with plausible rationale as to why $10 million is a good result for him. But at the point I say this, I really don't know for sure whether I can get the defendant up to $10 million, although I feel I have a good shot at it—and, after all, I'm not guaranteeing success.

What sometimes happens here is that, after conferring with his colleagues, the plaintiff comes back and says, "I can come down to $10.5 million—that's as low as we can go." Although this represents progress, it's disappointing—not a number I think the defendant will agree to. I express this view to the plaintiff and am cogitating what to do next, when the plaintiff says something like, "You know, if you had told us that the defendant would accept $10 million, then maybe we could have done better."

Now I know what to do. I don't negotiate further with the plaintiff. Instead, I go to the defendant and say to her, "If you can get up to $10 million, I can put the full force of my mediator's role behind that to try to persuade the plaintiff to take it—although I must tell you, he's not there yet."

If the defendant says okay, then I can go back to the plaintiff and say, "Based on my sense of the defendant, I'm confident I'll be able to get her to $10 million—so I'd like you to rethink this. And don't worry, I won't tell her you're there (if you are)—just that I'm hopeful I can get you there." If the plaintiff then okays the $10 million, I go back to the defendant and tell her she's got a deal—then whisk back to the plaintiff and tell him the same.

The tougher case would be if the defendant says, "I can't get up to $10 million, only to $9.5 million"—but she also hints that "if I knew the plaintiff would take $10 million, that might affect my thinking. . . ." At this point, it would be wrong for me to reply that the plaintiff will definitely take $10 million—all he said was that he might do so. So I respond with, "I'll see what I can do," and whisk back to the plaintiff with this message:

> "I can't tell you that the defendant will pay $10 million, but I can tell you that if she were persuaded you'd be willing to come down to that figure, she'd be much more amenable

to the concept. So, is it all right for me to tell her something like, 'I think I can get the plaintiff to go there . . . ?'"

Here's another technique I've used. Let's say the plaintiff, who was initially claiming a lot more, has come down to asking for $11 million—and I suspect he will go a little (but not much) lower. The defendant has come up from lower numbers to $9.5 million, and I sense she has some more to give. Here's what I say next to the defendant:

"Although the plaintiff hasn't come down this far yet, my sense is that if the dispute is going to get settled, the number will be in the 10's. Their CEO is traveling and will be calling in, but we can only reach him this once; so I think we have just one shot at accomplishing a deal today—there won't be any further negotiations. The good news is that they would like to settle this before we break for the holidays.

"I want you to give me the highest number in the 10's that you're willing to pay. I won't tell the plaintiff it's your number. Rather, I'll take it to him as my number for where I think a deal can be made today—a good place to settle the dispute.

"In choosing your number, there are two related things you should keep in mind. First is that the higher in the 10's you go, the more persuasive I can be in my pitch to the plaintiff that he should accept it. Second, your chances of success here depend to a great extent on the number you choose. If, for instance, you choose $10.9 million, I rate your chances of success at 90%. On the other hand, if you choose $10.1 million, I think your chances are only 10%. For each hundred thousand dollars above that, you increase your chances of success by 10%—so, for instance, at $10.5 million, I think you've got a 50% chance."

I consider this a good way of getting across to the defendant the tension that exists between saving a few bucks and undermining the ultimate objective of reaching a compromise settlement.

I recall just such a case where the defendant came back to

me with the number equivalent to $10.6 million in the above example, along with this stern admonition: "You realize, Jim, that we're providing you with a 60% chance of success—so don't screw it up!" I smiled, wiped my brow in visual acknowledgment of the pressure now on me, and worked with the defendant to construct the best arguments and rationale on the issues for arriving at $10.6 million, while comparing it favorably to other possible compromise scenarios. (P.S. I sweated profusely, but got the job done at that level.)

The Climax of The Put Case

Now let's return to The Put Case. Having reported back to Executive that Parent isn't willing to make the contingent deal, I do what any smart negotiator should do at this point—I shut up. Sure, I know what the next step has to be, but I want it to come from the parties, if possible, rather than be initiated by me.

Although my "wish list" at this point is that Executive or Parent would suggest a reasonable compromise on which they're willing to settle, my aspirations are more modest. What I'm hoping for is that both sides—or at least one—will ask me to suggest a fixed dollar compromise number today to resolve the dispute. (Remember, in this hypothetical, the mediation agreement does *not* contain my now customary provision, referred to in Chapters 5 and 14, calling for a mediator's proposed resolution if all else fails.)

My silence works; Executive makes the request. I reply that I'm willing to proffer a settlement number, but only if Parent also wishes me to; and I ask Executive whether he has any objection to my telling Parent that Executive has requested this. My reason for proceeding in this fashion is that, although neither of them will be agreeing in advance to accept the number I put forth, the pressure on each to do so will be heavy indeed following a joint request.

Executive approves my approach to Parent on that basis. Parent is more wary, but also accedes. My sense is that Parent may be feeling a tad guilty after torpedoing the creative compromise, and isn't inclined to be procedurally obstreperous now.

139

Still, Parent makes a point of noting that it's not promising to be bound by my suggestion.

If neither side were to ask me to do this and all movement toward a final solution had halted, then it would be up to me to raise the subject. Earlier in my career, I would have put the question to each of them as to whether they wanted me to proffer a compromise. Nowadays, I would suggest more forcefully that my doing so makes a lot of sense at this point. This is another juncture where both parties have to consider the mediator to be fair-minded. If they do, then after all the travail they've been through, they'll probably go along with the idea.

For the mediator, it's a little like jumping out of a plane with a parachute the first time—I have just one shot at getting this right. I need to choose my number carefully and then put my mediator's weight behind it as the fitting outcome of this dollar dispute. It should require each side to make a final move; but since neither party knows exactly where the other is, the sizes of their final moves don't have to be equal. I'll present it to each side separately, since the rationale supporting the compromise number won't necessarily be the same.

If possible, I'd like to have my number prepared in advance, so I can trundle it out without much further delay. Why so? Because I'll be trying to emphasize the *inevitability* of the number. If I have to go off and think about it for a long while, then somehow it might seem a lot less indisputable.

I'm contrasting this situation with what I do when the mediation agreement provides for a mediator's proposed resolution (what I call a PROD), and the parties—unlike here—are quite far apart as the mediation concludes (discussed in Chapter 14 and elsewhere). There, I take a week or so to give a fully considered recommendation to each side separately.

I consider it important to explain to the parties how I arrived at the number—and I always like to do this before I trot out the number itself. The reason here is obvious; once I announce the number, no one listens to anything else. Besides, this placement has the advantage of underlining that the number is the product of my reasoning—not something I backed into and am now trying to justify.

Anyway my number is $6.8 million. I go through the calculations (previously discussed) that got me there, which include slightly different components for each side, although ending up at the same place.

This is also the time to trot out any arguments I've saved (or even ones I may have used previously) as to why it's in a party's best interest to settle rather than fight. So, with Executive I emphasize how desirable it is for him to make a deal during the Year from a tax standpoint. I also stress how much higher this price is than he could have possibly anticipated at the time he signed the contract. With Parent, I counsel these top officers on how important it is to get this matter behind them without any negative publicity from a lawsuit; how undesirable it is to be litigating with the chief executive of a subsidiary; and how financially injurious this litigation could be if the jury reads the contract literally and comes in with a high-priced verdict.

When I encounter initial resistance, I resort to pointing out the relative insignificance of this final move. For Parent, the $200,000 increase called for is only about three percent of the deal. "Come on," I say, "if you're willing to do the deal at $6.6 million, what's the problem with $6.8 million?" (Well, they say, we have to draw the line somewhere—which is the usual, though rarely a devastating, rejoinder.)

I also encourage the parties to think about the perils of having to second-guess themselves. "Listen," I say to Executive, "if you don't make the deal, and then the jury buys most of Parent's arguments and comes in at $4 million, aren't you going to feel terrible that you didn't grab the $6.8 million?"

Of course, no one wants to be the first to agree to the compromise. So, in communicating my number to Executive, I make it clear that, if he's agreeable to it, I won't apprise Parent of that fact. I'll simply tell Parent that I've proposed the same number to the Executive, who is reflecting on it.

After much apparent soul-searching, Executive agrees to accept the compromise. Now, I go off to try to sell it to Parent. I also tell Parent's officers that if they're willing to agree to the number, I won't reveal this to Executive unless and until Executive has signified his willingness to settle at that figure. The Parent officers back and fill for a while, but finally agree to accept the number, and the deal is made.

It's critical that the final move appear to be a real wrench for all concerned—even if it's not—in order to make for a tight deal. In The Put Case, I don't have to worry about this. As he's agreeing to the $6.8 million figure, Executive makes an impassioned speech that he won't take a dollar less; and the Parent officers certainly imply that their purse is bereft of further coin. You never know for sure, but it appears that no one has left any appreciable dollars on the table.

After I tell each side that we have a deal, I encourage them to meet and shake on it. They do—and this time, each proffered hand is firmly clasped. By the end of the day, the parties sign a simple settlement agreement drafted by their lawyers, with the closing to take place on New Year's Eve.

And that's an example of how mediation can work in a one-shot dollar dispute. Nothing fancy—and clearly, the place where the parties end up isn't remarkable in itself. The noteworthy feature is being able to get there in a day and a half, given the litigation backdrop and the bad feelings previously engendered.

So, if you have a thorny conflict involving money that has resisted previous attempts at peaceable solution, you ought to consider the mediation alternative. The combination of a constructive climate and a neutral negotiator may be just what's needed to unlock the impasse and achieve resolution.

12

WHAT IF . . . ?

The Put Case is what I call a one-shot dollar dispute, in which there's not much for a mediator to move around to resolve matters, other than the dollars in issue—and as to those, what's better for one party is worse for the other. (The Art Case, to be discussed in Chapters 13 and 14, is of the same ilk, but the parties there are less constructively motivated.)

If I were to change just one fact in The Put Case, however, it casts a new light on things—at least in the endgame, if not throughout the proceedings. Can you guess what it is? What fact would you change in order to convert The Put Case from a one-shot dollar dispute to a dollar dispute that also might include a relationship between the parties extending beyond resolution of the dollars at issue?

The obvious answer here is the possibility that Executive stays on as CEO of Company for some period (or even indefinitely) after the purchase of his shares. You'll recall that, in presenting the fact situation of The Put Case, I emphasized that Executive had no desire at all to stay in office beyond the end of the Year, and Parent had no interest in having him remain. So that possibility was effectively "off the table" in the mediation and thus didn't enter into any of the strategy or negotiations.

But in the real world, stranger things have happened—and assuming the parties could forgive and forget their fracas over pricing the shares, Executive's continued presence is not out of the question. So, because it serves to illustrate some of the possibilities raised by a continuing relationship (or even just the desire for it by one party), I've included this chapter.

Four Possible Continuing Relationship Scenarios

I can see the possibility of Executive's retention arising in at least four different ways, each calling for different handling by the mediator. In this section, I'll briefly describe each of the scenarios; in the next section, I'll examine their differing (or common) characteristics in terms of how they interact with the negotiation of the basic dispute.

Scenario #1—"Have You Considered . . . ?"

Under this possibility, the mediation begins and proceeds just as in the basic Put Case, with neither party exhibiting any interest in the prospect of Executive staying on after the purchase of his shares. But then things bog down in the endgame—movement stalls, and agreement on a resolution seems unlikely. As the mediator, I'm searching desperately for something to break the impasse. Then it comes to me. I try things out first with Parent:

> "I'm worried that Executive has locked himself in place here. His pride (or whatever) keeps him from showing the flexibility needed if we're going to get this resolved—even if it means he'll have to pursue his remedy in court, which he doesn't seem reluctant to do.
>
> "In the hope it might loosen Executive up, would you be willing to keep him on as CEO of Company for some period of time after resolution of the stock purchase—perhaps a year or two? I have a hunch that such a show of your confidence in him might ease some of that doggedness he's feeling over not getting what he thinks he deserves on the stock."

To my surprise, the CFO of Parent replies, "We'd certainly be willing to consider that possibility. The only reason we never raised it ourselves is that Executive's employment contract terminates this December 31, and he made it clear he had no intention of staying beyond then."

That's all I have to hear. I'm up out of my chair and heading across the hall to Executive's small conference room, where I proffer something like this:

> "I just had a thought. I'm worried that, for whatever reason, Parent has dug in deep here, and appears unwilling to move to a point you'd consider a satisfactory compromise—even though they realize you would then press your suit in court. I'd like to introduce a new factor into the equation—something to try to loosen them up and bridge the existing gap between you.
>
> "Would you consider the possibility of staying on as CEO of Company for some period—say, a year or two—after selling your stock, under a new employment contract or an extension of the old one? If so, this would definitely give us something additional to work with. . . ."

To my surprise again, Executive replies, "I have no problem with that, assuming the terms are reasonable. I always thought I'd extend for a few years after my contract was up. The reason I put the shares to them now is because the price was very attractive, and I couldn't predict the future. Once we got into our dispute and the lawsuit over the price, it was the wrong time to talk about extending. I've always liked running the Company, and notwithstanding our litigation, I have no animus against those guys. But I seriously doubt that they'd be interested in me staying on, after what we've been through. . . ."

I stand up to leave, saying, "Let me see what I can do on that score in the other room. . . ."

Scenario #2—"I'd Like To, But . . ."

In this scenario, the mediator finds out during the mediation session that Executive would indeed like to stay on beyond year-end. Parent hadn't previously expressed any desire to renew or extend his contract, which was why he put his shares to Parent well before his term was up. Once the fighting started, the subject of his continuing in place hasn't been raised by either side.

So, when things begin to bog down, I ask him: "Would you

145

still be interested in staying on, assuming we could settle the price of the put—or has the litigation and mediation experience soured you on the Company?"

Executive smiles. "Hey, our fight is 'just business' to me. Sure, I'd like to stay on, since at this point I don't have any other employment prospects. But I seriously doubt those guys would want me around."

I file this away for possible use later on. Now, it is later on, and negotiations are at a standstill. So I decide to trot it out with Parent.

> "I've got an idea as to how we might inject something new into the discussion that could loosen up Executive from that hard-nosed position he's taking. Have you guys ever considered the possibility of Executive staying on as CEO of Company for some period—say, one or two years—after the terms of the stock purchase are agreed upon?"

The Parent team is decidedly cool to the idea. "We don't litigate with our employees. Once Executive went into court, that was it, as far as we're concerned." Not an encouraging response, but a mediator never takes the first "no" for an answer.

> "Well, if that's the way you feel, okay. It's just I have a sixth sense that Executive might like the idea of staying on—and if that turns out to be the case, it could give you some real leverage here. In return for you agreeing to that, I think I could get Executive to be more accommodating on the valuation issue. . . ."

SCENARIO #3—"We'd Like Him To, But . . ."

This possibility is the converse of the one under #2 above. Here, it's the Parent that wants Executive to stay on ("We don't really have an adequate replacement at this time"); but the Executive, feeling mistreated and "nickel-and-dimed" on the put, wants out—that's why he's selling his shares.

When things bog down and I decide to raise the point, I ask Executive whether he's made other employment plans. He replies that he has some feelers out, although nothing is firm. "But those damn guys in the other room [and, here, his face turns a little red and his voice rises] have now shown their true colors—" I interrupt the nascent tirade.

> "Calm down and hear me out. You've got some potential leverage here that you're not using. These guys would like you to stay on. They're willing to forgive and forget, so why aren't you? After all, you've said some nasty things about them, too. If you're agreeable, then not only can I use that to stimulate some movement from them on the put, but I might be able to get you better terms on your future employment than you now have. . . ."

SCENARIO #4—"Of Course, Executive Will Stay On . . ."

In this scenario, it's understood by both sides from the outset that Executive is going to stay on beyond the Year, and that the terms of his continued employment will be one of the issues to be actively discussed in the mediation. The reason he's putting his shares now is because he needs the funds to buy a new house.

Under this friendlier scenario, the parties would probably not even be before a judge—having decided to try to resolve the valuation of the shares through an amicable mediation before going to court. As the mediator in such a case, I would be thinking about how to tamp down any negative emotions right from the start. I might not even hold that first joint session, where the parties snarl at each other. And as for the terms of his continued employment, I might carry proposals back and forth or even allow the parties to talk directly to each other—especially if the leverage doesn't seem to be tilted one way or the other.

This possibility—which, in my experience is unlikely to arise—gets into the deal-dispute mediating that I'll be covering in detail in Part III, so I'm not going to dwell on it here.

Effects on the Mediation

Putting aside for the moment Scenario #4—in which the terms of the contract extension would be on the table right from the start—the other three scenarios introduce the possibility of Executive continuing on at an advanced stage of the mediation, when bargaining arteries over the put have hardened. An obvious question then is, once the extension issue is raised, how should I handle the "new face"? A number of possible variations come to mind, but here are three likely courses it could take:

> *Course A.* Once I get both parties on board as to the new possibility, I conduct the negotiations on the term of the extension apart from the put issue, making no attempt to trade off between them.

> *Course B.* This starts out like A, except that now I do suggest to the parties some possible swaps between the terms of the put and the terms of the extension. So, for instance, since Executive will no longer own shares in the Company (which had previously served to incentivize him to produce good results), he should probably receive a bonus keyed (directly or indirectly) to earnings. The better the terms of the bonus, the more he may be willing to back down on the put price—the more inflexible he is on the put, the more it might cost him on the bonus.

> *Course C.* The possibility exists of taking a more imaginative approach. One candidate is the deferred contingent valuation of a portion of the share price—the gizmo I suggested to the parties in Chapter 11, but that didn't get any traction there with Parent's team. Executive's willingness to extend might make that suggestion more attractive to them now.

If Executive doesn't need all the funds from the put today, how about splitting up the shares involved in the put? Parent could buy the major portion of them now at a compromise price that each side can live with. Then we can negotiate an agreement regarding the balance of the shares—perhaps a sale to take place at the conclusion of Executive's extended employment.

Of course, under that last possibility—and assuming the price for the deferred shares isn't fixed but reflects intervening events—the agreement needs to be a lot more clear about certain items, so the parties don't again end up squabbling over the price two years down the road. So, for instance, they'd have to designate a specific index to provide the needed multiple. They ought to agree in advance on procedures for handling accounting issues that proved troublesome the first time around. The agreement might provide for a designated CPA to act as an arbitrator, ruling on any contentious issues that come up.

I'm not going to go into the various issues of an employment contract (term, salary, bonus, fringe benefits, etc.), except to say a few words about one matter that illustrates a broader point. The point is that no matter how things are papered over, the fact is that Executive and Parent have lately been adversaries instead of allies, and this is bound to cause some level of distrust going forward.

So, the termination provisions in the contract extension, which might otherwise not arouse much more passion than the boilerplate in the back, now become something for the parties to fuss over. How do you define "cause"? What constitutes "good reason"? How much severance is provided? How does early termination tie in with the sale of the remaining shares (under that Course 3 alternative above)? General words and phrases (like "materiality"), used to compromise issues that negotiators prefer not to get too specific over, now require more well-defined content—with each side conjuring up its parade of horribles as to the nefarious deeds the other side is capable of. The mediator has to take care that negotiations over a relatively minor matter such as this don't get too heated—as they sometimes have a tendency to do, when you're negotiating against the backdrop of the other side's prospective bad faith—and then, all of a sudden, the whole mediation falls apart and the parties go back to war.

Raising the prospect of continued employment in a late round of the mediation may also butt up against the problem that conflicting plans have been made, or are already in place. Executive might have lined up other employment to begin January 1. Parent may well have selected a replacement for Executive going forward. If there's anything legally binding about those other arrangements, canceling them might require a dollar outlay; and then those dollars need to be factored into the resulting terms of the mediation.

Just a word about the importance of leverage here. I see a major difference in result between Scenarios #2 and #3. In dealing with #3, where Parent wants Executive to stay on but he's not especially keen on it, I'm going to be pushing Parent hard to agree to terms satisfactory to Executive on the put, so as to induce Executive to stay. I can just hear myself going at it with them:

> "You don't want a guy running your subsidiary who feels he's been screwed by the powers-that-be. The dollars on the put are pretty close—now's the time to stretch a little and bring a happy camper into the fold."

Whereas in #2, with Executive wanting to extend but Parent leery about the prospect, my pitch to Executive would be:

> "Look, those guys are hung up on the put price, but your positions aren't that far apart. If you're willing to go along with them on the put, I think I'll be able to negotiate terms for you on the extension that will make up for anything you 'left on the table' with the put—and without all those legal fees you'd be paying if you had to litigate this."

In each of Scenarios #1, #2 and #3, my inclination would be to keep the parties in separate rooms for the resulting negotiations. Although there are times when supervised direct negotiations between the parties may be warranted (such as with a highly technical subject matter), here I'd prefer to control the negotiations. I'm afraid that if I let them go at each other in person, one or the other side might slip up and revert to form—presenting a proposal or displaying an attitude that so turns off the other party as to imperil the entire mediation.

After all, these are the same guys whose previous direct negotiations ended up in a rush to the courthouse! However, I might vary my technique here and—at least with respect to several terms of the extended contract—transmit proposals between them.

You'll witness a much more extended treatment of a mediation that contains a number of issues to resolve (many of which don't directly involve dollars) in the deal-dispute materials of Part III.

13

THE ART CASE

Now I want to take you through an abridged version of a more troublesome mediation—a one-shot dollar dispute in which the parties don't engage as constructively as they did in The Put Case, and where the merits aren't so balanced. Every mediator has had cases of this type—they come with the territory. Once again, we'll view this from the mediator's perspective—posing the issue of what I need to do to have any chance of brokering a resolution. I call this hypothetical "The Art Case."

The Facts

Mr. Sella, a well-to-do individual in the throes of a temporary cash bind, decides to part with a valuable oil painting ("Portrait") from his impressive collection. He enters into an agreement to sell Portrait to a well-known (but not always well-heeled) collector named Ms. Byre for $5 million. The agreement is drafted by Byre's nephew, a third-year law student, and reviewed by Sella's brother, a lawyer-turned-novelist. A closing is set for six weeks hence, to give Byre a reasonable period to raise the necessary funds.

Upon signing, Byre gives Sella a check for $100,000, which the agreement states is non-refundable should Byre fail to complete the acquisition of Portrait for any reason, "including, without limitation, Byre's inability to finance the purchase." The agreement also contains a separate provision that if Byre "defaults," Sella will be entitled to $1 million as "liquidated damages." This latter provision contains no specific reference, one way or the other, to the possibility that Byre's failure to close may be due to her inability to raise the necessary funds.

Sure enough, Byre taps out on the financing and is unable to close. Sella demands the $1 million of liquidated damages, less the $100,000 already paid. Byre refuses to pay, arguing that the $100,000 is the limit of her responsibility. Direct negotiations between the two parties go nowhere, and each hires a capable litigator. The respective lawyers engage in some fruitless byplay, following which Sella sues Byre for $900,000.

As legal fees start to mount up, a mutual friend of the two litigants suggests they mediate their dispute. Neither of them has any prior experience with mediation, and both are skeptical, but they decide to give it a try. I'm selected as the mediator.

I ask the lawyers to give me brief submissions containing the arguments for their positions. Here's a paraphrase of the principal points they make.

Sella says the liquidated damage clause is clear—if Byre "defaults," I'm entitled to the $1 million, and Byre did default. And, by the way, the fact that the clause says "$1 million (less the $100,000 non-refundable deposit)" shows that it applies in a failure-to-finance situation.

Byre says no, no, all Sella is entitled to is to keep the $100,000 earnest money. The language you quote in the liquidated damage clause is meaningless, since the $100,000 is deducted from the $1 million in a real default, which this one isn't. The earnest money provision specifically refers to my "inability to finance the purchase" in making it non-refundable; the liquidated damage clause, by omitting those words and using the verb "default," was meant to apply only to my willful breach. But that's not the case here—I'd like to be able to close, but just can't raise the funds. And Sella knew full well I'd have to finance the purchase—that's why it's a condition of closing.

Wait a minute, says Sella—that last reference, which is to the phrase "closing conditions (including financing) having been satisfied," only occurs in the section that sets the date for the closing to occur—it's just a timing matter. And besides, there's a covenant that requires Byre to use her best efforts to obtain the financing. I don't think she did—and if she didn't, then whatever "closing condition" Byre is talking about isn't effective.

Byre replies, it's a real closing condition (not just a matter of timing); I did use my "reasonable best efforts" (the agreement language); and even if I didn't, it wouldn't undercut the closing condition. But more to the point, this isn't a valid liquidated damage provision, but instead is an unenforceable penalty— citing applicable cases to support Byre's argument.

Sella responds that it's a perfectly good liquidated damage provision, citing other applicable cases to support Sella's argument.

So now—the parties having failed to resolve their differences and poised to litigate in earnest—it's up to the mediator to see if some rationality can be brought to bear in order to settle things, without having to go through an expensive gut-wrenching trial.

The Merits

As we gather for the initial all-hands session, it's easy to see there's plenty of animosity between Sella and Byre. It erupts in their opening presentations, even after I urge them to keep the tone civil.

Sella is outraged that Byre, who sweet-talked him into making this deal in preference to other potential acquirers, "welched" on her agreement. Byre is furious at Sella's attempt to apply the clause regarding liquidated damages upon "default" to her inability to secure financing, which wasn't her fault. The back-and-forth accusations in the lawsuit have exacerbated the situation. So, too, have the combative natures of their respective lawyers—who, from what I can observe, aren't simply reflecting their clients' feelings, but really don't like each other at all.

I can see I'm going to be in for a long day—these are not the pragmatic businessmen and constructive lawyers of The Put Case.

I separate the parties and start to caucus with each side. I begin with Byre, who even in private isn't giving an inch. My attempts to engage her go nowhere. "Sella's got his 100 grand," she says, "and that's all he's entitled to under the contract." To which her lawyer adds, "And besides, it's not a valid liquidated damages clause but an unenforceable penalty."

155

I don't fare too much better in Sella's room. When I suggest that, at best, the contractual language is ambiguous, he resists the notion. "It's clear, and it runs my way. Do you see any exception for failure to finance in the liquidated damage clause?" And his lawyer has plenty of arguments and authorities for the validity of liquidated damages here.

In a case like this, where a prime issue is contractual language, one key element is whether the language is clear on its face (so that all a court would look at and attempt to construe is the language itself), or whether it's ambiguous (in which case the court would also examine extrinsic evidence to help ascertain the intention of the parties).

I'll make a confession here. Sure, I might come out differently on this issue if I were a judge called upon to render a verdict; but as a mediator, I'm generally inclined to treat disputed language as ambiguous. I can't help thinking—why else would they be here? To be sure, as I noted in Chapter 6, a mediator can't be a fact-finder—but the probable facts of the matter often do affect the approach I take.

So I tell Sella that a court could well consider the language to be ambiguous—and as a mediator, I'm inclined that way—and ask him to give me some factual content regarding the situation at the time of signing. After much urging, I do get something useful from him—although it doesn't go to resolving the contractual language, but rather bears on the liquidated damage issue. It also illustrates an important facet of mediating that's worth mentioning.

Assume that under applicable law a principal issue in determining whether something constitutes a valid liquidated damages provision or an unenforceable penalty is whether the provision is indeed an honest attempt to liquidate the damages. Further assume that two criteria for this determination are (i) whether the damage actually suffered by the aggrieved party upon breach of contract is likely to be difficult to calculate (the greater the degree of prospective difficulty, the more it resembles an enforceable liquidated damages clause), and (ii) whether the provision could be applicable to a wide range of breaches, some serious and some not (which cuts toward penalty status).

Byre has argued strongly on this second point—"It could apply to just about anything, so it's not valid."

Now Sella—apparently in an attempt to rebut that argument of Byre's on the second point—tells me that, prior to contracting with Byre, he attempted to sell Portrait to another well-known art world figure, Mr. Curator. "Think about this, Jim," he says to me. "Byre is arguing that it's not clear whether, if she breached, I would have sold Portrait or kept it or donated it to a museum or whatever—and that each of these is a different damage situation. But the fact that I tried to sell it to Curator before Byre came along shows my real intention—it's good evidence that the clause was really only applicable to a single type of damage."

Aha, I think to myself, this may be one of those moments where a big mouth can get a negotiator in trouble. In this complex world we inhabit, operative facts are multi-faceted. Propositions that, upon first glance, seem to cut in a party's favor, have an annoying propensity to turn against that party. Double edges abound; the argument you make that's beneficial for one aspect of the problem may work to your detriment on another—and the detriment may just outweigh the benefit. As a mediator, this is something I always keep in mind, because I'll sure as hell use the blunder if I can.

So I say to Sella, "Well, if you end up in litigation and this comes out, Byre will undoubtedly depose Curator and ask him what he was willing to pay for Portrait. How much was that?"

And now Sella, who doesn't realize the trap he's heading into (while his lawyer, who's fiddling with his BlackBerry, is asleep at the switch), answers, "He offered $4.7 million." I then ask, "Is Curator still around with the money?" Sella replies, "I guess so—I decided not to contact him while this lawsuit was going on."

This, of course, is a potentially devastating fact against Sella on the *other* issue—the relative difficulty of fixing the damages in advance. The knowledge that a third party exists who was willing to take Portrait off Sella's hands at a specified price means that the potential extent of Sella's damage (the $300,000 differential between Byre's price and Curator's offer, plus incidental expenses) was readily cognizable—and thus no liquidated

damage clause was needed. But perhaps of even more significance, this gives me some prime ammunition to use when I get
down to evaluating the case.

The Dollars

After much discussion on the merits, I now turn the parties to
the dollars involved.

In The Put Case, where the parties were basically constructive (in terms of "let's get this settled"), you were able to see how
the dollar discussions work when everyone is on the same page,
albeit at odds on some of the numbers. By contrast, when the
parties aren't behaving constructively, the dollar discussion is
going to be rough sledding. At this point in the mediation, after
discussing the merits, I can generally tell which type of mediation it's going to be—and The Art Case is definitely in that
second category.

In Chapter 9 of The Put Case, you'll recall, I worked out my
mediation strategy prior to engaging in dollar discussions. In
The Art Case, however, I want to get some more feel for how
tough each side will be on the numbers before devising my
mediation strategy.

In a case like this, I generally begin the dollar discussions (as I
do here) by asking each side in private, "Well, now that it's time
to settle this case, what do you have for me?" And what I usually get are very modest concessions from their initial positions.

In The Art Case, Sella says, "If I have to litigate with Byre to
get my $900,000—and I certainly will, if we can't resolve this
here, and I'll win—then I'll have some legal fees. So I'm willing
to settle this for $850,000 today."

Byre tells me, "I've already given this jerk $100,000. He
knows he's not entitled to more—I don't even think he'll press
his lawsuit if we can't settle here—so legal fees shouldn't be a
problem for me. But just to get it off my back, if we settle today,
I'll reimburse him for his expenses to date, up to a maximum
of $25,000."

My usual reaction, upon hearing this kind of thing from each
party, is to shake my head slowly from side to side to visually
express my disappointment at the paucity of the proposal. At

times, though, I have to admit I go further—saying something along these lines:

"You've gotta be kidding! What kind of concession is that? I thought we were here to try to settle a contested matter. Instead, you're looking for unconditional surrender, and you know you're not going to get it. Why did you bother to go to mediation in the first place, if that's all you have to offer?"

Well, that's a little strong—although I don't consider it so terrible to let the parties hear the frustration I'm experiencing. But whether expressing disappointment, dismay or outrage (which might depend on one's personal style, as well as on how pitiful that first proposal is), a mediator does need to provide a negative reaction. Otherwise, a party may mistakenly think he's getting close, since he doesn't know where the other side is.

By the way, this is a prime example of one reason I don't transmit proposals between the parties. Here are two adversaries who are already sore at each other. For Sella to hear that all Byre is willing to do is cover some of his expenses with a cap of $25,000—for Byre to hear that Sella's only concession from his exaggerated demand is $50,000—will just serve to further enrage both of them. Each will focus on the adversary's penuriousness, using it as a spur to reciprocate in kind. Instead, I want to focus each individual on his and her own situation—"What makes sense for you in order to get this thing settled?"

Sometimes my reaction (which might conclude with, "Can't you do better than that? You have to, if you want to settle this.") will produce a slightly better number—Sella might go down to $800,000, Byre up to $50,000—but often it doesn't. And with time at a premium in a one-day mediation, I can sense that pressing them to voluntarily improve upon those first tight-fisted offers won't amount to much—in fact, it will just dig them in deeper at unacceptable numbers.

So, in an attempt to move things along, here's what I've taken to doing to begin closing a big gap like this. I present each side with a number that represents a reasonable move in the direction of compromise, although clearly not a number the other side would agree to.

Here, for instance, I might say to Sella, "Look, this won't be acceptable to Byre, but I assume *you* would be willing to do a deal at $700,000 today, wouldn't you? That's over 75 percent [or, a better wording for this purpose, "almost 80 percent"] of the amount you're claiming."

With Byre, I might say, "Look, this won't be acceptable to Sella, but would you at least be willing to settle this for $150,000? That's $50,000 for his liquidated damage argument, $50,000 for his lack of best efforts argument, and $50,000 for his expenses? That would be a good settlement for you."

If it works, then at least I've got them into a $700,000 to $150,000 range. It's still daunting, but a lot better than where they are—and it represents movement, which is an important ingredient in one of these controversies. Then I can take a crack at slightly better outside numbers—perhaps $600,000 and $200,000.

But my experience has been that even when the move I suggest to a party is modest—and represents a level at which that side should be delighted to make a deal—its response usually doesn't come all the way to my number. Sella might move down to $775,000; Byre could go up to $100,000. Still, what I get is usually better than what would have been offered had I left the parties completely to their own devices.

I seldom suggest a number to either side that appears to have been just pulled out of the air. Rather, I attempt to support it with some plausible rationale. Note, I said "plausible"—it doesn't have to be (and rarely is) convincing or—at least with regard to intermediate numbers—even persuasive. But I believe plausibility is crucial—I like to say that it furnishes a litmus test as to whether the position being taken is defensible.

My advice to deal negotiators has long been that if you can't support a position with a plausible rationale, then don't take the position. Even if you back into the rationale used to buttress the number you want to proffer, there has to be some logic for your stand. And in my view—although apparently not in the view of many of the parties I deal with—the same goes in a mediation.

In lieu of rationale, I sometimes use percentages, as I did here with Sella. When (unlike here) percentages are used to evaluate a claim, they can create a false sense of certitude about an inherently uncertain determination. Still, they do convey a simplistic meaning in otherwise complex circumstances, and that can prove helpful.

My goal, of course, is to get the parties into an appropriate range within which a resolution might take place. Feasibility is my byword here. What I ask myself—and keep asking, because it can change as more information is revealed—is whether a number somewhere in this range is likely to be acceptable to both sides. Then, without revealing to them what I have in mind, I work on getting each side to its outer edge of the range. If I can't at least accomplish this much, then the mediation session is unlikely to produce a resolution.

Sometimes one side gets there, but the other doesn't. I thank the compliant party but tell him that his adversary isn't in the ballpark. If, as can also happen, neither side gets to its outer edge of the range, I tell both of them what I tried to do and failed to accomplish. Sometimes, this might spur a party on; at other times, they just give me one of those looks that translates as, "Well, Jimmy boy, it is what it is."

Dealing with Unreality

It's time now for me to go off by myself to assess my true feelings about the merits of the case and to consider where a feasible resolution might take place. If I determine the merits to be about equal, I'll be aiming them somewhere in the broad middle of the spread between their positions.

That's not, however, the way I feel about The Art Case. I've seen and heard enough to conclude that the merits here favor Byre. I think the contractual language cuts Byre's way; I have no reason to believe that Byre (who from everything I can tell was anxious to buy Portrait) didn't use her reasonable best efforts to get the financing; and I view the $1 million figure as more of a penalty than a real effort at liquidating the damage.

And here (as in many situations of this type), it's not only the merits that point in that direction. From what I've observed of Byre, she's not going to cough up a big sum for Sella in a case where she and her counsel clearly believe they have the merits—and where she feels, in a self-justificatory way, that she already paid through the nose (the $100,000 earnest money) for any problems caused by her being unable to close. As for Sella, although I hear a lot of bravado coming at me from his direction, and he hasn't yet turned up his cards, I don't sense the same rigidity as to outcome—I think, deep down, he knows he's holding a weak hand.

So this is a case where both the merits and the apparent feasibility point to a settlement figure much closer to the positions Byre has taken than to Sella's—let's say something in the $200,000–$250,000 range. Put another way, for there to be a settlement, Sella is going to have to move a much greater distance than Byre. Or, viewing it from another perspective, while Byre's figures are relatively realistic, Sella's figures are unrealistic.

In a case like this, persuading the unrealistic party (Sella) to move that much greater distance is hard work—partly because the mediator, in acting as the agent of reality, runs the risk of appearing to side with the realistic party (Byre). And when the realistic party indignantly refuses to move further toward the middle, the mediator can't persuade Byre that Sella (who hasn't moved down) isn't acting unrealistically, since the mediator believes he is! It's a difficult predicament.

This is another reason why I don't transmit proposals between the parties. It's not only that I want them focusing on their own concerns rather than on the paucity of the other side's proposals. But it's also the fact that in cases when I have to move one side a lot more than the other, it's to my advantage that the big-move party doesn't know what's going on in the other room, so he doesn't feel he's being discriminated against.

At any rate, this unequal situation poses added problems for the mediator. When this happens—and after re-checking my calculations—I try to determine why the unrealistic party is so far from home. How to deal with this difficulty may depend on the underlying reasons, and these can differ. Although I'll never know for sure, being able to make an educated guess is important. Here are some of the possibilities—and the answer may be that more than one of them applies.

The first occurs when the parties are companies (unlike in The Art Case), and the representatives of the unrealistic party have been given limited authority to settle, which they don't feel free to exceed. When I learn that someone's settlement authority is minimal, it infuriates me—especially since each side has assured me (in our first telephone conversation, and then again in the mediation agreement) that the representatives attending the session will have full authority to settle.

If I hear this as the excuse for minimal movement, after expressing my aggravation, I tell them to pick up the phone right now and get some more authority. This may work, but often they'll say that the people they need to contact are not available, or "We need to hold an internal meeting" on this, or such. I then probe with them whether they think they'll be able to get additional authority later on, so that a second session down the road might make sense—but I can see that we're going nowhere today.

The second possibility is that the unrealistic party just doesn't want to resolve the matter at anything approaching its true settlement value. Sure, if the other side were to surrender unconditionally, they'd accept that—although in most cases they know this isn't going to happen (but see the fourth possibility below). Sometimes, they adopt this position because it's to their advantage to keep the dispute bubbling—perhaps providing a competitive business advantage or leverage for another purpose. Or they may be sitting in the mediation because they've been ordered to by a judge, or required to participate by a contractual provision, but they have no intention of using the mediation to reach a compromise settlement. This mediation just isn't going to work.

The third possibility is that the unrealistic party absolutely believes he can't lose in the resulting litigation if the dispute isn't settled, so he's not prepared to provide (or accept) anything dollar-wise in the mediation except for what he terms "nuisance value." Here, the mediator has to interject some reality into the proceedings—hoping to change the equation by apprising the overconfident party just how far off-base his views are, and acquainting him with the risks he'll be facing in litigation.

That's different, however, from the fourth possibility. Here the unrealistic party knows his case isn't that strong—but he believes that if he hangs tough, the other side will fold. This may be what's going on with Sella in The Art Case. Unfortunately, however, people like Sella seldom voice that motive, but rather try to puff up the strength of their own cases. So the mediator has to figure this one out for himself, and then say to the Sellas of the world, "Look, if you're taking this absolutist position on the theory that the other side is going to fold, just forget it!—I'm privy to their thinking and, take it from me, that's not going to happen."

A fifth possibility I sometimes infer is that the lawyer representing the unrealistic party really wants to try this case and not be robbed of his day in court by some mediated settlement. The worst motive for this—which I'm very reluctant to ascribe to quality litigators—is the temptation provided by the much larger legal fees resulting from a full trial and the resultant appeals. More likely it stems from a feeling that he has a strong case—and since litigation is his life's work, he wants a chance to go to trial and win. Whatever the reason, though, the lawyer may not be giving totally dispassionate advice to the client regarding the relative gains and risks of settling vs. litigating.

If I sense this problem exists, I try to find a way to talk over the lawyer's head to the client. Where a company is involved and inside counsel is part of the team, I may pitch my appeal in that direction—since he or she is presumably looking out for the company, and will be aware of the risks, concerned about the expenses, and cognizant of the other problems of litigation. (Notwithstanding, I've encountered some real warriors in the GC chair.) As far as the executive in charge of the team, I'll sometimes trot out the speech I use (see Chapter 1) in my proposed resolution presentation about not "outsourcing the outcome."

A sixth possibility is that the unrealistic party thinks the extreme position he takes throughout the mediation will influence my views, and that this will cause me to push the other side further than I might otherwise do. A mediator has to be alert to this, needs to ensure that he or she is not giving off vibrations of malleability, and must make it clear this won't happen.

Finally, the seventh possibility is that the unrealistic party may just be an ornery negotiator who has to be dragged kicking and screaming for each yard of progress that's made—which can be the toughest of all these mediation assignments.

Regarding Sella in The Art Case, I surmise that his unrealistic stance is a combination of the fourth reason (that Byre will ultimately fold), the sixth (that Sella's inflexibility will influence me), and, unfortunately, the seventh (ornery negotiator). I'll need to address these as the mediation proceeds.

This may be a good time to take a gander at Appendix A— "The Mediation Morning Line"—which measures the negative effects of unreality (and also indifference to compromise) on the chances of achieving resolution in the mediation.

Termination vs. Adjournment

But alas, my best is not good enough; and it becomes obvious to me as the afternoon wanes that I'm not going to make any more significant progress today. This can and does happen— and not only in a mediation like The Art Case, where one of the parties is unrealistic. It can also occur in the equally common situation where *both* parties are unrealistic.

At this point, I have a decision to make—whether it makes sense to terminate the mediation (subject to making my mediator's proposed resolution) or just adjourn it, with the possibility of having a second session or some other form of proceeding down the road. If I thought there was some real benefit to be gained from continuing the process, I would recommend the latter course.

Occasionally I do see that benefit. If, as I've mentioned, one or both of the parties lack authority to move into a zone where a resolution could take place, and I've received some encouragement from the party or parties that such additional authority might be forthcoming ("when the CFO gets back from his vacation"), I might recommend that a second session be held— provided I'm notified in advance of scheduling the session that additional authority has indeed been obtained.

Another reason for a second session is where the case involves disputed facts that weren't clarified at the mediation, but could become clearer through further digging in the weeks ahead. Sometimes the initial session reveals that some vital information hasn't been furnished, and I've asked one of the parties to produce it for me and the other side. Depending on what the information proves to be, a second session might be productive.

At times, when the initial mediation session hasn't gone anywhere, and the parties are too far apart to bridge through a mediator's proposed resolution—but I sense they have substantially more to offer—here's a way I've tried to narrow the gap.

I acknowledge to the parties the difficulty of reaching agreement, which will require "creative approaches" by both sides (as well as by me as the mediator). So I ask each side to think about it for a week and then present to me in writing (but not to the other side) its own suggested compromise resolution of the dispute. It should be accompanied, I tell them, by rationale as to why this resolution makes sense and why the other side ought to be willing to agree to it. And I tell them that, on the basis of these proposals (and other factors), I'll then make a judgment as to whether I think it would serve a useful purpose to have another session, or just go straight to the mediator's proposed resolution.

I consider this a good idea, but I have to admit that the results haven't exactly been encouraging in terms of receiving a workable proposal. What I end up getting is some movement and even a little rationale, but it's generally swamped by additional justification for their original positions. And as for why the other side should be willing to agree to this formulation, well, forget it—there's no way either side would agree to anything approaching the other side's proposal. So, I usually end up going right to my own proposed resolution—the Mediator's PROD. But the process is still of some value, since I usually learn certain things that come in handy in devising my resolution. And I tell the parties that it wasn't a waste of time, because I'll be incorporating some of the thinking displayed in their proposals into my final one.

By the way, there's an interesting technique that Dennis Ross has used in mediating disputes between nations and factions (discussed in Appendix B). At some point—not prematurely— he asks each side to explain what *it thinks the other side can accept.*

He has received useful input from parties who recognize this as a way to reveal something sensitive about what *they* might actually be able to accept, but without having to say anything about themselves. I've tried this a few times, albeit with meager results, but I'm not giving up on it.

Most of the time (and The Art Case falls into this category), I can tell that the mediation isn't going anywhere—today or at a later date. So, now it's time to move to the next step—my last chance to broker a resolution between the parties.

THE MEDIATOR'S PROPOSED RESOLUTION

A number of the dollar dispute mediations I conduct don't get settled at the session itself, for reasons I've previously discussed.

In mediations where the parties have dug in at levels that still leave a large gap between them, and the mediator's efforts at getting them to move prove unavailing, I give it a good college try—but if I'm convinced things are going nowhere, I don't prolong the agony. I decide to terminate the mediation, subject to my proposed resolution.

In some cases, one of the parties is prepared to negotiate constructively, but it becomes obvious to me after a few forays that the other side isn't moving in any appreciable way. Since I don't transmit proposals back and forth, the constructive party doesn't necessarily know that the non-moving party has fossilized—so, in theory, I could continue to press the constructive party further toward a compromise. But I don't do that. I consider it unfair to the constructive party to ask him, in effect, to bid against himself. And I tell him so: "I'm not getting anything out of your adversary; so in fairness, I'm not going to ask you to go further *today*"—implying, of course, that I realize the constructive party has more to give, and I'll undoubtedly be asking him for it at a later date (which will occur, if not earlier, in my proposed resolution).

How it Works

As I noted earlier, there's a provision in my mediation agreements (which, for the reasons given in Chapter 5, I've dubbed the Mediator's PROD) that says if the mediation doesn't result in a mutual agreement, I will then recommend a specific over-all resolution to the parties for their acceptance or rejection—but not for further negotiation.

My method of arriving at this non-binding determination is not as an arbitrator might make an award, but on a compro-mise basis appropriate to a mediation. I tell the parties, in an annex to the mediation agreement, that it will likely be a com-posite of several elements, including my views on the merits of the disputed items, partially discounted by the degree of uncertainty as to whether such a result would be reached in court; what I've learned or inferred from my private sessions with each party; the business and financial realities and con-siderations involved; my sense of the negotiating factors and relative leverage; the feasibility of it being acceptable to both sides; and other appropriate elements that enter into a compro-mise determination.

I realize that a lot of mediators shy away from doing this, and I'll discuss in a moment some possible negatives to including such a provision in the agreement. But the fact is that I don't insist on my PROD—I tell both sides in advance that if either party doesn't want it, I won't include it. In all the years I've been doing this, only one party has objected to its inclusion—and, as I surmised then (and had confirmed for me later), he was in the mediation only because a judge ordered him there; he had no intention of settling short of unconditional surren-der by the other side.

Everyone else appears to welcome it—or at least doesn't ob-ject to its inclusion. I think they recognize that if the mediation exercise is going to be valuable and solve this problem (that the parties haven't been able to do on their own), then they might as well have an experienced neutral's view of the juncture where a compromise might be struck that will satisfy both sides. Most people who opt for mediation don't want to see it fail. And they're fully aware that if they don't like my recommendation, they don't have to accept it—and neither my number (or for-mula) nor their reaction to it will be disclosable in court.

Typically, where significant dollars are at stake in a complex case, I don't present my PROD right at the end of the mediation session, but rather a week or two later, so as to have time to prepare properly. (But compare the situation in Chapter 11 of The Put Case, where I considered it important to move to this exercise promptly.) I make sure, though, that I hold a private *post mortem* with myself right after the mediation session concludes, while everything is still fresh in my mind. At that time, I make notes as to the range I think my proposal should fall within and how far I think each side may be willing to go; I record some interesting things that were said in caucus; I develop potential rationale to support my resolution, and so on. I consider it foolhardy to rely on all this coming back into my head a week or so later.

Some mediators who make settlement proposals to parties do so in the form of a single written document delivered to both sides that contains both the proposal and their reasoning. That's not, however, the way I go about it.

Although my ultimate number (or settlement formulation) is the same for both sides, I schedule separate half-hour phone calls with each party to deliver my PROD. (I advise the parties they are free to make an audio recording of my remarks; and I do confirm the number or formula, but not the rationale, in writing after the calls.) The reason I discuss it privately with each side is that I go into detail as to my rationale for reaching the result and why it makes sense for that party to accept. Since the circumstances aren't the same for each party—and each side isn't in possession of the same information as the other, given the confidentiality of the proceedings—what I say privately to each party will necessarily differ.

A good example of this would occur if I learned (as mediator) that plaintiff Mr. A is subject to a significant negative leverage factor (say, the need to get new funds quickly to pay off pressing debts), of which defendant Ms. B is unaware. Neither Mr. A nor I would want Ms. B to learn of (and be emboldened by) this state of affairs; and yet I would definitely use it as one means of persuading Mr. A to accept my recommendation—a proposal that perhaps contains less dollars than he'd like to receive, but enough to pay off the debts. (See more on handling negative and positive leverage in Chapter 27.)

To be candid, the way I get to my ultimate number sometimes

differs as between the two parties. That's not to say I'll tell Mr. A he's a loser on a certain issue while also telling Ms. B she's a loser on the same issue. My judgment as to the "winners" and "losers" has to be the same for each party, but the weight I accord particular issues in my calculation can and sometimes does differ.

Here's an example. Let's say a claimant (Mr. A) is vigorously demanding interest on a payment that should have been made at an earlier time, but the defendant (Ms. B) is absolutely adamant that she won't pay any interest. What I might do then is, for Ms. B, have my principal number work out precisely to my proposal number, without adding any amount for interest. For Mr. A, however, I'll have the principal number work out to somewhat less than my proposal number, and then add in a difference-splitting interest factor that brings it up to the proposal number.

I don't announce to both sides that I'm doing this, although I do inform them in more general terms that what I say privately to both sides will differ. If Ms. B knew that I was formulating it to Mr. A with interest, she shouldn't mind, since it's to her benefit for me to get Mr. A to accept the resolution. And if she learned that she was being asked to pay "more" by way of principal than Mr. A, my reply would be that the principal number I gave her was the right one—but I had to discount it for Mr. A, in order to throw in some needed interest.

Another good reason to speak to each separately is it enables me to tell the party who has to make less of a move from his last position to my number that I'm asking the other party to make a greater move from his last position. Disputants like to hear that less is being required of them. As for the party who has to make the larger move, well, I simply don't mention this subject. Sometimes I get lucky, though, and am in a position to tell the defendant that the plaintiff has to make a greater *dollar* move, while being able to tell the plaintiff that a larger *percentage* move is required from the defendant. (This is a negotiating point I previously discussed under "Put Case Strategy" in Chapter 9.)

Neither side is going to be overjoyed with the compromise number, so I have to be persuasive as to why they should accept. It's important for me to get my PROD right—something that *both* sides can accept—because it's not subject to further negotiation in the mediation. (There's nothing to stop one side from later calling the other directly, but my experience is that this seldom occurs.) Each side can either accept or reject my number, and both have to accept for it to achieve the settlement.

You may be wondering whether, in a situation where my proposed resolution is accepted by Mr. A but rejected by Ms. B, I'd be tempted to urge Mr. A to give a little more (or take a little less), in order to incentivize Ms. B to accept the revised terms. I'll plead the Fifth on the question of whether this has ever in fact occurred, but I do know this much: the minute that the Ms. B's of this world think there's a chance of receiving better terms than I'm proposing, my not-to-be-negotiated recommendation loses a lot of its leverage. As a result, I make it very clear that no party should reject my proposal on any premise other than "litigation, here I come."

It's a challenge, but one I enjoy rising to—even more than if I were delivering a judgment that both sides were forced to accept (as in arbitration). It's the ultimate application of the dealmaker's mentality, given its emphasis on rationale and persuasiveness. And because I've been successful with it most of the time (but not always)—having seen the provision work in a number of cases where the parties were far apart at the end of the mediation—I believe in its potential efficacy.

A fair question to ask is, why does a mediator's proposed resolution have a chance of working—which it definitely does—in a situation where one or both parties have been so resistant to compromise during the mediation session? I often ask myself this while preparing one of my PRODs, to which I reply by recalling Samuel Johnson's venerable dictum, "Nothing focuses the mind like a hanging." True, there's no noose here, but it is a critical juncture, where the parties need to stop posturing and spouting invective in order to directly confront a serious prospect. What I'm telling them is something like this:

> "I know you don't give any credence to what the other side is arguing, but this isn't the other side talking—this is the neutral mediator, free from self-interest in the outcome.

cause if both of you don't accept it, this dispute is going to end up in a messy, time-consuming, nerve-wracking and expensive litigation."

For disputants who take seriously the future course of their commercial affairs, this does tend to focus the mind.

A Suggestion to Parties and Their Counsel

In some cases I mediate, the stinginess of the concessions on the part of one side (or more often, both sides) is what I might have expected if they were swapping proposals with each other through the mediator (which is one reason I don't proceed that way). It does *not* represent the more realistic postures that I'd hoped would emerge from my confidential process. I think I know one reason this sometimes happens, although no one has ever confessed it to me. Let me explain by using a hypothetical example.

Let's say a claimant is seeking $10 million, and the defendant's position is that the claimant is entitled to zero (a common state of affairs in my line of work). Assume there are some merits to each side's case, and some different possible damage outcomes. So it's unlikely the claimant will be able to get $8 or $9 million by way of settlement, and equally unlikely that the defendant will be able to settle it for $1 or $2 million. The likely zone of possible settlement is between $3 and $7 million—still a big range, and certainly worthwhile for each party to shoot for the end of the range most favorable to its side.

What I sometimes find in one of my mediations—in which neither side knows where the other side is, so no one's acting out of pique or retribution—is that the claimant (Mr. A) moves down to, say, $8.5 million, but no further, and the defendant (Ms. B) moves up to, say, $1.5 million, but no further. They both know they won't be able to settle at those numbers. But, even though I urge each side to get more constructive, they don't—and so it comes down to me proposing a number.

Now, it's possible this happens because each of them is privately predicting that the mediation session isn't likely to result in an agreement, so my Mediator's PROD will be called into play. And Mr. A thinks that the higher the number he's at when we break—and Ms. B thinks that the lower the number she's at—the more it will influence me to proffer a proposal that's a lot closer to where he (or she) is than to where the adversary is.

I can't wait until Part V (where the bulk of my advice to parties and their counsel appears) to say the following to a party or lawyer who's thinking that way: Hey, you're way off-base. When the only thing I receive from a recalcitrant party is an unrealistic number—even if they tell me, as sometimes happens, that it's their "bottom line"—I simply throw it out as being of little use to me in devising my PROD, and start from scratch using my own sense of things.

On the other hand, I would really sit up and notice if, for example, the claimant (Mr. A) were to say:

> "Jim, I understand that my $8.5 million number is unrealistic in terms of a mediated resolution, and that if I want to achieve that much, I'll have to litigate. I think I'd win, but I concede it's not without risk. I'd prefer to settle this, if I can do so at a realistic number that still gets me a big chunk of what I think I'm entitled to.
>
> "So I'm going to give you a real number that we'd be willing to settle this for, together with our rationale for considering it appropriate. I hope you can achieve that number, or at least get a comparable realistic number from the defendant that would create a zone within which you might be able to effectuate a settlement today.
>
> "But even if you can't, and you have to present your proposed resolution, I'm hoping that my number and its rationale will influence you as you go about making your determination. Not to "split the difference" between my realistic number and the defendant's unrealistic one—I know you're too smart to be lulled into that, Jim—but because the rationale I'm about to present may convince you that [say, $6.5 million] is a rational place to settle."

(Or a comparable speech from the defendant, Ms. B, proposing a settlement at [say, $3.5 million].)

175

To my mind, that's the smart way for a party to proceed. Assuming the rationale were compelling, I would indeed be influenced. And I wouldn't use it against them to construct a loaded bid-asked spread and then split the difference. If I could get the other side to do something similar, maybe we could even resolve things at the mediation, obviating the need for me to present my PROD.

And maybe some day (wishful thinking!), someone will actually come up with something like that. . . .

The Proposed Resolution

Here's what I do in one of these single party telephone calls to present my recommendation. After reiterating the process I've followed, I turn to my proposal and the rationale for it. But I make sure to state that if a party disagrees with my reasoning, or finds some mathematical or other fault in it, the bottom line number I'm providing is still my proposed resolution.

I review the positions the parties have taken on the key issues. It's important for the mediator to show he's taken into account all their arguments, good and bad. Then I give my own views of the merits. I express a reaction on everything (even if it's just, "This one could go either way.") and I try to say—usually in words, but sometimes in the percentage likelihood of a party prevailing—how I feel each issue will fare in litigation.

Now let's see how this plays out in The Art Case. I start by dealing with the contractual language. I tell Sella that I don't agree with his position, and I don't think the court will either. Byre's inability to close because he can't raise the financing shouldn't be deemed a "default" within the meaning of the liquidated damage clause. That reference in the agreement to "closing conditions (including financing) having been satisfied" is more than just a timing matter. And, I tell him, you've given me no compelling reason to believe that Byre didn't use his reasonable best efforts to get the financing.

With Byre, I come out the same way, but I put it a little differently. I tell her I think she has the better interpretation on the contractual language, and that a court would probably find for her. But I'd probably add, "It's too bad, though, that there wasn't an express provision making financing a condition of Byre's obligation. And it would have been better if the liquidated damages clause had contained a specific reference to the inability to finance as not coming within the meaning of 'default'. . . ." As for best efforts, here's what I might say: "I haven't seen any actionable lack of best efforts on your part here—although in litigation, you can never tell what Sella and his lawyer might come up with . . . And I must say, I don't agree with your position that if you failed to use your reasonable best efforts it wouldn't undercut the financial condition. "

Then I deal with the liquidated damage provision. To Sella, I stress that his backup bid from Curator makes calculating the damage not that difficult, thereby undermining a principal requirement of enforcing the provision. To Byre, I'm less specific—I can't pass along what Sella told me in confidence about Curator's bid—so I just tell her that, in my view, she has the better of the case here (although I can't resist adding, "I do think, though, it's difficult for a party to ask the court to rule that a contractual provision she was willing to live with at signing is really a penalty that shouldn't be given effect").

I'll come back to The Art Case presently, but first let me make a few general observations. When I complete my review of the merits, I move to the numbers. At this point, I generally tell each side where the other side ended up in the mediation session if (as is so often the case) they ran out of gas early. (I would not tell Party A where Party B ended up if Party B has proposed to me in confidence a really constructive compromise.) I want them to see that the proposal I'm presenting not only requires their own movement but also a substantial concession by the other side.

In a case where both sides have been less than forthcoming in terms of providing true compromise proposals—let's say the plaintiff is still seeking in excess of $20 million, while the defendant has offered less than $5 million—I might start this part of my presentation with something along these lines, to set the stage for what will follow:

[I'm speaking to plaintiff here; a statement to defendant would be along comparable lines] "My sense is you'd like to settle this for an amount in the $15 to $20 million range, hopefully toward the upper end of the range.

"My sense is that the defendant would like to settle this for an amount in the $5 to $10 million range, hopefully toward the lower end of that range.

"Both of these wishes obviously can't be fulfilled—not even at what each of you considers the worst end of your desired range.

"And so, because I'm trying to arrive at a feasible positive outcome for this mediation, I'm going to be recommending a number in the range that lies between your two hoped-for ranges—namely the range between $10 and $15 million.

"I recognize this is less than you'd like to receive, but given the situation as I analyze it for you, I'm hopeful you'll give it due consideration.

"As for the defendant, I knew it's a lot more than she wants to pay, and she may well be unwilling to accept it, although I have some good arguments to make to her as to why she should. . . .

"What each of you needs to do is balance the adverse comparison of my number to your desired outcome with the favorable comparison of my number to the much worse result you'd have to live with if you were to litigate this and lose."

Speaking of balance, there's a balancing act here that I'm always acutely aware of. On the one hand, each party prefers to think that my proposal is requiring even more of a move from the other side. On the other hand, I sense in each party a certain wariness about accepting my proposal unless he thinks the other side will also accept. So whenever I stress to Party A how far my proposal requires Party B to come, I try to conclude on a reasonably optimistic note—that I have good arguments to make to Party B, which I'm hopeful will influence her to accept my proposal.

Now I take each party separately through a mathematical calculation as to how I've reached my number. I don't tell them the number first, but hold it back—not only to keep their interest, but also to support the unspoken thesis (which is accurate for the most part) that the number emerged from the mathematical exercise and wasn't just plucked out of the air.

Obviously, the ideal resolution for a mediator to propose, if it's available, is one where the reasoning is clear, simple and relatively unassailable—where, once all the dueling contractual and valuation arguments are stripped away, something stands out as a compelling compromise for both parties to accept to avoid litigation. In the dozens of proposals I've proffered, such a resolution has revealed itself to my eyes maybe twice. The rest of the time, I've basically had to scrounge around.

In the typical dollar dispute mediation, I've found there to be various reference points—outcomes that either could conceivably prevail in court (such as the "litigation" positions each side comes in with, or a more rational variation thereof) or make sense as a basis for settling the dispute. These reference points—some advanced to me by the parties, some that I've derived myself; some that favor one party, some the other, several more neutral—are the basic building blocks I use in coming up with my proposal.

I then go through them, awarding each a percentage likelihood of success in court or meaningfulness to me, and multiplying that by what the particular result would produce in the way of dollars. At the end, I add up the numbers and arrive at my resolution number. (It also may contain a compromise amount of interest if the dispute is about a long overdue contractual obligation.) Sometimes, it's possible to come at this several ways that all fall into the same general dollar area, which adds credibility to the valuation.

So, in The Art Case, here's how I start out with Sella. "In order to recover $900,000 here, you have to win on both issues—the contractual language and the validity of the liquidation damage clause. Byre only has to win on one of them for her to have no liability. And I consider both of those issues to be losers for you."

This is an important point to make to any party who has a double burden like this. Even if both of the issues were a 50-50 proposition, for Sella that means his chances of winning both are only 25 percent. When the odds are against him in each—say, one-third/two-thirds—his success rating drops down into the teens.

I then tell Sella that the stronger of the two issues for him is the validity of the liquidated damage clause, on which, however, I give him only a one-third shot at winning. On his weaker contract language issue, his chances go down to 20 percent. One-third of $900,000 is $300,000; 20 percent of $900,000 is $180,000 ("which I'll round up to $200,000"). I add the $300,000 and the $200,000 to get $500,000—then divide by two (since he has to win both), which brings it down to $250,000. He'll have at least $50,000 legal expenses to try the case, "so subtract that, and you end up with $200,000, which is my proposed resolution."

I might have come out higher here—perhaps $250,000—if I hadn't learned about the $4.7 million bid for Portrait by Curator. If that offer is still available, it suggests that Sella's maximum damage here is $200,000 (the $300,000 spread between $5 million and $4.7 million, minus the $100,000 earnest money he's already pocketed) plus expenses. And, of course, I point this out to Sella, with the thought (express or implied) that I could well have come out at even a lower number—since that $200,000 is the *maximum*, and I think his chances of achieving it in court are dubious.

I might get to that $200,000 number somewhat differently with Byre—especially since I can't reveal the existence of the Curator bid. I tell her she has a 25 percent risk of losing on the contractual language (applied to $900,000, that's $225,000), and a 40 percent risk of losing on the validity of the liquidated damage clause (applied to $900,000, that's $360,000). The average of the two numbers is $295,000 ("say, $300,000"), which I divide by two (since Sella has to win on both) to get $150,000—to which I add $50,000 for the saving of legal expenses, coming out at $200,000.

After presenting my number, I try to persuade each party that it's in his or her best interests to accept it. For the more realistic party, I like to point out how much further the unrealistic party has to move. So, I may say something like this to Byre: "In the mediation, Sella only reduced his demand to $850,000. I know $200,000 will be a stretch for you, but look how far Sella will have to come down from his number."

For Sella (as well as for any other claimant who has already received part of his payment in the transaction—but never for the other party who has paid it), I include that amount in making reference to his percentage recovery. ("You'll be getting 30 percent here—the $200,000 I'm recommending plus the $100,000 earnest money you've already pocketed—on a dubious claim that you would likely lose on in court and still have to pay your legal fees." And, of course, I often add to both sides the caution (which may indeed be a reality) that "I couldn't go lower [or higher], because then, even if you would accept, the other side wouldn't."

Like most mediators, I always stress the legal and other expenses a party will have to face if the dispute goes to trial. Sometimes I factor this into my computation of the settlement amount (as I did here); other times, I simply refer to it as one of the key factors for the party to weigh in deciding whether to accept the recommended settlement.

Another factor that (when applicable) falls into this latter category is an embarrassing disclosure that would emerge from a public trial. I don't attempt to put a dollar value on this, but I emphasize to the party at risk that it's definitely something for them to take into account when evaluating my proposal.

And with corporate defendants, I never fail to make the point (see Chapter 1) about "outsourcing" the possible company detriment to outsiders (like a judge) over whom you have no control—"while my settlement proposal is good risk management."

It's only a hypothetical, so I'll never know for sure, but I like to think that Sella and Byre—after a good deal of grumbling—bite the bullet, accept my proposal, and settle their dispute.

So that's it for a dollar dispute from the mediator's point of view. In succeeding chapters, we'll examine a deal-dispute mediation containing other issues than just dollars, a multi-party mediation, and representing a party.

PART

DEAL-DISPUTE
MEDIATING

I turn now from the often stifling confines of a one-shot dollar dispute to a situation that presents a blend of "dispute" and "deal" factors—what I call "deal-dispute mediating." Here the mediator helps make a deal between adversaries that not only resolves their prior disputes (some, but not all, of which are over money), but also achieves agreements between them on current and future issues (relating to assets, liabilities, transactions, and conduct). The similarities and contrasts between deal-dispute mediations and one-shot dollar disputes are described in Chapter 15.

This kind of situation I have in mind here is a prime example of the words "Other Commercial Conflicts" in the book's sub-title. It can arise in a number of different contexts—for example, a corporate joint venture that has soured, or a financially troubled company (with too many mouths to feed) that is attempting a turnaround to avoid bankruptcy. I've always seen this as a logical direction for the practice of mediation to take—away from narrowly-defined litigable disputes and toward a more comprehensive approach to resolving conflict in fractious business controversies.

To appreciate what's involved in one of these deal-dispute mediations, we need to focus on a specific scenario. The hypothetical situation I'm using here is a mediator's-eye view of the breakup of a business between partners—colleagues who were once on the same team but have lately become adversarial. I call it "The Split-Up Case."

I've divided the analysis into five chapters, as follows. Chapter 16 sets forth the facts of the matter, discusses some preliminary considerations, and presents an inventory of the parties' grievances. The mediator's task in getting a handle on all this, and then in developing and presenting to the parties a realistic basis for resolving matters, is the focus of Chapters 17 and 18. In Chapter 19, the mediator goes about narrowing the gaps between the two sides, plus there's some scrutiny of the lawyering for the parties. The final steps to a handshake, a written agreement in principle, and a binding contract are covered in Chapter 20.

The primary viewpoint of this Part III is still that of the mediator. (The view from the standpoint of the lawyers involved in a mediation is covered in Part V.) Many of the techniques utilized here by the mediator are useful in any mediation where the conflicts and grievances between the parties extend beyond mere dollars; and as we go along, I'll call your attention to the broader applicability of what's being illustrated in The Split-Up Case.

CHAPTER
15

THE CONTRAST WITH ONE-SHOT DOLLAR DISPUTES

In the one-shot dollar dispute examined in Part II, if the parties are unable to reach a negotiated agreement through mediation or otherwise, they end up in court where a judge or jury decides the matter at issue. So, the litigation alternative forms the backdrop for the mediation negotiations—the measure against which the parties evaluate any proposed resolution.

By contrast, in the kind of deal-dispute mediation we'll examine in this Part III, although specific items are in dispute (or even the subject of active litigation), other vital issues separating the parties aren't litigable at all. Rather, they're business matters, not involving claims of legal wrongdoing, that must be resolved for final agreement to be reached.

This is a prime reason why a mediated resolution is preferable to the alternative of leaving things to the courts. It's not easy for judges to resolve disputed issues of business judgment, and they can't impose the kind of resourceful business solutions the parties should be able to fashion with the mediator's assistance.

By the way, just because some of these issues aren't litigable, don't assume that the level of ferocity over them between the parties is diminished. Quite the contrary, I've found that ill will and bad feelings in a deal-dispute mediation may be at even a higher pitch than in a one-shot dollar dispute, because the parties here aren't just quarreling over past events but about stuff that's happening currently—new grievances occurring on a daily basis. Multiply that by the high level of distrust each side feels toward the other with regard to anything with forward-looking consequences, and the resulting emotions can approach those in testy protracted marital squabbles.

There are both similarities and contrasts between what works for the mediator in the one-shot dollar dispute and what's needed in a deal-dispute mediation. Some techniques I use are comparable, such as the desirability of caucusing privately with each party in lieu of joint sessions, for reasons similar to those contained in Chapter 4. There may be advantages to bringing the parties together in certain other deal-dispute mediations—such as a turnaround situation—but not usually in the business divorce example used here.

I also believe that the activist, judgmental approach I use in one-shot dollar disputes is the best way to proceed in deal-dispute mediating. I'm sure many facilitative mediators would disagree with me here, and I do acknowledge that this is more fertile ground for their talents than when there's nothing to move around but cash. But that's just not my style. As a mediator in a case like the business divorce, I'm all over the place—pushing, resisting, cajoling, expressing my views on the merits, and proffering compromises.

Once again, however, this does not mean that the mediator should try to impose on the parties his or her own preferred solutions. Rather, the mediator must help the parties find their own mutually acceptable resolutions. So, while the mediator may have strong personal views on the merits of the various issues, he or she has to factor into any proposed resolution a healthy dose of feasibility—what is possible to achieve.

So, for example, the merits may clearly point A's way on an issue, but a resolution totally in A's favor just won't work—B isn't buying it and is unlikely to be converted. On the other hand, to "split the difference" on the issue will greatly offend A, who is legitimately convinced his cause is just. The parties have tried but failed to bridge the gap. So, if agreement is to be reached, the mediator will have to come up with a solution—pragmatic, often business-oriented, at times imaginative, and usually something a sitting judge would be constrained from considering.

On the other hand, some of the techniques I use in deal-dispute mediating differ from what I do in one-shot dollar disputes. For instance, in the latter (as discussed in Chapter 4), I usually stay away from transmitting proposals back and forth between the parties. In a deal-dispute mediation, however—especially in fashioning the deal terms on a business matter that hasn't yet become an adversarial disputed issue—I may well invite a compromise proposal from one party, suggest a few revisions, and then pass along the revised proposal to the other side.

As we proceed here, I'll refer periodically to the dollar dispute model, pointing out contrasts and similarities. What should be obvious, though, is the need for mediators to recognize that each controversy has its own characteristics, which may call for differing techniques.

There is one constant, however, that I believe pervades all forms of mediated proceedings—the mediator has to be a good negotiator. If anything, this skill is even more vital in the deal-dispute area. Unlike an arbitrator, the mediator has no authority to impose an outcome on the participants—they have the ultimate decision-making power. So, the mediator's ability to persuade, willingness to bargain, mentality to conciliate, and knack of devising creative solutions to problems—these remain the keys to resolving impasse. I'll say it again—a mediation is simply another form of negotiation, in which a prime negotiator is the neutral mediator.

CHAPTER 16

THE SPLIT-UP CASE

N ow, I want to show you how deal-dispute mediating plays out in a specific hypothetical situation. Although The Split-Up Case[23] (as I will refer to it) is entirely fictional and the characters exist only in my imagination, I have dealt with the kind of factors and motivations you'll observe at work here— they're grounded in reality. For the sake of clarity, I've kept the facts basic and the business dimensions small, but the principles and techniques expounded are equally applicable to large-scale complex scenarios.

The Facts

My evidence is purely anecdotal, but I'll wager that across the face of America there exist a slew of business partnerships whose partners can no longer stand the sight of each other. These unhappy proprietors are locked into commercial marriages that have soured, causing emotional stress, inhibiting effective communication, and stunting the operations of the enterprise.

When life together for business partners becomes unbearable, they—just like their husband-wife counterparts—have to confront the prospect of a divorce. But breaking up a business is no cakewalk. Actually, that shouldn't come as a surprise. Hey, if the partners have been unable to communicate and act rationally in connection with their *shared* interest in *promoting* the business vehicle, how can they hope to forge mutually agreeable solutions to their sharply *diverging* interests in *splitting it apart?*

The answer is: many of them cannot. When bad feelings run rampant, it's tough for the parties to discuss the thorny issues involved in a business divorce. While lawyers and other advisors can sometimes be helpful, at times these agents simply take on the emotional coloration of their principals, which does little to bolster rational discourse.

I'm convinced that the best source of help for estranged partners is an independent mediator—someone who can serve as a buffer and escort them through this sticky transition. But even though effective mediation greatly increases their odds of working things out, success doesn't come easily. This is no garden variety mediation, and there's rarely any instant gratification.

So here are the pertinent facts of The Split-Up Case, which you need to absorb in order to appraise the mediator's strategy and tactics.

Michael ("Just call me 'Mike' . . .") and Robert own a management consulting business operating under the name "Corporate Advisors, Inc." (the "Company"). They started the Company together fifteen years ago and have always been equal partners (or, since its incorporation ten years ago, equal shareholders). Although each was initially engaged in all aspects of consulting, over time Robert has become much more focused on employment and compensation issues, while Mike advises client businesses on the strategic and marketing directions they ought to take.

In recent years, the two of them have disagreed over a number of matters, many of which remain unresolved; and their relations have progressively soured, to the point where it's difficult for them to hold a civil conversation, let alone formulate business strategy for Corporate Advisors. The most recent disputed issue has been whether or not the Company should take out a large bank loan in order to expand the business by opening offices in two nearby cities. Mike is pushing the expansion; Robert opposes the move.

The Company's board of directors consists of three members—Mike, Robert, and the Company's lawyer, Larry. The certificate of incorporation of Corporate Advisors, Inc. provides that decisions concerning certain important items of business (such as the sale or dissolution of the business) require unanimity among all three directors for passage; other matters can be decided by majority vote. As a strictly legal matter, it's unclear whether the expansion decision comes under the unanimity requirement.

When this decision came to a head at a board meeting, the vote was two-to-one in favor of taking out the loan and expanding—Mike having convinced Larry it would be a good idea. Mike and Larry treated this as the requisite approval, contacted the bank and began taking other steps related to the planned expansion. Robert countered with a lawsuit to enjoin them from going ahead in the absence of a unanimous vote. Feelings were running high, and the two partners rarely spoke to each other.

The judge assigned to the case called in the parties and addressed them and their lawyers in the following vein (which I'll paraphrase): "The issue before me—whether or not unanimity is required for the loan and expansion—is a legal matter, which I can certainly decide if you wish me to. But whatever way I decide, it's not going to resolve your larger problem, and will probably only serve to further exacerbate your relations. The two of you are trying to jointly run a company, but you're not even talking to each other. So, I recommend that, before I rule, you seek out a mediator who has experience in business-related matters, to help you find a way out of this morass you're in— which might then make a judicial resolution of the voting issue unnecessary."

As a result of the judge's recommendation, the parties have asked me to serve as the mediator. I have a preliminary meeting with the lawyers for each side—Kyle representing Mike, and Brenda representing Robert. (Larry, who is clearly conflicted, is not involved on behalf of either party.) From this meeting and the court papers they furnish me, I become aware of a number of matters other than expansion that are agitating the parties.

In order to reach any resolution between them, I'll have to deal with such historical issues in dispute as: (i) allegedly unauthorized actions by one partner on behalf of the Company, not disclosed to the other partner until discovered independently, which actions have turned out badly; (ii) more generalized charges by each regarding the other's mismanagement of the Company's business to its financial detriment; and (iii) transactions by one partner with the Company that were not authorized by its board of directors, resulting in the depletion of Company funds. In addition, if a split-up proves to be the best way to go, there will be all the "deal" issues of dividing assets and liabilities, as well as developing a road map to keep the ex-partners from clashing in the future.

I'm interested in the challenge posed by The Split-Up Case and decide to take on the role of mediator to help the parties come up with a satisfactory resolution. I know full well (and warn the lawyers) not to expect instant gratification here, but rather to envision a possibly lengthy process, where success is not foreordained. (Because each situation is different, I can't quantify the duration for the reader; but in my experience, it's more likely to be a matter of months than days or even weeks.)

Before beginning the mediation, I urge the parties (through their lawyers) to reserve sufficient time from their daily chores to see this through with expedition—pointing out that the shorter the period, the better it is for the business. I also want their clients to understand that neither will get everything he desires—that both will be called upon to make concessions and compromises. It's a point I'll be emphasizing with the parties when we meet. For now, I ask Kyle and Brenda to report back to me that they've conveyed my words to their clients, who have confirmed their willingness to actively participate.

Threshold Matters; Categories of Issues

Before getting into the mediation itself, I want to touch on some preliminaries of note.

There are two threshold matters that the mediator must confront in a business divorce. (Analogous thresholds exist in other deal-dispute situations.) First is whether the situation is indeed ripe for a split-up. This is the initial determination a mediator ought to help the parties make—is divorce the best solution? Can the partners' relationship be improved to the point where no divorce need occur? Or, even if a dramatic upgrade in relations appears unlikely, is the *status quo* preferable to a messy split-up?

This may not be an easy call for the mediator. After all, he or she is viewing the principals in a carpeted conference room, rather than "on the job." The real questions are how they relate in *their* office and whether they can run the business, given the friction between them. Still, unless the parties come to the first session having already made the decision to part company, I want to form my own judgment as to the *status quo* alternative and help the parties explore their options. For purposes of this Part III, however, let's assume the rupture can't be healed, and I'm convinced the parties should go their separate ways.

Once a divorce outcome is evident, the second threshold question is what form the split-up ought to take. The laws, charter documents, and agreements governing the business enterprise may well provide for its dissolution, but these rarely lay out a detailed road map for both parties to follow—and few partners would relish getting a judge involved in overseeing the distribution of their assets and liabilities.

One obvious possibility is for the partners to sell the business to a third party, distribute the proceeds, and go their separate ways. This only works, however, if the third party doesn't require their personal services following the acquisition. Alternatively, one partner may buy out the other's interest in the business, with the seller taking early retirement. Here, the main concern is to reach agreement on a mutually satisfactory price and other terms for the buyout—a resolution where the business divorce and dollar dispute come closer analytically.

My working hypothesis, however, is that in many business-divorce situations, *both* parties want to remain at work, and that's often the best solution. It satisfies each partner's need to continue pursuing what he or she has built up over the years. Moreover, it minimizes the significance of the tough valuation issue in a buyout by one partner—what's the business worth? Where the business is divided between the parties, many matters can be resolved on the basis of relative entitlement rather than absolute dollar amounts. So, for purposes of this Part III, I've assumed that finding a way to keep both partners in business forms a crucial element of the mediation.

The issues in a business divorce—as well as in other deal-dispute mediations—typically break down into three general categories: those related to the past, the present, and the future.

Past issues are usually of the who-did-what-to-whom or who-milked-the-company variety. Each party is indignant over what the other has done (or failed to do). Although some of these deeds may require righting, perhaps by moving dollars around, not all of them will. For example, those in the nature of mis-management may be impractical to resolve. A central role for the mediator in a deal-dispute situation is to strike a workable balance here. The partners need someone impartial to tell them that, in one instance, A should pay B to make up for A's misfeasance, but in another case, B just has to swallow hard and get on with his life.

The present day issues involve how to divide the assets, liabilities, employees, and customers/clients of the business between the partners. The split should be both equitable and practical. The partners may be less than candid as to their wants and needs—afraid that by showing interest in getting something, they will raise its ante, or by seeming disinterested in an item headed for the other partner, they diminish its worth. The mediator's ability to find out privately from each party what he or she needs or really wants is crucial to brokering a deal between them on these matters.

Issues concerning the future are of two general types. Some arise because the former partners will now become competitors. The mediator should explore ways to minimize direct competition between them. Perhaps there are two non-competitive businesses, where partner A can take one and partner B the other. Or a geographic split may make sense—one partner conducting operations west of the Mississippi and the other east. Or they can agree to a division of existing customers or clients.

The other future aspect relates to matters that cannot be totally resolved at closing—an asset with substantial unrealized potential or a liability of uncertain dimension. The mediator has to keep in mind that solutions contingent on future events raise bothersome concerns and should be kept to a minimum. Likewise, the unsettling aspect of one partner looking over the

other's shoulder can only lead to more recriminations down the road.

Initial Steps; The Open Session

The initial steps of a deal-dispute mediation are similar to those spelled out in Chapter 5 for the one-shot dollar dispute. I'll restrict my comments here to certain aspects of particular importance.

The parties in deal-dispute mediations need to agree not only to refrain from pursuing their court case while they're engaged in the mediation (as is equally true in dollar disputes), but also not to take actions relative to the business that might upset the applecart. In this case, I insist they put the disputed expansion on hold, pending the outcome of our process.

The most crucial ground rule of all in a deal-dispute mediation is that the parties themselves personally commit to active involvement in the process. This isn't something Mike and Robert can delegate to their lawyers or business advisors. Reaching any kind of accord with the parties right there on the premises is tough enough; but if they're not around—and thus free to sharpshoot at whatever is decided—little lasting progress will occur.

I spoke at length in Chapter 14 about the provision in the mediation agreement calling for a mediator's proposed resolution if the mediation doesn't otherwise produce agreement. Although it makes a lot of sense to have this also in deal-dispute mediations, let's assume for purposes of The Split-Up Case that the agreement has no such provision.

On the subject of what I can and cannot do with information conveyed to me privately, here's the compromise I propose. As to allegations that one party is making against the other (or replies to those allegations), I intend to assume (unless specifically advised otherwise) that I'm free to relate these to the other side. After all, if such charges are intended to influence my thinking, then the other side should be given an opportunity to respond. In the most crucial area of confidence, however—a party's private sentiments about the *resolution* of an issue—I'll keep these confidential unless receiving explicit permission otherwise. I tell the parties that if they have any doubts as to which category something falls into, they ought to label it clearly.

As usual, I probe with the parties their prior negotiations on the issues before us. I used to do this when they were together; now, I'm more likely to do it with each in private, for the reasons described in Chapter 6. In The Split-Up Case, no movement to speak of towards a negotiated resolution has taken place. The sole reason the parties are in my conference room is because the judge suggested it made sense. So, there's little help here; but at least we don't have any prior unreasonable demands or spurned proposals that could impede future progress.

As in the dollar dispute, I've asked each party to furnish me (and the other side) with a written statement, setting forth his views on the issues in dispute, and appending copies of any key documents involved or authorities cited. These are helpful in preparing me for what is to come. My sense is that a mediator who takes too long at early sessions to understand what's involved can lose the confidence of the parties—I want to be constructive right from day one.

At the outset of any mediation, I favor letting the parties and their counsel present affirmative statements of their positions on the disputed issues in an open session with everyone present. In the one-shot dollar dispute, this usually takes the form of the litigators (who are about to go at each other in court) arguing why the outcome of the mediation should be favorable to their client. I'm sure that some mediators—especially those who utilize a facilitative approach—would skip this step in a deal-dispute mediation, as just exacerbating the bad feeling already present. But as I noted in Chapters 5 and 7, I still consider this useful for psychological reasons (both sides are able to say they gave it their best shot), for the possibility that one side's statement will influence the other side's decision-maker, and for such insights into relative strength and weakness as the mediator might gain through the parties' choice of issues and effectiveness of presentation.

In this phase of many deal-dispute mediations, there is less discussion of the merits of disputed issues and more generalized comments about how aggrieved each party feels over the other's shortcomings and depredations. This does not serve to influence the other party, who listens with fists clenched, itching to reply in kind. I also find it less useful from the mediator's standpoint, except for one crucial item: this is my sole chance to observe in person how the partners interact with each other.

In The Split-Up Case, the diatribes I hear from Mike and Robert and their lawyers are about what I expect. There is precious little talk about the unanimity provisions of the Company's certificate of incorporation or even the merits of expansion; instead, we're treated by both sides to a rash of invective about what a scoundrel (and how incompetent) the other partner is. Any sign of conciliation is missing—there appears to be a total failure of communication between them. My first impression is that these people are no longer capable of being partners, but I reserve judgment on that score until I can speak to each privately—perhaps they'll display a different coloration outside each other's presence.

Hearing Grievances in Private Caucus

The next step, which I consider necessary, is not pleasant for the mediator. This is where each of the parties, in private, lets down his hair about what a rogue he has for a partner—and, incidentally, what a reasonable person the speaker is. (Such venting isn't limited to partnership situations, but is endemic in many deal-dispute mediations.) As a mediator, you may be tempted to cut this short, or term some matters irrelevant, or ask for a synopsis; but my advice is to sit there and listen to the entire exposition.

It's important for both parties to feel you've heard and absorbed whatever they have to say—it increases their comfort level with the process. Although I sometimes ask clarifying questions, I don't usually take issue with their version of the facts at this time; and I save any comments about significance until later on.

After hearing both sides out fully, I then go back to each of them with a synopsis of the other party's differing version of particular events (having confirmed everyone's willingness to share this information). I take care to emphasize that what I'm conveying is not *my* reaction. At this early stage, I don't think the mediator ought to be critical of or endorse the allegations he's transmitting and should guard against inadvertently giving that appearance. Successful mediation ultimately depends on building trust, calling for the mediator to exhibit a sense of even-handedness for the hard work ahead.

Although this step in the mediation usually evokes some outcries of rage and incredulity, things could even be worse if the mediator doesn't exercise some restraint in telling tales. I don't consider it necessary to transmit every gratuitous slur and innuendo that comes my way. Purely personal stuff, for example—the ire displayed over perceived insults to kith and kin—can usually be excluded. After all, the mediator isn't merely a tape recorder; a bit of judgment is appropriate in deciding whether something is pertinent or simply inflammatory.

I see this step as serving at least five purposes:

(i) letting the parties get everything off their chests once and for all, so that afterwards they can get down to the hard work of devising a rational resolution to their impasse;

(ii) providing the mediator with relevant information to factor in to his developing views of the merits on some contested issues;

(iii) clearing up any actual misunderstandings by the parties, to turn them into non-issues;

(iv) giving the mediator some clues as to whether the lawyers or other advisors who attend these caucuses with their principals are likely to be helpful, harmful, or neutral in bringing the parties together; and

(v) (with particular reference to The Split-Up Case) laying the basis for the mediator's advice to the parties as to whether (a) it will be possible to save the Company in its present form, (b) the status quo is better than the alternatives, (c) the Company is a candidate for a sale to a third party or for one partner buying out the other, or (d) (assuming both want to stay in business) a split-up of the Company is feasible.

What I learn from Mike and Robert is that the specific dispute over expansion—the decision that led to the litigation and subsequent mediation—is much less on their minds than are a collection of grievances, real and imagined, occurring over the years. It's the sum of these grievances that has brought the two of them to this unhappy current state of affairs.

They go through the motions on the expansion decision: Mike wants to add the new offices but without Robert looking over his shoulder; Robert doesn't want to be worried that Mike's "grandiosity" (Robert's term) will ruin the Company. I sense that neither is really anxious to discuss with me the merits of this decision, which I take as a tacit confirmation that they both see this mediation as leading to a split-up—in which case the expansion decision will become irrelevant. Perhaps they also realize that, insofar as the business merits of expansion are concerned (as contrasted with the legal issue of the necessary vote), they're much better equipped to make that decision than I am to give advice on it.

So, instead of that, each prefers to regale me with tales of corruption, venality, and incompetence on the part of the other. Mike, for example, harps on Robert's mismanagement of his portion of the Company's business, comparing it (with obvious relish) to the greater profitability of Mike's own segment. Robert dotes on the cost to the Company of Mike's unauthorized venture into real estate, proudly contrasting his own purity of purpose. "That's sheer hypocrisy," cries Mike on hearing about this, and he proceeds to regale me with a tale of Robert's fraudulent use of Company funds to finance renovations to his personal residence—and so on.

One of the recurring themes I encounter (and hear more of as time passes) is this sort of remark from Robert: "I'm finding out new information every day—things Mike is doing that I don't know anything about and that are terrible for the Company." I only half believe these protestations of innocence. They come from both sides, though, and the shifting informational sands make it difficult to pin things down for a settlement.

This is part of a broader general problem in deal-dispute mediation, especially in a case such as a business divorce. In the one-shot dollar dispute, what's at issue is generally historical; the facts are fixed—it's their significance that needs to be assessed. Here, however, the business is ongoing while the mediation is in progress; something new happens every day, creating fresh problems.

To be sure, the parties can and do reach a "standstill" understanding on specific matters, such as holding off on the litigation and not pursuing the loan and expansion while the mediation is ongoing. They can agree not to clash over the disputed matters other than through the mediation, limiting their business contacts to what's required for the Company's routine operations. But when the mediation takes a long time, it's difficult to hold things constant during the entire period.

As the process of venting and reply takes place, I can't help observing certain personal characteristics of the parties. Mike is bolder, while Robert is more risk-averse. Mike paints with a broad brush; Robert tends to be precise. Mike is more comfortable on the offensive—not so much attempting to defuse the charges against him as hurling new ones back against Robert. By contrast, Robert goes to great pains to make me understand just what he did and why he did it—a catalog of detailed self-justification. This kind of personality observation is important for a mediator to make, and I have a hunch it will prove useful to me as things proceed.

I also begin to form some impressions about the lawyers who are advising Mike and Robert. Mike's lawyer, Kyle, tends to be bombastic, overstating the facts, demeaning Robert at every chance—he sounds like a badly written, argumentative litigation brief, even on non-litigable issues. By contrast, Robert's lawyer, Brenda, appears better suited to what we are undertaking. She presents her points firmly, but in a less contentious manner, and avoids belittling Mike. I have a feeling she'll be helpful in devising ways to resolve some of the sticky issues. At any rate, I keep an open mind here, because we haven't yet gotten down to the hard part of the process. Kyle may simply be mirroring his client's attitude or just showing off for him— perhaps I'll be able to do business with Kyle on a one-to-one basis later on.

It's now time to resolve the threshold questions I mentioned previously. I've concluded that Corporate Advisors is a ripe candidate for a business divorce. The enmity between Mike and Robert is such that they're unlikely to be able to work out their differences and remain together. The Company is being damaged by their scrapping and lack of communication. Because consulting is a business that's dependent on their personal services and contacts, I don't envision a third party stepping up to buy the Company without them. Mike might be willing to buy Robert out, but Robert definitely wants to continue his employment consulting and wouldn't agree to give up his clients. Because they operate primarily in separate business areas, I see a real possibility for a successful split-up of the Company here.

I share this conclusion privately with each of the parties at the end of this step. It doesn't appear to come as a surprise to either of them. My guess is that it independently validates what they've suspected for a long while now. They each agree to work with me toward this goal.

CHAPTER 17

THE MEDIATOR AT WORK

Now I want to focus on the mediator who has to sort all this out—to bring structure to what he or she has learned, and to lay the necessary groundwork for the succeeding steps.

The mediator's guiding principle in such a case—in what's often a highly emotional scenario, sometimes with a degree of bitterness akin to that in a failed marriage—is to see that rationality rules. The mediator has to make the feuding partners realize that what's at issue here is a business, and they have to dampen their emotions in order to work out rational, commercially reasonable outcomes. Sure, the ultimate resolutions will rarely go as far as each party would like (in terms of favoring himself and penalizing his partner), but they constitute the keys to accomplishing the split-up—enabling both parties to get on with their lives, while salvaging the existing business.

Assessing Priorities

In the exercise of good judgment, I feel that the appreciation of significance plays a crucial role. Sorting out what's primary from the pack of applicable factors is the key to effective lawyering, smart negotiating, and almost anything that involves decision-making. It's especially pertinent for a deal-dispute mediator who has been inundated by the parties with their respective grievances.

So while the tirades and allegations are still ringing in my ears, I make some preliminary determinations (not yet shared with the parties) as to *their priorities*. In the first exuberance of their venting, everything seemed to take on uniform importance. The issues are not equal, however, and it makes sense for the mediator to rank them in terms of significance.

Please understand, this isn't a question of the mediator's own priorities. I have to examine every issue from the respective standpoint of each party. Their priorities on particular issues may differ, but this—far from being a source of concern—is just what I'm looking for. If Mike feels strongly about issue X but attaches much less importance to issue Y, while Robert is hung up on Y but not on X, the basis exists for resolving both matters—something that would be harder to pull off if each were dogmatic on the same issue.

For instance, I can see that Robert is furious about Mike's real estate foray. About two years ago, Mike had Corporate Advisors buy as an investment a small commercial building, subject to a mortgage. Although the transaction clearly required unanimous board approval under the Company's certificate of incorporation, Mike did this on his own without consulting Robert. Then, at the next regular board meeting, he asked for a ratifying vote. Robert, although distressed by Mike's audacity and equivocal about the investment, didn't want to have a direct confrontation with Mike at that time. Faced with a *fait accompli*, Robert simply abstained on the vote.

About six months ago, the largest tenant in the building failed to renew his lease, the space could not be relet, and the rental income no longer covered the mortgage payments. The Company's negative cash flow from the investment appears unlikely to be stemmed in the near term. In Robert's bitter words: "If Mike had asked for my consent *before* committing to the deal, as he was obligated to do, I'd never have given it. As a result, we wouldn't have made the purchase and be in the hole we're in today."

Mike professes to be unruffled by this—"All that was two years ago, so why is Robert making a fuss about it now?" Unless I miss my guess, though, beneath his bravado, Mike seems a bit abashed over his conduct on the real estate—in contrast, say, to the indignation he mounts in replying to some of Robert's other allegations, such as those concerning a certain venture capital investment. I sense that I may be able to recommend at least a partial reparation with regard to the building.

In contrast to Robert's fire and brimstone over the real estate, Mike's attack on Robert for using Company funds to renovate his residence has almost a perfunctory air to it. My suspicion is that over the years Mike has probably had some work done on his *own* house at Company expense without Robert's knowledge! Meanwhile, Robert has mounted a furious defense against the charge. He's outraged that Mike is questioning these expenditures, "because, Jim, the sole purpose of the renovation was to make my residence more conducive to conducting business meetings on the premises—something designed to benefit both of us equally." I think all Mike really needs on this one is a face-saver to justify his real point—which is that Robert is no saint.

So I go about trying to rank the importance of the various issues to each party, knowing that this will come in handy later on. Along the way, I note an element akin to what I observed in Chapter 6 about dollar disputes containing two kinds of issues—straight dollar ones and those where, for at least one party, a seemingly sacred principle lurks underneath the dollars. In a business divorce like this, the historical disputes that agitate a partner deeply are usually those where he feels most violated by the other: "What Robert did there was *unforgivable!*"—"*How dare* Mike not have sought my consent prior to putting our hard-earned money into *real estate?*" These high priority irritants, however, may *not* be the big ticket dollar items.

So, when an issue of "violation" involves a modest amount, I may be able to arrange a trade: say, Party A's acquiescence on the small dollar violation issue that vexes Party B, in exchange for Party B's concession on a larger dollar issue that ruffles Party B's feathers a lot less.

Determining Which Wrongs Won't Be Righted

My crucial task now—even more important than assigning priorities—is to decide which of the historical dispute issues agitating the parties are capable of being resolved through some adjustment, and which are not. I've found this to be a vital aspect in deal-dispute mediating—the realization that not all perceived wrongs can be righted. It's a conclusion, I must say, that the parties are unlikely to arrive at on their own. They will only accept this if persuaded it makes sense by an impartial mediator.

For example, I'm well aware of how annoyed each of them is at the other's alleged mismanagement. This is especially true of Mike, who never misses a chance to remind me that his segment of the business is more profitable than Robert's—which, Mike says, "is no accident, because Robert is a lousy manager."

A few years ago, Robert tried to expand his employment consulting into advising companies on their relations with trade unions. This was expensive—the Company had to hire experienced personnel and make certain commitments—and it proved to be a total bust. Mike, who was aware of this initiative but had let Robert "do his thing," now cannot stop second-guessing the futility of it all. Robert, while disappointed at the results, still feels it was an appropriate opportunity to pursue. "And if Mike wants to talk about that kind of thing," Robert says with scorn, "why don't you ask him about the time he tried to break into the insurance industry . . . ?"

I quickly realize that allegations of past mismanagement or errors in judgment cannot be rectified in this mediation. Here's how I break the news to the partners:

> "Look, I have to assume that each of you was trying to perform as well as possible with the business you were running. If things had worked out better, both of you would have benefited as equal partners. So, when a business initiative didn't work out, that's too bad—but it's not anything we can remedy today. Don't expect any satisfaction on this score."

Along with charges of mismanagement go accusations of "goofing off." Neither partner has ever worked as hard in the business as the one speaking does. "Robert takes long vacations . . ."; "Mike's out on the golf course every Wednesday . . ." Just as with mismanagement, the idea behind charging one's partner with sloth is to prove that the fifty percent return Lazybones has been receiving over the years constitutes gross overpayment. Well, too bad—we can't rectify this now and, deep down, they both know it.

Another anguished theme I'm subjected to is one partner's failure to disclose to the other something that was going on. "He never told me . . ." or "He never said a thing about it"—I hear this refrain again and again.

Take, for example, the venture capital investment in telecommunications I mentioned earlier. Mike proposed that the Company invest in this at a board meeting several years ago, citing the fact that the underlying business had some natural tie-ins with certain of the Company's consulting clients. Robert thought the idea sounded interesting, and it was unanimously approved. What Robert alleges that Mike did *not* disclose—although Mike says he did—was that Mike was transferring the investment to the Company from his personal investment portfolio (at his original cost). Robert also claims that Mike knew at the time of the board meeting—although Mike says he did not—of a capital call from the venture that would be coming up a few months later.

When Robert finally focused on this (in the course of the next year-end audit), the once promising investment was looking a lot less rosy. With the clarity of hindsight, Robert now alleges that it was a sense of impending doom and the imminence of the capital call that caused Mike to transfer the investment to the Company—whereas, Robert fumes, if everything had been hunky dory and there was no need to put up more funds, Mike would have just kept the investment in his personal portfolio.

Mike vigorously disputes this. He says he had every expectation of success for the investment, and claims he only transferred it to the Company because Robert had previously expressed concern that Mike might take "corporate opportunities" for himself.

This quarrel offers a good example of a crucial limitation a mediator faces in all kinds of cases, not just deal-dispute situations. It's very difficult to "find the facts" here. The mediator—lacking discovery, testimony and such—is not really equipped to sit as a judge of differing factual narratives. I also realize that to probe into this too deeply may erode the parties' trust in my impartiality.

There is, to be sure, a self-dealing transaction with the Company here, and I'm not without suspicion about Mike's conduct; but I cannot simply assume Robert's scenario—and proof is hard to come by. If it were clear that the price the Company paid Mike for the investment had been inflated so it provided him with a profit, or if there was evidence that his cost basis no longer reflected a proper valuation, then I might recommend a retroactive price adjustment. But the stuff I hear regarding past value and what Mike knew at the time is just too murky to reach that conclusion.

Without profit to Mike or clear-cut base motives on his part, the case becomes one of alleged non-disclosure of pertinent information—namely, that the investment was coming from Mike's own portfolio and thus constituted a self-dealing trans-action with the Company. But as with bad business judgments, non-disclosure of information from one partner to the other is not something as to which I can ordinarily recommend a cash adjustment. Bottom line, if I'm not pretty sure about something, the more prudent course is not to push hard for an adjustment. I'll admit, though, that this one leaves me feeling uneasy.

I also lack sympathy towards complaints about past wrongs that are now being raised vociferously for the first time. I realize why this is so—the impending divorce has made both partners realize they better speak up now or stand forever mute. I don't doubt that some of these grievances have gnawed at the parties over the years, and I can understand that they may not have wanted to rock the boat as relations went from bad to worse. Still, from my viewpoint, deferred indictments turn pounds of flesh into ounces; and I'm well aware that any satisfaction one party may gain from delayed retribution will be more than off-set by the other's indignation at having this "afterthought" in-flicted on him.

So, here (paraphrased) is what I tell both parties and their counsel about this:

"No matter what grievances you may have about your partner's past mismanagement or failure to disclose or slacking off, these will just have to go by the boards. What I propose for us to deal with—in addition to prescribing a rational basis to divide the business and to resolve the forward-looking issues—are matters of self-dealing or other transactions that resulted in one of the partners personally profiting and the other not profiting (or profiting less), or one of them profiting at the expense of the entity."

I want them to know how I feel on this subject *before* I ask for their proposals. Although no one steps forward to congratulate me on the rationality of my exclusions—and Kyle mutters something in protest—I take the absence of loud dissent from the two partners as a tacit endorsement of my position.

Carrots and Sticks

My other mission now is to prepare the parties for the negotiating to come. I take two different approaches here—what might be termed the carrot and the stick. Let's start with the stick.

In many mediations, one of the parties is just too cocksure for things to work effectively. I've got one of those in The Split-Up Case, and his name is Mike. Sure, he'd like to resolve this and get Robert out of his hair, but I sense he's not willing to bend over backwards to do so. If the mediation doesn't succeed, Mike appears prepared to live with the *status quo*—he's less concerned than Robert at the prospect of continued confrontation.

In part, this is a matter of his personality, and I can't do anything about that. But I think the larger cause is his belief that, with Larry at his side, he'll be able to accomplish most of his agenda. In particular, he seems convinced (presumably based on what Kyle has been whispering in his ear) that if they wind up back in court, he'll win on the majority vote for expansion—a prospect he's really excited about, whether on his own or still in business with Robert.

I'm concerned that this attitude can impede the kind of reciprocal concession pattern that will be needed to successfully resolve the situation. So (and this is where the stick comes in), I decide to do something about it—make an attempt to tamp down Mike's self-perceived positive leverage.

You should understand, I only do this kind of thing where I

feel such cocksureness is both unwarranted and adversely affects the likelihood of getting a deal done. When positive leverage is justified and doesn't burden a deal (i.e., the deal will still get done, albeit on terms favorable to the more powerful party), the mediator can continue to negotiate and point out essential considerations, but he or she has to be wary about minimizing the imbalance. Here, however, for reasons I'm about to explain, I don't consider Mike's high level of bravado to be warranted, and I see it as potentially obstructing the deal.

So I have a heart-to-heart talk with Mike and his lawyer Kyle. Here's a paraphrase of my pitch:

"I'm getting the impression, Mike, that you don't much care whether this mediation works out—but I think you should care. The court case is not a slam dunk your way by any means. The language of the certificate of incorporation may be favorable to you on its face, but I know this judge, and he's likely to be concerned that allowing a majority vote to govern such a crucial Company decision will emasculate the unanimity requirement. However, I don't want to argue the legal question—let me turn to the more important practical considerations.

"If you go to court and win on the vote, Robert will still be your partner. I'm sure the bank will want his personal guarantee on the expansion loan, along with yours. But you can bet that Robert will refuse to sign a guarantee, and no one can make him sign it. Then, even if the bank could make do without Robert from a financial viewpoint, his refusal will alert the bankers to the rift that exists between the two of you. And they'll feel very uneasy about making a big loan to a business that is trying to expand at a time when the principals are actively feuding.

"Moreover, you may think that your vote and Larry's can carry the day on most issues, but if I were Larry, I'd be worried. Brenda might well advise Robert to hogtie Larry with a lawsuit alleging breach of fiduciary duty—the Company lawyer taking sides in a dispute between equal partners. And Robert could be so angered if this isn't resolved that he sues you on the unauthorized real estate investment and perhaps some other stuff. Meanwhile, it's a sure thing that Robert will get himself more involved in the running of the Company—insisting on formal procedures and documentation, and generally making your life miserable.

"So my advice to you is to care a little more that this mediation turns out to be successful. . . ."

Kyle blusters for several minutes in response, but I notice that Mike doesn't say much. I don't want to get my hopes up, but this "stick" might possibly have made Mike more amenable to a settlement than he was before.

Now for the carrot. Deal-dispute mediating, as I've said, is no walk in the park; a business divorce like this may take a long time to accomplish. As a result, a sense of frustration often pervades the atmosphere. To combat this, the mediator should look for opportunities to obtain agreement between the partners with respect to even minor matters that come up along the way. These can provide encouragement to the parties that something positive may eventually occur.

In The Split-Up Case, for instance, Robert has been making a lot of noise about that venture capital investment. He wants to see all Mike's documents and records from his original investment. Mike, who insists that nothing was amiss, is resisting Robert's demand. So, in a private caucus with Mike and Kyle, here's what I say about this to Mike:

"Hey, Mike, if I were being charged with wrongdoing on something where I was innocent—as you say you are here—I'd want to lay out all the books and records for the other side to see, so as to rebut the charge. The more you refuse to do that, the more suspicious Robert has a right to be."

The clear implication of my remark—although I don't say it—is that the *mediator* is also getting suspicious! Maybe that's why my coaxing works, and Mike agrees to disclose certain pertinent information. Although the non-disclosure issue on the investment doesn't go away, this allays some of Robert's worst suspicions (as well as my own); and it demonstrates to the partners that the enterprise we're engaged in isn't totally hopeless. I hope this will encourage them to make some reasonable proposals in the next round.

Requesting Proposals from the Parties

At this point, my format for mediating a deal-dispute scenario such as this business divorce begins to diverge from what I do in a one-shot dollar dispute. Upon reaching this juncture in a dollar dispute (as explained in Chapter 8), I move into private discussions with each party over the merits of the issues underlying the dispute. Rather than asking each side for a proposal, I tell each side my reactions to the various issues—hopeful that this will keep the parties from digging themselves into their wish lists and that my neutral views will have a moderating influence on their private attitudes.

In The Split-Up Case, however, I want to hear each side's proposal regarding a reasonable basis for the business divorce, uninfluenced by my own recommendations—other than my excluding from consideration such issues as past mismanagement and non-disclosure. Here's my reasoning for this different approach:

(i) The issues in a business divorce are more commercial and multifarious than in a money dispute, and there are a lot of different ways to skin a cat. They know their own business much better than I do, and I'm loathe to inhibit their imaginations.

(ii) Now that (hopefully) the bulk of the ranting and posturing is out of the way, I'd like to know how realistic (or unrealistic) each of them is, in order to determine what still has to be overcome for them to reach final agreement.

(iii) By observing the weight that the parties themselves place on various issues (explicitly or implicitly), I'll be better equipped to set priorities.

How about those two reasons I had in the dollar dispute for not letting the parties tell me what they wanted? With respect to the possible loss of flexibility, I try to keep them from digging in to particular positions by phrasing my request to each in terms of, "What do *you* think would be a good compromise resolution?" Because I'm asking the other side the same question, the clear implication is that there will have to be substantial movement on both sides before a final agreement is reached. As for wanting to let them hear my thoughts, I realize that this mediation has a long way to go—there will be plenty of time for that down the road.

In requesting their private views, I tell each side that I won't convey this to the other side without express permission. I'm hopeful that privacy will encourage them to be more forthcoming than if, for example, Party A knew that Party B would learn of Party A's concessions before Party B had agreed to give up anything in return.

In my book, *Smart Negotiating*[24], I point out how important it is for a negotiator to react on the spot to the other side's proposal, especially when some aspect of it is really wide of the mark. Where a buyer, for instance, consciously makes a lowball bid on property you own, he'll be anticipating a strong negative response from you; if, however, you don't react that way, he may infer that the skimpy price he offered didn't strike you as being that far out of line. My advice to negotiators is to never let your absence of reaction be misconstrued. Besides, this presents an ideal opportunity to send a signal to the other side—a signal that can't be delivered as effectively later on, when it lacks spontaneity and carries a "manufactured" label.

Well, in my mind, this advice applies equally to a mediator who's smack in the middle of what's likely to be a tough negotiation. So, although I'm listening carefully to whatever each party proposes, that doesn't mean I am mute. If a party's proposal contains a clearly overreaching or unattainable element, I believe in reacting negatively to it on the spot—or at the latest, soon after hearing the balance of the proposal. I want him to know right off the bat that this element of his proposal will have to be altered.

Mike tries one of these. They are both in agreement that Mike ought to keep the office lease and that Robert will move his operation to new quarters. But Mike then takes the position that the cost of the move should be totally at Robert's expense. I react immediately—"Come on, Mike, that's clearly over-reaching."

There's another advantage for the mediator in doing this. By observing how a party responds to my negative reaction, I gain insight into how firmly the party feels about the particular issue. If he backs right off, then my legitimate inference is that he's merely testing me and, if flagged, doesn't intend to press it further. If he resists vigorously, though, then I know I have more of a problem on my hands. Here, Mike quickly retreats to the notion that the expenses be paid by the Company prior to the split, which in effect means the partners split it fifty-fifty.

Other than a spontaneous negative reaction of this kind, I refrain from negotiating their proposals at this time. I don't want to cross swords until after I've gone through the crucial exercise described in Chapter 18. If a party's proposal happens to contain a quite reasonable element, I consider it appropriate to provide positive reinforcement (without going overboard, because even more may ultimately be required from him). So, I utter a few words of approval—my favorite phrase for the purpose being, "That's a constructive provision."

The Parties' "Compromise" Positions

Let me set forth at this point the positions each party takes on certain major issues involved in the split-up, so you'll be able to follow how I go about trying to bridge the gaps.

Both parties subscribe to the notion that the business be divided neatly into the kind of strategic consulting that Mike has been doing and the employment consulting that has been Robert's forte. To keep this hypothetical as non-technical as possible, I'm not going to discuss the corporate and tax mechanics necessary to accomplish this with maximum efficiency. This, however, doesn't mean that such matters are unimportant. Quite the contrary, they may be essential; and the mediator either has to understand them or bring in someone who does (an accountant, for example), in order to provide the needed assistance.

Other than two employees (Emma and Edward) that both

partners want to take, most of the Company's employees fit logically into one camp or the other, or have a clear allegiance to one of the partners, or don't matter much. But the parties disagree over what's to happen in the future regarding current employees. Mike doesn't want Robert ever to hire any of "his people." Robert is agreeable to each partner not soliciting the other's employees to leave for a period of a year; but, he says, if an employee leaves one partner's employ without being solicited by the other, the other partner should be free to hire that individual. My surmise here: Robert is convinced that Mike will antagonize some of his own good people into leaving, in which case Robert doesn't want to be precluded from hiring them.

Because Mike is staying on the premises, it makes sense for him to keep the furniture, fixtures, and equipment. Both agree he should buy Robert's half-interest in them, but then there's the question of price—depreciated book value? current market value? As for the costs of Robert's move to new quarters, which Mike is now willing to split, Robert thinks Mike ought to pay the whole thing—"After all," Robert says, "Mike's just staying put."

The office lease that Mike will keep is neither favorable nor unfavorable, so there's no advantage either way. The real problem on the lease is that each of them is an individual personal guarantor; and the supposition is that the landlord (who has not yet been approached) will refuse to let Robert off the hook, even after they divide the business and he moves out. Robert insists that, if this were to happen, Mike must personally indemnify him for any liability or expense he incurs with respect to the lease—a sensible position that Mike is hard put to oppose (although he says he'll "think about it" and "first wants to see where other things come out"). Robert goes further, however, asking Mike to escrow funds to secure his indemnity. Mike considers this nonsense and will have none of it.

The toughest issue here is over clients of the Company—existing and future. Take the existing ones first. They appear to fall into three categories:

(i)   a few old clients, dating back to before the partners divided up the work, for whom either Mike or Robert

does both strategic and employment consulting;
  (ii) a number of shared clients, for whom Mike does strategic consulting and Robert does employment consulting; and
 (iii) the balance of clients for whom either Mike or Robert performs his specialty but where the other partner (and the other's specialty) is not currently involved.

On the old clients in (i), I'm glad to see that both parties take a hands-off attitude—neither will try to hustle the other's meal ticket. I was concerned that one of them would get greedy here, leaving blood on the conference room carpet. It's nice to know there can be such moments of unexpected satisfaction in an otherwise huffy mediation; unfortunately, they're often few and far between.

On the shared clients in (ii), Robert's position is that each partner should be restricted in the future to his specialty. "That's all right," says Mike, "except if the client asks one of us to take over the other's specialty." "No, no," says Robert, "no exceptions." He appears worried about Mike's clout with these shared clients, knowing that immediately after the split-up Mike will add someone to his staff with employment consulting expertise.

On the clients in (iii), where only one of the partners is engaged and is performing his specialty, Robert wants the second partner to be free to compete for the client's other business. (Apparently he distinguishes this category, where he has nothing to lose, from the situation with the shared clients in (ii); Robert must believe he can sell employment consulting services to some of Mike's clients, and he appears not too worried about Mike coming after his clients on a strategic consulting basis.) Mike says no to this, because "it would be too disruptive." (Mike must want to be able to cross-sell his new employment expert to his existing clients without having to compete with Robert; I guess he's not interested in going after Robert's clients for strategic consulting business—probably because, I suddenly realize, he has already pitched them for the business and failed to land it!)

Turning now to prospective clients whom neither partner

represents, Robert—again with nothing to lose—is in favor of unbridled competition. With these, however, Mike's position is that each partner should be restricted to his area of expertise. At first, this strikes me as inconsistent with his desire to go after the employment consulting business. After a little probing, I realize Mike must be concerned that Robert will utilize the analytical tools and other techniques Mike has developed over the years to compete with Mike for new strategic consulting business. After all, Robert is still capable of this—witness his long-term clients who fall into the (i) category. So now it begins to make sense—with all his bravado, Mike is more concerned about Robert eating his lunch than he is confident about selling employment consulting services to future clients through his new expert.

Oversimplified, there is $200,000 cash (and other liquid assets) in the Company till and $100,000 of bank debt. If they were liquidating the business, they would use the cash to pay the debt and then divide the $100,000 balance between them, $50,000 each (as befits their fifty percent shareholdings). Here, however, they're not liquidating—rather, the segment of the business representing sixty percent of the current earning power is going to Mike, with the balance to Robert.

As a result, Robert thinks he should be entitled to more of the cash to offset this. Kyle, though, starts quoting corporate law provisions that he claims mandate a fifty-fifty division; and Mike, for his part, says that if the bank loan is not paid off immediately and he has to carry it, he should get more of the cash to offset this. I get the impression that no one's position on this potentially troublesome issue has been thought through in depth or is set in stone.

Robert wants Mike to take over the losing real estate property—"That's his baby; he didn't even consult me before buying it." Mike is willing to do so; the question is one of valuation. It's carried at $40,000 (net of the mortgage) on the Company's books, but its present value (though uncertain) is presumably a lot less. Mike doesn't want to pay anything for property that is currently a losing proposition with a costly mortgage to carry. But Robert wants Mike to pay the Company the amount of its original cost for the property, plus interest to date. (His theory is that because the original purchase was unauthorized, the property should be replaced by the funds the Company would have in its coffers today if Mike had not overstepped his bounds.)

On the relatively unpromising venture capital investment, Robert reasons that because Mike initially foisted it on the Company, he should now buy it back from the Company for its original cost plus the amount of the subsequent capital call. Mike is unwilling to lay out any cash for this, although he doesn't seem averse to letting Robert share in any profits that might eventually come from it.

There is another asset—a patent on software that Mike has developed, using Company funds (but on a fully disclosed and mutually approved basis). Both parties agree this could be a real winner some day. Robert wants to retain his half-interest. Mike would like to buy it from the Company now at its cost basis—arguing that because he's going to have to expend time, effort, and funds to make it worth something, Robert shouldn't be entitled to a residual half-interest.

So, these are the kind of issues that a mediator encounters in a deal-dispute situation—issues that will have to be resolved before this split-up can take place. You can see what a far cry they are from the narrow unanimity-vote question on expansion that triggered the litigation—no wonder the judge washed his hands of it and sent the parties off to mediation!

18

THE MEDIATOR'S
REALISTIC EXPECTATION

It's now time for the deal-dispute mediator to develop a realistic expectation as to the overall terms upon which the contretemps might be resolved—in The Split-Up Case, to effectuate the business divorce. This is something I also do in the one-shot dollar dispute (see Chapter 9), but with this significant difference: in the dollar dispute, I don't share my realistic expectation with the parties (at least not until the final hours of the mediation), whereas in the business divorce, I'll be presenting it to both sides in the very next step.

Developing a Feasible Resolution Model

I see my mission at this point as forcing the parties to take a hard-headed look at what they can feasibly expect to achieve from the mediation. For this chore, I need to have in hand my own comprehensive proposal. Sure, I'll have to keep reassessing the situation as the mediation progresses, and I recognize that my expectations may well be modified along the way. At this juncture, though, I've learned enough to take a first cut at the task.

My expectation has to be realistic—a resolution that I believe is feasible to achieve. It's almost never either party's desired outcome, but that's not the test. I'm looking for something that *both* parties will be willing to swallow—a compromise that each considers preferable to the alternative of returning to court and then continuing to run the business in confrontational fashion.

In my book, *Smart Negotiating*[25], I discuss how each side in an unassisted two-party negotiation develops his or her realistic expectation. My method there is to construct an amalgam of what I term "aspiration" and "feasibility." Aspiration is where the party would like to come out, but on a realistic basis (not a pipe dream or wish list). For the buyer of a house, for example, it represents the objective value of what's being purchased (measured, say, by comparables), modified by any special element of subjective worth (the house is only three blocks from the kids' school).

This aspiration is then leavened by feasibility, factoring in a combination of what the other side's underlying views are likely to be (notwithstanding his current posture) and the leverage that's present in the deal. (So, if the seller of that house needed to close quickly to pay debts, he'd be at a real disadvantage; but if he were able to generate competition from several buyers, he could shift the leverage back to his advantage.)

In an unassisted two-party negotiation, each party generally has (or certainly should have) good information as to his own aspiration, imperfect information (at least at the start) on what the other party really wants, and a mixed bag of information on how the leverage is operating in the transaction (because leverage often depends on appearances, and these can be deceiving).

By contrast, when I'm a mediator trying to determine a realistic expectation to guide my efforts, I know less about each party's own aspiration than the party himself (unless the party has leveled with me completely, which would be unusual); but I know more about what the party on the other side is likely to accept (unless the other party hasn't leveled with me at all, which is too discouraging to contemplate). Still, a crucial ingredient in assessing feasibility—a factor that the mediator simply cannot ignore—is the relative leverage present in the situation. The mediator is just going to have to dig this out, because it's unlikely to be handed to him on a platter.

There may be a number of leverage factors at work in a typical deal-dispute mediation, but I see it often coming down to one key factor—*desire*. In The Split-Up Case, who wants the business divorce more, and how much more does he want it? So I try to figure out, on the basis of what I've learned and observed, who is being harmed more by the existing situation, who is more likely to prevail in the judicial arena, who is under severe financial or time pressure, and who has the greater opportunities obtainable through a split-up?

In a regular two-party negotiation, *negative* leverage (such as financial necessity or adverse time pressure) is greatly increased if the other side is aware of it—although it still exists even when that's not the case. So here I also have to assess whether information connoting negative leverage that I've learned in confidence from the partner subject to it—which I won't pass on to the other partner—is nevertheless known to the other side.

In Part V, when we view mediation from the viewpoint of the lawyers, I'll address some ticklish questions as to how the parties deal with the mediator on both negative and positive leverage factors.

In The Split-Up Case, I've become aware of certain factors that may prove significant. I have previously discussed Mike's seeming hubris and my attempt to tone it down. As for Robert, it's becoming clear to me that he really wants out of the Company, the sooner the better—and I can't say that I blame him. He's feeling increasingly powerless, especially since Larry began siding with Mike; the constant confrontations seem to disturb Robert more than his partner; and Robert is uncomfortable with the risks posed by Mike's expansionist posture.

Robert has also complained to me that Mike, who apparently has more outside sources of income than Robert does, is squeezing him financially by keeping cash distributions from the Company at a lower level than Robert would like. (In response to this, Mike says he's merely keeping a cash cushion in the Company to weather any economic downturn and to support business expansion plans.) I also get the clear impression that Robert would like to go after new strategic consulting business. This is what he started out doing for a living—he considers himself fully as competent as Mike in this area—but he has been under wraps for many years because of the way the two of them have divided up the new business initiatives.

So, all in all, I sense in Robert a stronger desire than Mike to reach a negotiated accommodation on a divorce, but not so strong that Robert will be willing to give in completely on those issues that are most important to him.

At any rate, I come up with a realistic expectation on each of the key issues. Let me enumerate these, because the determinations I make in The Split-Up Case illustrate various ways a mediator might go about shepherding a resolution in other types of deal-dispute mediations.

For instance, on issues where no fault is involved and the merits don't point clearly one way or the other, the mediator looks for solutions that have a logical basis and provide something to each party—albeit, not as much as he wants. Remember Emma and Edward, the two key employees coveted by each partner? Well, the fact that Emma has worked more closely with Mike, and Edward with Robert, suggests following that course (assuming it's okay with Emma and Edward) in dividing them up. Do I detect a snicker? Hey, I never said this was rocket science.

Wherever possible in deal-dispute mediations like the business divorce, the mediator should strive for resolutions that don't provide a breeding ground for disputes down the road. Take the issue of future hiring by one partner of the other's employees. Clearly, there should be some restriction, although I shy away from the kind of permanent ban that Mike suggests—two years feels about right. But Robert's idea to key the restraint to *solicitation* can lead to future squabbles over who approached whom. I prefer a prohibition on *hiring*, which is easier to interpret and enforce—although admittedly it might work more of a hardship on the displaced employees themselves.

The office lease guarantee presents a type of issue where the merits dictate the solution. If Mike cannot convince the landlord to release Robert from his personal guarantee of the lease, then Mike should clearly hold him harmless, because Mike alone will be utilizing the space. But Mike isn't penniless or a deadbeat, and will presumably be motivated to pay his rent on a timely basis; so I don't see a need for him to tie up funds in escrow to support his contractual indemnification.

The costs of Robert's move to new quarters demonstrate where "splitting the difference" can be useful. Please note, though, that on a dollar issue such as this, the split does not have to be fifty-fifty. Here, there are good arguments both for dividing the cost fifty-fifty (the position Mike has come to after

I reacted negatively to his original "let Robert pay it all" stance) and for Mike picking up the entire tab (Robert's posture from the start). So I'm going to advocate a split where Mike's share is seventy-five percent. Neither of them will be satisfied, but I think it can be sold to both.

When I find myself tilting toward one party on an issue, I often try to link it to another issue on which my tilt goes the other way. So, for example, in dealing with existing clients, I'm more comfortable with Mike's posture of restricting competition, although wary of perennial restraints. So I shoot for a five-year period (assuming that this will not be considered unreasonable under applicable law), during which: (i) on existing shared clients, neither of them can go after business in the other's specialty; and (ii) where only one of them is working for a client, the other cannot pursue the balance of that client's business (even if the client purports to want to use the other partner—there's too much possibility for subtle coercion here). The restriction minimizes future friction, and clients will continue to get the same level and provider of service they've had up to now.

On the other hand, I'm more inclined toward Robert's view of free competition with respect to other potential clients. I would let Robert go after fresh strategic business and Mike after new employment consulting clients; why should either be barred where there are no pre-existing interests? So, in presenting my views to the parties, I make a point of linking these two issues.

In dividing the business along functional lines, Mike ends up with the segment that has traditionally produced sixty percent of the Company's income and Robert with the forty percent balance. Inasmuch as they're fifty-fifty stockholders in the entire Company, I think this requires an adjustment running Robert's way.

Let's assume the value of the business is $1 million, a number each party has used illustratively in my presence. If they split it up equally, each would be entitled to a $500,000 portion; but here, what Mike is getting is presumably worth $600,000 and Robert $400,000. So, Robert's $100,000 shortfall (and Mike's $100,000 premium) have to be rectified.

My understanding is that the $100,000 bank loan will continue in place. Right now, they're each responsible for half of this ($50,000); but if Mike agrees to take over the whole loan and holds Robert harmless on his personal guarantee, this would increase Mike's responsibility by $50,000 while relieving Robert of a $50,000 debt. Further, assume they're dividing the $200,000 of cash and other liquid assets (net of payables); each of them would, on the basis of fifty percent stock ownership, be entitled to $100,000. Shift that distribution so that $150,000 goes to Robert and $50,000 to Mike and, together with the debt assumption, the $100,000 differential is resolved.

For this kind of solution to work, the parties need to agree on the valuation of the business. You can bet that Mike will be arguing for a lower valuation (and Robert will be contending for a higher one), so as to render the differential to be made up less (or more). Mike will also argue that he is getting less than sixty percent of the potential earning power, while Robert will contend that he is getting less than forty percent. And Mike will contend that he's entitled to keep at least some part of the sixty-forty differential because he developed the business. So, this will not be easy, and it may be necessary to consult accountants or third parties with expertise in valuation who can parse the division more expertly.

The real estate investment poses an issue on which I consider it appropriate to rap one of the parties on the knuckles—in this case Mike, because of its clearly unauthorized acquisition by the Company. The two of them should not continue as partners in this property; it will only lead to more friction down the road. The timing for a sale to a third party—given the absence of a major tenant—could not be worse. So, Mike ought to buy the building from the Company at some price higher than its current value (which value is definitely less than the original cost).

I decide, however, not to refine the resolution of this any further at this time—not suggest a number or formulation—but rather just present the general concept and see how the parties respond. This is well to keep in mind for a mediator formulating an initial realistic expectation in a deal-dispute scenario like The Split-Up Case—you don't have to present a final buttoned-down solution to every matter, but rather can test the water at this juncture.

I don't do a knuckle-rap, however, on the venture capital investment. There may or may not have been full disclosure, but there's no hard evidence that Mike knew then it would prove to be a bust; and his transfer of it to the Company to avoid any corporate opportunity charge makes good sense. So, my immediate reaction is to let them split the investment fifty-fifty to avoid valuation questions. It's trickier, though, if the investment can't be divided—because this may call for some joint judgments on their part down the road.

I contrast this investment with the software patent, which could be a real winner. Here, in order for it to flourish, Mike is going to have to expend considerable effort and funds. He's not going to be happy doing this if a big slug of the benefit ends up going to Robert. So, Mike has to buy this investment from the Company before the split—not at its cost (as Mike would like), but at a present value that reflects the patent's bright promise. We may need some outside help to determine this.

Robert's foray into trade union consulting doesn't call for any adjustment; but the funds used to remodel his home pose a tougher issue. Robert is so self-justificatory on this one that he'll climb the walls if I recommend him reimbursing the Company for the whole job. If I do nothing, however, Mike's blood will boil—even though I sense the issue isn't crucial to him.

In situations like this, I like to find a "token" to offer up to the aggressor with the weaker case. The key here is to convince Robert to isolate some fraction of the job that didn't benefit the Company—that had nothing to do with entertaining clients— and get him to reimburse the Company for that portion. This doesn't undermine his defense of the work's major thrust, but it gives Mike a token to "save face" on the aggressive posture he has been taking here.

Armed now with my own realistic expectation on the key issues, I end my temporary isolation and head back into the fray.

Presenting the Mediator's Split-Up Recommendation

Before presenting my proposal to the parties, I want to make a final reality check to see if I've been reading the situation accurately. For this, I visit each partner separately. Here's a paraphrase of what I say to Mike:

"As I look at the issues here from your viewpoint, Mike, they divide into three categories:

(i) First, the real keys for you—the most important things you would like to realize out of this business divorce. These include getting your segment of the business free and clear, ending up with the software patent, [and so on].

(ii) Second, other matters that, while not unimportant to you, are of a lesser priority than the keys. In this group, for example, would be how much you pay for furniture, fixtures and equipment, and what's to be done about Robert's home renovations.

(iii) Third, what I see as your big concerns going forward—such as not having Robert compete on your existing clients or look over your shoulder on jointly-owned assets."

I go through a similar exercise with Robert, detailing what I see as his real keys (getting adequately compensated for the unequal distribution of earning power, having the ability to compete for new business, and making sure that Mike's un-authorized foray into real estate is at least partially rectified); matters of lesser priority (disposition of the venture capital investment, the costs of his move); and ongoing concerns (not being responsible for debts and obligations of the business, having minimal contact with Mike in the years ahead).

The purpose of this exercise is simple. The proposal I'm about to make to them is fashioned to fulfill more of each party's keys than of his lesser priority items, and to address his major ongoing concerns. I want to make sure, however, that the partners rank these matters the way I think they do. So, I solicit each of their comments separately. Does an item belong in the first or second category? Are the concerns I've flagged really the major ones, or do some exist that I've overlooked?

They respond by giving me some further guidance. For instance, Robert says I should have included among his keys a vindication on the charge he bilked the Company for renovating his home. "It's more than money," he says, "it's a matter of real principle." Mike includes on his list of concerns the disagreeable prospect of having to tie up any of his funds to secure continuing obligations to Robert, who's making a lot of noise on this score. "If I have an obligation," says Mike, "I'll honor it—just like I always have."

After making any adjustments warranted by their reactions, I'm now ready to make a specific proposal for the business divorce. First, though, I have to make sure both parties want me to do that; I'm reluctant to proceed on this step without their mutual approval. They give me the go-ahead.

I present my proposal to the partners separately, in each case prefaced with a preamble which I'll now paraphrase:

> "Because you two don't get along or trust each other, my proposal provides for as little future interference by each of you in the other's affairs as possible.
>
> "In the absence of extensive and expensive litigation and discovery, the suspicions each of you has about the other and 'where the money went' will never be allayed. So you'll just have to take a pragmatic view of what's being resolved here, realizing it's necessarily imperfect.
>
> "As I explained earlier, I'm not going to try to rectify past business judgments or failures to disclose, where neither of you benefited or suffered a detriment different from your partner."

Then I orally present my proposal to each of them, which is along the lines set forth in the previous section.

The procedure I use here differs in two respects from what I do in the one-shot dollar dispute. First, the proposal I make in The Split-Up Case is, in fact, my realistic expectation, and it's the same for each of them. In the dollar dispute, by contrast, I don't disclose my realistic expectation to the parties. Rather, in order to leave myself bargaining room, I usually present each party with a different number, which I may characterize as a "valid settlement point."

The reason for the difference in treatment is because, in the dollar dispute, I encourage each of the parties to negotiate directly with me instead of with each other. In the business divorce, though, they'll be negotiating primarily with each other (albeit through me). Since each side will be pushing in a different direction, enough pressure will exist to obviate any need to give myself leeway going in.

The second distinction is that, in contrast to the specific numbers I present to the parties in the dollar dispute, my proposal here is, well, a lot mushier. It attempts to deal with each of the issues but is purposely fuzzy around the edges. I don't want to lock myself into any precise formulations at this juncture. What I want to do is gauge their reactions, discuss the issues in the context of the proposal, and prod them to engage in some constructive negotiating.

19

NARROWING THE GAPS

A s I mentioned previously, what happens next in the business divorce differs from the technique I favor for mediating a one-shot dollar dispute. There, I shy away from traditional positional bargaining between the parties. Rather, I work separately with each side to approach a resolution level at which each will feel comfortable and the dispute can be settled—but without either side knowing, until the end, just where its adversary stands.

Shuttling Back and Forth with Parties' Proposals

In the business-divorce case, however, I do shuttle back and forth on specific issues, telling each party where the other party stands (having received permission to do so), and trying to get both of them to help close the gap. It's more like a traditional positional mediation, but with certain special features, as you'll see. My dollar dispute method—which is well-suited to getting both sides to agree on a single figure that settles everything—just doesn't work when the parties are actively clashing on multiple business issues. In deal-dispute mediating, the parties and the issues have to be played off directly against each other.

Notwithstanding all the back and forth, though, I advise mediators to keep the parties in separate rooms. In part, this has to do with attempting to keep emotions under control, so reason can hold sway. But even if the parties were civil toward each other, I still believe this type of mediation is better handled in private caucus than in open session. Here's why.

First of all, the mediator can only function with the trust and confidence of both parties. They have to believe that he "calls 'em as he sees 'em," exhibiting no partiality or hostility. As I've said before, for an activist mediator like myself, this isn't easy to achieve with so much emotion flowing (both expressed and latent)—there's a strong sense of the-friend-of-my-enemy-is-my-enemy that pervades the atmosphere.

So, for me to side with Partner B on an issue in my private sessions with Partner A causes Partner A real distress—yet it has to be done. But just think how much worse it would be if it were occurring with Partner B present! Partner A would become even more hostile towards me. Partner B would gain a false sense of confidence, making things even worse when I go the other way on the next issue. Using the privacy of the caucus is not only for building trust—it's also for preventing the erosion of that trust, when the mediator is forced to take a hard stance counter to a party's interests.

But if all the mediator does is elicit a proposal from A, transmit it to B, receive B's reply and take it back to A, I doubt the mediator is going to get very far. Remember, these two partners have forgotten—if they ever knew—how to negotiate with each other. Hey, if they could handle it, they'd be out running their joint business and making money, or would have gone their separate ways—but in neither case would they need a neutral's help in talking to each other.

So, I feel strongly that the mediator has to help shape the party proposals he or she transmits, to ensure constructive movement toward an eventual agreement. (This is also the way I go about it on those infrequent occasions in a one-shot dollar dispute when I'm transmitting proposals from one party to the other.) To do this, the mediator can call on a variety of techniques. Let me briefly discuss several of them.

First is the use of the mediator's imprimatur. Assume I'm working on Mike to modify his proposal as to a certain issue. He's taking a hard line. I make it clear to him that he'll get absolutely nowhere with his position on this issue if I cannot get behind it. "Even if I'm able to support you," I remind him, "Robert might well balk—but *without* my imprimatur, forget it." Indeed, after that happens a few times, Mike begins to grasp my point.

So, for example, Mike and I are debating the issue of who pays for Robert's moving expenses. Robert has been firm in his demand that Mike pay 100 percent of them. To get Mike to move from the 50-50 (to which he's previously come) to the 75-25 split I've proposed, I tell him that I'll then be able to say to Robert, "I totally support Mike's compromise on this issue." And that, I say to Mike, is what will be necessary to get Robert to back off his 100 percent demand.

I further tell Mike that if he won't go above 50-50, then the best I'll be able to say to Robert is, "Mike's position is not unreasonable, although the matter is open to argument"—clearly a lot weaker endorsement, and one that's unlikely to move Robert. And should Mike revert to his opening position that the move ought to be entirely at Robert's expense, then my words to Robert would be, "I don't agree with Mike's position at all, but here it is"—which would certainly result in Robert's posture becoming cast in concrete.

I consider the mediator's imprimatur—arrived at and used judiciously by a disinterested neutral whom the parties trust—to be one of my strongest weapons. Obviously, though, there's no way this can be accomplished if everyone is sitting together in the same room.

A second technique—also illustrating the advantage of working in private caucus—is the mediator's ability to adopt a party's constructive suggestion as the mediator's *own*—as if the mediator had thought it up. This makes it a much easier sell to the other side. Here's an example.

Robert is balking at the idea of having no continuing interest in the software patent once Mike buys it from the Company. I've been focused on the concern Robert has expressed over missing out on an eventual bonanza down the road. Now, assume I'm discussing this issue in caucus with Mike and his lawyer, Kyle. Mike is adamant—he'll be doing all the work and putting up the funds, so Robert shouldn't reap any of the profits.

Suddenly, much to my astonishment, Kyle breaks in with a constructive idea. "Perhaps what's really bothering Robert," he says, "is the worry that after buying the patent from the Company, Mike will turn around the next day and sell it to a third party at a big multiple of the price Mike paid the Company.

Maybe Robert's real fear is of 'being had.' But Mike has no intention of flipping the patent, so why don't we propose that if Mike does resell it at a profit within a year, Robert will be entitled to fifty percent of the profit?" Incredibly, Mike concurs—"That's okay with me"—which shows me how much Mike relies on his lawyer.

Well, I think to myself, this may not solve everything, but it's a fine idea. The problem I see, however, is that if this is presented as coming from Mike's team—and especially from Kyle, whom Robert and Brenda don't much care for—then Robert will immediately be suspicious. I can just hear him—"They must have something up their sleeve." He'll worry that Mike does intend to sell the patent, but in thirteen months; or that he'll sell it next month for a phony low price, while raking in the real bucks in some other form that Robert will never see. (I generally stay away from using pejorative terms like "paranoia," but believe me, this kind of thinking can run rampant in a business-divorce situation; and the mediator can't afford to ignore its corrosive effect.)

So, I ask Mike and Kyle if they have any objection to me presenting Kyle's idea to Robert as if it were my own—a mediator's attempt to resolve the impasse by protecting Robert against a legitimate concern. Then, I tell them, at least Robert won't have a reflexive negative reaction—as he would if he knew where it really came from. He'll be able to assess whether it meets his needs strictly on the merits. Mike and Kyle are agreeable, and I do it that way.

Well, it mollifies Robert somewhat—he was, in fact, apprehensive about this possibility, although he hadn't articulated his concern. And because the suggestion emanates from me, he doesn't get hung up on thirteen months or a faked bill of sale. But he's still not comfortable giving up his entire share in the patent's long-term future value, "which may be much more than what it's worth today." So, back to the drawing board. . . . Well, no one ever said this stuff was easy. A mediator has to have a lot of patience in working through conflict and overcoming the frustration.

So now I try a different approach on the patent—one that can be useful to mediators in all sorts of situations. I decide to take into account the differing personal characteristics of the parties. I mentioned earlier my observation that Mike was the bolder of the two parties, with Robert more risk averse. The time has come to put this perception to use.

I go back to Mike and tell him that I support his position on this issue—that, assuming he's willing to pay a reasonable price for the patent and to give Robert protection against his flipping it, then Robert's interest in the patent should end. I tell Mike that I've come to this conclusion because I appreciate that the development of the patent will require Mike's time and attention, as well as substantial financial resources; but, I say, although I've made this point to Robert, he doesn't seem to appreciate its reality.

So, then I trot out to Mike something along these lines:

"Let's make the realities of this more dramatic. Why not offer Robert a significant share of any ultimate profits on the patent (although less than fifty percent, since you'll still be doing the work) if Robert is willing to commit to put up close to half the development funds?

"Now, I realize, Mike, that you don't want Robert as a partner on the patent, so this offer will involve some risk to you—the risk of Robert accepting. But I can see that you're a born risk-taker; and my perspective on Robert is that he's likely to be risk-averse with his own funds.

"If you concur in that, then the odds are Robert won't go for it—won't want to commit now to put up what might be a large sum of money on an uncertain venture that you'll control. But your offer—which I'll endorse—will make it clear to Robert that 'you have to pay to play.'"

Mike ponders this for awhile. I know what he's thinking, so I anticipate the point.

"Look, Mike, I could present this as my idea, which would give you the ability to disavow the proposal if it seems to interest Robert. But I think it would serve the purpose better if it came directly from you."

Mike, who deep down understands Robert even better than I do, gives me the go-ahead.

I deliver the proposal to Robert, who mulls it over and, as predicted, ultimately declines to accept. The issue of Robert's long-term interest in the patent is effectively resolved. The stage is now set to shift the negotiations on this back to the price Mike will have to pay and the short-term flip protection.

Like any negotiator, a mediator has to know when to talk and when to keep his or her mouth shut. Let me give you an example.

On the issue of hiring the other partner's employees, you'll recall that Mike started off wanting a permanent ban on hiring. I've told him that I'm on board with regard to using hiring (instead of solicitation) as the criterion, but it has to be for a defined period. Okay, he says, how about ten years? "Come on, Mike," I reply and recommend a two-year restriction. Mike moves down to five years. I leave it at that for the moment, and we turn to other issues.

Meanwhile, getting Robert to relinquish soliciting for hiring is tough, but he's finally willing to do it—for a period of six months. "Much too short," I say, "come on, be reasonable—how about my two-year recommendation?" After a lot of tugging and hauling, he finally gives in—"two years, but not a day more."

So, do I now run back to Mike and say, "Hey, great news, I've got Robert to agree to a two-year ban on all hiring?" Absolutely *not*—Mike is still at five years, and two years won't clinch a deal at this point. I still have a lot of work left to do with Mike in terms of shortening his view of the appropriate period. I'm not going to discuss here how that's done—there has to be some mystery left to this process!—but I'll tell you this much: it won't be possible to accomplish the task if Mike knows that Robert has given up on solicitation and has already come to the two-year duration.

The Role of the Lawyers

Sometimes I sense that things might be achieved through the lawyers that cannot be accomplished with the parties themselves. So, let's briefly examine the role of the lawyers in The Split-Up Case. (I'm saving more general observations about lawyers, and advice to them about participating in mediations, for Part V.)

Early in the shuttling process, I convene a meeting of just the two lawyers and myself to see if some progress can be made on a specific issue—preferably one with some legal content, so as to validate the rump session. Whether or not this works is a matter of how constructive each lawyer is, the chemistry (or animosity) between them, how tight a leash their clients have them on, and so forth. I consider it worth a shot, though. A recommendation to a party from the impartial mediator is powerful; when the recommendation comes from the party's own lawyer, it's even stronger. (Remember how quickly Mike went along with Kyle's flip-protection idea a few pages back?) If the joint lawyers' meeting works in this instance, I'll undoubtedly try it later on other discrete issues. If it fails, not much will have been lost.

In The Split-Up Case, the issue I've posed to them concerns the unauthorized real estate investment. But the lawyers' meeting proves to be unproductive. Mike's lawyer, Kyle, takes an adamant stance that Mike did nothing wrong (even though he clearly did) and should not have to pay; while Robert's lawyer, Brenda, is presumably under strict instructions to bring home the bacon. There is some value to hearing them bang heads on this issue—it lends credence to my observation to Mike that if the split-up isn't resolved, Robert might sue him on this issue—but in the end, no overt progress occurs.

This, however, is where a good lawyer can make a big difference in a mediation, and Brenda happens to be a good lawyer. As I discuss in Part V, a prime task of the lawyer is to get the mediator favorably disposed to her client's side of an issue and then to persuade the mediator to let the other side know it. In my overall proposal, I did come out favoring Robert on this realty issue, but I was wishy-washy on exactly how to deal with it. Brenda must have realized that this undercut the impact of my imprimatur. And given the tone of our recent lawyers' meeting, it certainly did little to persuade Mike and Kyle.

So now Brenda—who may be worried that I'm waffling a bit after the unavailing session with Kyle—goes to work on the mediator. Her aim is not only to convince me that my initial instinct as to Mike's misdeed was correct, but also to make me see what an unrealistic position Mike and Kyle are taking on the issue—and, by implication, why I have to do something about that. Here are some of the techniques that Brenda (and good lawyers generally) use in this kind of situation.

First, in our private caucus, Brenda presents the strongest case as to why Mike was in the wrong here. She has all the facts of the original situation at her command. When I play devil's advocate to dispute some aspect of the matter with her, she is primed to respond.

So, for instance, I might ask her, "Why, when Robert first learned about what Mike had done, didn't he complain more vociferously? Also, why didn't he vote *against* ratifying the purchase rather than just abstaining?" Brenda is ready for this. "I'll tell you why," she says, and proceeds to quote me chapter and verse on the unstable situation that existed between Mike and Robert back then, just when they most needed to pull together to land some major new clients—a scenario that makes Robert's reluctance to take Mike on forcefully more understandable. As for the abstention, she reads me the accompanying explanation in the board minutes, which clearly shows that Robert did state his disapproval of what had occurred.

Second, Brenda tries hard to convince me that Mike—perhaps spurred on by Kyle—is acting unrealistically here in resisting some kind of reparation. She reminds me of what I should know myself—that only by my letting Mike and Kyle know how much stronger I consider Robert's posture on this issue will there be any chance of getting Mike to move off the dime. For this purpose, and because she knows the operative facts a lot better that I do, Brenda arms me with ammunition to do battle with Mike and Kyle—supplying me with rationale, analysis, key documents (such as the board minutes), and so on.

Third, just in case I might say something to Mike and Kyle from which they'd infer that Robert might ultimately turn out to be a pussycat on this issue, Brenda instructs me as to what I should tell the other side about Robert's posture here—that, in

her words, "he's dug in" and "there's not much room at all for him to move."

Fourth, Brenda realizes—and this is a crucial realization for any lawyer participating in a mediation—that even if you have a winning case, your client has to be willing to compromise. Although she clearly has the best of the argument here, Brenda understands that Robert has to move a little if he wants me to push Mike to move a lot more.

So now Brenda goes to work on her client Robert, who is hung up on his formulation of how to remedy the damage done here. He wants Mike to buy the property from the Company at its original cost (which is a lot more than it's worth today) plus the interest paid out to date—in effect, replacing the unauthorized property with the funds the Company would have in the till today if Mike hadn't gotten out of line. Brenda helps Robert see that if its original cost is reduced by an appropriate depreciation figure and if the interest element is foregone, the resulting price will still be a lot more than the property is worth today; and Mike will effectively be holding the company harmless from the diminution in value of the real estate.

Well, armed with all this, how can I miss? Ultimately, I do manage to pull it off—but the success is mostly attributable to Robert's lawyer Brenda who, as you can see, did a lot of the heavy lifting.

Another technique I sometimes use here—especially when a lawyer's client is taking an unreasonable stand on an issue—is to deal with that lawyer separately, outside the presence of both his or her client and the other lawyer. For example, assume that Robert suddenly executes an about-face and now wants to be able to compete on those long-term clients for which one of the partners does everything. Before passing Robert's new position on to Mike, I take Brenda aside for a little chat.

"Look, Brenda, this is really foolish of Robert. Not only will it be seen as reneging—which it is—but it's throwing the gauntlet right in Mike's face on those old clients he's very sentimental about. And even if Robert were to prevail—which he won't—there's little chance of it producing any practical economic benefits for him.

"Get him to back down on this. If he does, I'll work harder to overcome Mike's unreasonable position permitting competition with a shared client who asks one partner to take over the other's specialty—an invitation to backdoor pressure that could end up really hurting Robert."

Brenda gives me a nod—I can tell she understands the practical aspects of my message—and says she'll see what she can do. Later I learn that she has managed to turn Robert around on this point.

Progress Slows to a Crawl

I go back and forth on the various issues, trying to narrow the areas of difference. I make some progress, but often of the two-steps-forward, one-step-back variety (with the "two" and "one" sometimes reversed!). I realize why this is, although there's not much I can do about it.

In mediating a one-shot dollar dispute, I make a real effort to reach a resolution in one or two sessions. There may be a brief interval—some breathing space that hopefully works to our advantage—but I try hard not to lose any existing momentum. By contrast, in a deal-dispute mediation such as this business divorce, the negotiations are usually not continuous. There are frequent breaks in the action—after all, as these people remind me, they still have a business to run. This elongation of the mediation does not work in its favor.

What happens instead is that the parties rev themselves up during the intervals and come to the next session loaded for bear, itching to plead their case. At best, this stalls any productive movement. At worst, one of them retreats to a more extreme position on an unresolved issue than the more accommodating stance he came to in the heat of last week's activity.

A mediator can live with stalled movement but not this sort of retrenchment. When it happens, I speak up on the spot—I call a renege a renege—and let the retreating party know, in no uncertain terms, that this kind of behavior is anathema to the process. A mediator has to hold the parties to the concessions they've made on earlier occasions; otherwise, the settlement castle he or she labored so hard to construct is just made of sand.

The other reason for lack of movement and backtracking in a business split-up like this is the ambivalence one or both of the parties may feel about getting divorced. Even though they can't stand the sight of each other, they worry about change. I can almost visualize what is going on inside a partner's head.

"Am I doing the right thing? We fight like hell, but we've worked pretty well as a team over the years; will we be less successful on our own? How will our clients perceive and react to our split? Am I getting snookered on the terms of the deal? How would I do in court if we went that way—can I achieve what I want from the judge?"

A party who's not sure he wants to end up signing a split-up agreement is unlikely to undertake the movement necessary to cause it to happen.

On the other hand, as more and more time passes without things being resolved, this fact itself can sometimes motivate the parties to push ahead. The mediator can help here. Assume one partner complains to me about the time this is taking. I reply, "Well, it's because you and your partner aren't being more forthcoming on the issues." He protests that it's all his partner's fault. I respond, "No, both of you are responsible. If you become more flexible, I'll be able to use that to motivate your partner to do the same." Maybe, if I'm lucky, the logjam breaks.

In a protracted deal-dispute mediation like this, what usually happens is that, at some point, only a few issues remain open, but progress will have slowed to a crawl. Even though the issues may be small ones, they will be couched as matters of "principle."

This is just what happens in The Split-Up Case. We get down to three open issues—involving the venture capital investment, guarantee of the bank loan, and Company clients for whom one partner performs services. (I'll describe these controversies in Chapter 20.)

Now, on the theory that you have to know when to push and when not to, I decide that there's a better way to proceed at this point than just continuing to bang heads. Keep tuned.

CHAPTER
20

FINAL STEPS

We come now to the final steps a deal-dispute mediator has to take to settle the disputes and seal the deals.

Preparing a Draft Agreement in Principle

For the reasons set forth below, at this point I draft a written agreement in principle (sometimes referred to as a letter of intent, memorandum of understanding, or heads of agreement between the parties), which I submit to both sides simultaneously. It contains the outcomes of the resolved issues, identifies the issues that are still open, and makes clear that nothing is agreed to until there's agreement on everything. I don't ask the parties for permission to prepare this document, although I tell them I'm doing it—the idea being that if either has any strenuous objections, he'll have an opportunity to be heard.

One real advantage of having a draft agreement in principle on the table at this juncture is that it serves as a written record of the accords the parties have already reached on the resolved issues. I tell the partners to let me know immediately whether they disagree with my description of these accords; otherwise, I imply, *forever hold your peace.* This memorialization feature is important to avoid any eleventh-hour reneging when we recommence the mediation sessions. I also ask them whether they consider any issues to be open other than the ones I have so designated; this way, there's less likely to be any last-minute surprises.

A collateral virtue of the draft agreement in principle is for the parties to see in black and white how many more issues we've been able to resolve than the few items on which they're still at odds—and also how much more basic the resolved issues are. Because we're spending a lot of time now on the open items, they tend to take on a weight that's out of proportion to their actual importance in the business divorce. I reinforce this by characterizing what is left as "relatively minor stuff," coaxing the partners into a more receptive mood to resolve them—"hey, it's not such a big deal."

After identifying particular issues that are open, the document contains my proposed resolutions for them (clearly identified as not having been agreed upon by the parties). I'm sure that some mediators might feel more comfortable requesting permission from the parties to offer recommendations here. Given the activist role I've been playing all along—and, let's face it, because I very much want to voice my views on resolving these last few items—I don't ask permission. I do, however, tell the parties in advance that I intend to present these recommendations, listening for cries of anguish (and not hearing any here).

My aim at this juncture is to take a page out of the dollar dispute notebook and turn the negotiations on these open points from Mike vs. Robert to a composite of Mike vs. me and Robert vs. me. I purposely did *not* do that earlier when presenting my oral recommendations. Back then, I wanted to stay more flexible—not dig in too early. Now it's time to take a stand.

Here are my three rules of thumb for this penultimate step. First, don't resolve all open issues in the same direction, even if one partner is acting more reasonably; believe me, each of them has to take something away from the endgame process. Second, if feasible, placate each party on what he feels strongest about and disappoint him on what he can most afford to give up. Third, strive for solutions that are logical and hard to argue with—outcomes the mediator can get solidly behind.

I try to follow my own advice on the venture capital investment, proffering a logical swap of upside potential for downside protection. Clearly, this should not be a major issue, but it shows how minor issues can take on outsized importance in the endgame because they have to be resolved in order for the deal to move forward. It also illustrates what can sometimes be a major sticking point with vying parties such as these: namely, the desirability of having in place an agreed-upon mechanism to govern joint decisions that need to he made down the road.

Assume it proves to be impossible to divide this investment, thus forcing Mike and Robert to continue as fifty-fifty partners on it. As contrasted with the patent, they have no future work to perform on this, but they may well face a joint decision down the road—whether to sell their investment or continue to hold it. Robert is concerned that when decision time comes, Mike will want to retain the investment, which will thereafter decrease in value. For his part, Mike does not want to be forced to sell it too early—he sees a long run to daylight here.

Since we can't depend on the two of them sitting down when the decision time arrives and discussing it rationally, there needs to be a mechanism in place to handle the possibility of disagreement. This calls for a compromise that can appeal both to someone who is risk-averse (like Robert) and to a risk-taker (like Mike). The solution I propose might seem a bit complex (although most transactional lawyers would be comfortable with it), but sometimes that's just what is needed to get both sides to buy into it.

(i) If, when the decision arises, Mike decides it's time to sell, then they sell. (Because they're splitting the proceeds equally, Mike should have no reason to try to harm Robert through a premature sell decision.)

(ii) If, at decision time, Robert wants to sell but Mike does not, then Mike will have a choice:
(a) either Mike buys out Robert's half interest right then, at a price equal to one-half of what they could have realized if they had sold their joint interest; or
(b) they continue to hold the investment jointly—but then, when they finally do sell it, Robert will be entitled to get (in part from Mike, if necessary) the higher of (1) one-half of the sale price or (2) the value Robert would have received if Mike had bought him out at the earlier date, plus reasonable interest from then to the date of sale.

A basic assumption of this resolution is that Robert will not need the money at the time of decision, but will be satisfied as long as he's protected against a subsequent diminution in value. If, however, cash flow turns out to be a concern for Robert, I have a further twist in my back pocket. Assuming Mike elects the (ii)(b) option, then Robert will have the right to put his half interest to Mike, but at a discounted price from what Robert would have received under (ii)(a). This will put Robert in funds, but it's not a choice he would presumably make unless he's under real money pressure at the time.

The broader point here is that while it's desirable to resolve every forward-looking issue in the course of a deal-dispute mediation like this business divorce, it may not be necessary to do so. If there are some items which defy current resolution, the mediator may be able to help the parties construct an effective mechanism for dealing with these issues down the road. Nevertheless, on the premise that the less contact the two partners have in the future the better, the mediator should try to keep this sort of thing to a minimum.

On the bank loan guarantee, I take a tack that sometimes works when there's little merit to a party's refusal to budge on an issue. I devise compromise provisions that (for other reasons) may be sufficiently onerous to the no-budge party that he finally accepts the more straightforward solution he has previously been rejecting.

The facts here are that Mike's part of the business will take over responsibility for repaying the $100,000 bank loan. He'll get full credit for this against the disproportionate distribution the two parties receive (that makes up for the fact that Mike's segment of the business is more valuable than Robert's). Mike refuses, though, to hold Robert harmless on the latter's existing personal guarantee of the loan. Robert, quite rightly, wants to be off the hook. Mike's argument is that, unlike the forward-looking situation with the office lease, here both of them have *already* had the use of the funds represented by the loan. Mike is willing to repay the loan from the business; but if, for any reason, he's unable to do so, he wants the two of them to be equally liable to the bank for the shortfall.

I cannot fathom Mike's position here. Among other things,

it undercuts the full value he's being awarded for the loan assumption in the disproportionate distribution. But he has dug in his heels on the point, and I haven't been able to budge him. I sense that Mike must have another agenda here; for some reason, he doesn't want Robert to be a free agent vis-à-vis the bank. Maybe Mike thinks the continuing personal guarantee will diminish the line of credit available to Robert when he begins to compete with Mike for future business. . . .

So, what I do here is construct an alternative approach to the simple hold-harmless provision—an approach that has a rational basis, but that I sense Mike will not want to be saddled with. I won't go into the details, but it's a combination of tagalong rights, keeping some of his money in escrow to apply to loan repayment, limiting the cash distributions he can make from the business to himself until the loan is paid off, and a formula for reducing the credit he receives toward the disproportionate distribution under various contingencies. I realize this would be a mess to police, but my hope is that it will bring Mike to his senses.

The third issue involves Company clients with whom one partner is doing business in his or her specialty. Robert wants to be able to go after the other segment of that client's business; Mike wants it protected, presumably so he can cross-sell the services of his new employment consulting guru. I came out Mike's way in my realistic expectation; but Robert has been so rigid on the point—he must have his eye on one or two of Mike's clients that are ripe for employment consulting—that I need to reassess my expectation. This situation calls for a creative compromise that will somehow enlarge the pie enough to satisfy both parties.

Here, I slip up, though—something that can happen to an activist mediator. The solution I devise suffers from defects so obvious I really should have known better. It involves one partner referring certain types of business to the other, in return for which he gets a placement fee, with a formula that is keyed to— well, let's mercifully leave it at that. I can't understand what I was thinking about. A creative solution should flow naturally from the situation (which this one did not) and have some attraction for the parties. My idea that one partner might actually help another out is bound to prove so anathema to both of them that it will never get off the ground.

Be that as it may, I now present the parties with my draft agreement in principle, hoping they'll sniff the imminence of closure that awaits them just beyond these few remaining uncertainties.

Negotiating the Agreement in Principle

Now begin the final agonizing negotiations. The open points may be relatively few and minor, but the mediator (as well as the parties and their counsel) should never lose sight of the fact that the whole thing could blow up at any time. Even in a friendly deal, as agreement nears, emotions tend to run high—and this is no friendly deal. "The hell with him—let's go back to the mattresses!" is the kind of sentiment a mediator often encounters from one or both of the parties in navigating their ship back into the harbor through the last couple of buoys.

At any rate, after some back and forth, each of them signs on to my proposed venture capital investment compromise. On the bank loan, Kyle who seems to have undergone a rite of passage during the mediation, is instrumental in pointing out to Mike how onerous it would be to have to comply with my complex alternative provisions; and Mike finally sees the light here, agreeing to hold Robert harmless on the loan. As to handling clients, as I should have expected, neither is at all attracted by my clumsy creativity on this issue of some potential consequence.

Fortunately, my judgment now returns and I come up with a different compromise that makes a lot more sense—a basis on which, in fact, I can actually see them settling. First, however, I want to pause to examine some pertinent facets of the endgame, from the standpoint of both the mediator and the parties.

Assume we're down to this one issue, for which the mediator has devised a resolution. The mediation has been quite protracted; and although the mediator is sensing paydirt, the situation remains potentially explosive. The mediator is concerned that if he proceeds on a business as usual basis, his resolution may be pondered critically by each side for days, with each of them ultimately returning to the fray with six-shooters blazing. The question for the mediator is how to avoid this happening.

That's the situation in The Split-Up Case, and my answer to the question is that now may be the time to apply some pressure. So, I schedule a mediation session, letting the parties know in advance that I have devised a better way to deal with the open client issue. But I also tell them, "This is it—either we reach a deal today or let's forget about it. Nothing else is going to happen in the weeks and months ahead that will change anything." Here's the other ground rule I impose for the final session: "I don't want to hear anything negative from either of you about your partner. I've been listening to that refrain for months—today, I want only constructive thinking."

This now-or-never strategy is a bold gesture, not to be used lightly because it could backfire. I would probably refrain from imposing this pressure if the proceedings had not been so protracted or if a number of matters were still open. Here, however, given the long duration of the mediation, my fear of the parties backtracking, and the fact that we're down to a single issue, I consider the risk to be reasonable.

We're back together now, although the parties are still in separate conference rooms. Before offering my resolution, I lay the groundwork by speaking separately to each side on two subjects. First is the relative insignificance of this one point, as compared to the dozens of issues they have managed to put to rest. Second is the compelling rationale as to why it makes such sense to effectuate this business divorce, compared to the perils (which I enumerate at length) of going back to war if agreement is not reached.

Then I present my new compromise to each of them separately. It's a little complicated, but still understandable—and it has something for everyone. (I'll state it here in terms of Mike's strategic consulting clients, but it's reciprocal for Robert's employment consulting clients.)

- Mike furnishes Robert with a list of his clients who fall into this category.
- At the closing, Robert designates which of Mike's clients

Robert wants the right to go after for employment consulting business.

- Robert will be barred from soliciting those he does not name for five years.
- If during the five-year period Mike gets the employment consulting business of someone he doesn't name, Mike will pay Robert as an override a certain percentage of the fees he realizes (thus creating an incentive for Robert not to name everyone).
- As to the clients Robert does name, Mike has the right to "protect" any of them, thus restricting Robert from soliciting them also for five years.
- If Mike then gets employment consulting business during that period from a protected client, he has to pay Robert an override which is double the percentage he pays him on the clients Robert has voluntarily elected not to go after.
- As for the clients Robert designates that Mike does not protect, they can each solicit these; and if Mike gets the business, Robert is not entitled to any override.

Well, after some fussing back and forth and attaching a few bells and whistles to my suggested resolution, they actually do reach agreement on the client issue. Hurrah!

I've anticipated this happening and have prepared in advance a revised agreement in principle that requires only a few changes to be in form for signing. I ask each of them to stick around while I make the changes. I want them to sign before leaving the premises, to obviate any changing of minds or forgetfulness the next day. And so they do. (Of the four participants, only Brenda says, "Thanks for your help.")

In a one-shot dollar dispute, when a deal is finally reached, I bring the parties together to shake hands. Here, frankly, I skip that step; I don't want to take a chance on any last-minute fireworks!

Going to Contract

In the one-shot dollar dispute, once agreement in principle is attained, there's little left for the mediator to do. The written agreement that embodies the resolution is usually rather basic—A pays B a certain sum of money and everyone exchanges releases. This is not the case, however, in a deal-dispute resolution like The Split-Up Case.

Going from handshake to binding agreement is almost never a simple matter in any arm's-length deal, even one between relatively civil contracting parties. It's one thing to reach accord on the general principle that governs an issue; it is quite another to apply the principle to the myriad of permutations and combinations that a resourceful lawyer can come up with to cover all the possibilities.

Achieving a written agreement is especially difficult where the deal contains a number of forward-looking issues. The transfer of current assets and liabilities is fairly straightforward, but to speculate on what might happen down the road lies in another realm entirely. There are so many conceivable eventualities. Even in an amicable deal, where the parties today have no reason to distrust each other, a careful lawyer is well-advised to include provisions that regulate tomorrow's breaches and defaults—as well as to face up to the prospective bad faith of the other party, just so the latter will not be tempted to get cute.

In The Split-Up Case, a number of provisions require amplification and many of them are forward-looking. What raises the level of difficulty is that the parties aren't friendly and don't trust each other. So, they're disposed to think the worst about what might happen—with respect to those shared clients, for example. This can lead to plenty of negotiating fireworks at a time when no one is legally bound by the agreement in principle. Make no mistake—the deal can still unravel at any time.

So, I urge the mediator of a deal-dispute scenario to stay actively involved during this sensitive period. There are many roles a mediator can play. She can influence the lawyer drafting the agreement not to draft egregiously; she can try to defuse the outraged reaction of the recipient of the nevertheless egregious draft; she can help the parties and their counsel interpret what the parties meant (or at least, what the mediator understood them to mean) in terms of the scope and effect of particular agreed-upon provisions; she can give her views as to how matters not considered during the mediation sessions ought to be handled in order to best effectuate the spirit of the agreement in principle; and so on.

I'm sometimes asked by one or both of the parties whether I am willing for the agreement to contain a provision by which, in the event a dispute arises under the agreement that they cannot resolve, the parties mutually consent to use my services to help mediate a resolution between them. Did one partner solicit a client that he or she should not have? What about this asset (or that liability) of the Company we failed to consider? The parties don't want to be back in court over new issues, but they realize they are still going to have difficulty talking and resolving differences. The mediator knows the terrain, and the three of us did work together successfully in reaching this agreement. I can see why this might make sense for them, so I'm inclined to oblige on this score.

On the other hand, when I'm asked to act as an arbitrator of any dispute they cannot resolve—where I would be handing down judgments that each would agree in advance to respect—I say "no." I don't think that a mediator, who has encouraged both sides to be utterly candid with him, has any business getting himself into a situation where he can impose his will on the parties—there's just too much risk of conflict, to say nothing of the possibilities of rancor and criticism from the "losing" party.

Even after the agreement is signed, the mediator should remain available to assist the parties in getting to and through the closing. Troublesome issues can also arise at this stage and, as Yogi Berra reminded us, "It ain't over 'till it's over"—until the divorce is official.

So there we have it—a deal-dispute business divorce mediated to a successful conclusion. It's hardly elegant, and the resulting agreement won't come up for the National Book Award, but we got the job done. In the real world, where this kind of thorny situation can often arise, that's no small feat. These ex-partners can now get on with their lives. The lawyers can congratulate themselves on having helped their clients resolve an untenable situation. Finally, the mediator has the satisfaction of knowing how unlikely it would have been for the parties to be able to achieve this result without a neutral negotiator interposed between them.

PART

MEDIATING
MULTI-PARTY DISPUTES

In this Part IV, I'm going to complicate things by shifting the focus to disputes where more than two parties are involved. Many of the principles discussed in earlier chapters are applicable here, plus several added twists. But it's the execution of the process that's tricky, with each party pulling in separate directions that must be reconciled, and the resolution often calling for forward-looking provisions to be negotiated. Mediators who preside over multi-party disputes really have their hands full.

Chapter 21, which introduces the basic types of situations that arise here, makes the case both for settlement (as opposed to litigation) and for mediation (rather than direct negotiations) as the best means to accomplish that settlement. In Chapter 22, you'll meet the four parties involved in what I call "The Casino Caper" (the hypothetical situation I'm using to illustrate these mediator techniques), find out the facts of the controversy, and hear their disparate opening postures. Chapter 23 follows the mediator as he devises a strategy, gathers information, decides on a format for settlement, and then attempts to market it to the four parties—with some reflections on the mediation process along the way. In Chapter 24, I address the mediator's draft agreement in principle, the bargaining over the critical forward-looking deal aspects of the situation, and the denouement which includes the mediator's proposed resolution.

CHAPTER 21

THREE'S A CROWD

For business lawyers who negotiate, there's an ascending hierarchy of difficulty in the situations they face:

- When there are only two parties, and what they're negotiating is a deal, the bargaining may be spirited but it's relatively straightforward everyday stuff.
- If you add a third party (or more) to the mix, things become more complex—sequencing questions are raised, alliances may form—but at least the parties are all working constructively toward a common goal.
- Now go back to just two parties, but have the negotiations be about resolving a dispute instead of just making a deal—that's tougher sledding, as emotions, posturing, and the specter of a looming lawsuit cloud the picture.
- Then stir in both of the intensifying factors—multiple parties trying to resolve a dispute—and the problems escalate almost geometrically.
- And for the final level of difficulty, make it a multi-party dispute where not only do past injuries have to be rectified, but at least two of the parties need to cut a new forward-looking deal in order for the entire brouhaha to be put to bed.

It's the multi-party dispute, and especially that ultimate situation—the multi-party dispute *cum* deal—that's my subject in this Part IV. How do business lawyers, faced with a crowded, litigious and often chaotic situation, manage to create a workable framework and negotiate an overall resolution that terminates all litigation and allows everyone to walk away reasonably satisfied with the result? (Not ecstatic, mind you; if you're looking for ecstasy, try some other line of work.)

But don't worry, my purpose is not to wallow in the complexity of it all. Rather, I'm going to try to offer some constructive advice on how mediation can deal effectively with the issues these kinds of situations present. My perspective will be that of the mediator; and although the mediation aspects I focus on are particularly meaningful in multi-party situations, most of them are also applicable to the typical two-party dispute.

Let me begin by stating my underlying premises:

- There are plenty of multi-party disputes around.
- Quite often, these are not suitable for resolution by courts or arbitrators, which lack the flexibility needed to fashion workable results (while eating up lots of time and money).
- On the other hand, trying to resolve these disputes non-judicially by direct negotiations among the parties is hard work indeed.
- It's even more difficult when (as is frequently the case) some facet of the resolution requires negotiating a forward-looking deal.
- Under these circumstances, mediation is the best means of crafting a resolution that will satisfy all parties.
- But even in mediation, in order to reach an overall resolution, both the mediator and the party representatives must learn how to cope with the troublesome characteristics of multi-party disputes.

Just a word to any deal lawyers who may be reading this. Later on, in Chapter 26, I make an argument for how useful deal lawyers can be in dispute resolution generally. In the sort of case we're talking about here—featuring multiple parties and often calling for negotiations to craft provisions that guide future conduct—a capable deal lawyer's presence is even more requisite.

Some Examples of Multi-Party Negotiating

Let's begin by analyzing some relatively simple examples of what goes on in a multi-party negotiation. We'll start in the deal context where there's no pre-existing dispute. Assume a buyer (B) is negotiating to purchase a townhouse from the seller (S). B wants to use the entire house, but a tenant (T) occupies part of the premises and has a legal right to stay on for the next two years. T has let it be known, however, that he would be willing to move early if provided with an appropriate financial incentive.

So, if you were representing B, how would you go about negotiating here? The central question is, where will the money come from to get T to move—from S or from B? And no matter which one of them writes the check, how will this be figured into the purchase price negotiations being conducted between S and B?

Here's the negotiating problem from B's standpoint. He's trying to work out a deal with S on the price for the townhouse, but how can he commit to a price with S without knowing (i) who's going to take care of T, and (ii) if it's going to be B, what it will cost? So the threshold question for B is who to deal with first. Should B talk to T and find out the cost of getting T out of there, which B would then factor into his negotiations with S? (The alternative of B sending S to negotiate with T may not be so smart if B is the one who will be paying T, since S would then lack a strong incentive to negotiate hard with T—unless S were worried that the cost of the payment will reduce the purchase price he'll get from B.) Or should B first deal with S, so as to know whether the house can be bought at an acceptable price—perhaps phrasing his offer to S this way: "I'm willing to pay $4 million for the townhouse, provided I don't have to spend more than $200,000 to get rid of T."

So, although there are some sequencing decisions to be made, the situation is garden variety, everyone appears to be unemotional, no one's committed to anything, and no past wrongs have to be righted.

Now, envision a multi-party *dispute*, and you can see how things start to get tougher. Assume a plaintiff (P) is suing two defendants (D-1 and D-2) for damage P has suffered from a faulty thingamajig. One defendant designed it, the other manufactured it. P doesn't know which of them is at fault, but he claims he's been damaged to the extent of $1 million, and it has to be the responsibility of one (or both) of them.

You can bet there's likely to be some emotion here. P is mad at both defendants, while D-1 is pointing an angry finger at D-2 and vice-versa. And this kind of situation can put the parties in some uncomfortable positions. For example, what D-1 says in order to rebut an argument from P might actually strengthen D-2's hand vis-à-vis D-1.

Let's say you represent D-1, and your client wants to settle the claim without having to go through a court proceeding. D-1 acknowledges privately that P has been harmed (although not to the full extent of the $1 million P is claiming), and she's willing to pay some (but not all) of a negotiated settlement.

What do you do here? Do you begin by bargaining with D-2 over how to split up the cost of the settlement (although without knowing at this point what the actual bill will be), and then, having the split in hand, try to negotiate the total damage settlement with P? Or do you start by bargaining with P about the aggregate damages before dealing with the issue of how D-1 and D-2 will whack it up? What you don't want to happen is that you hammer out a difficult agreement with the first party, only to find the second party unwilling to accept terms that fit your first deal, thereby forcing you to go back and renegotiate it.

My general advice in these situations—which may not be applicable in all cases—is for the two defendants to work out their split first, as well as their mutual expectations vis-à-vis P, so that they present a united front in negotiating against P. This is easier if each defendant is willing to pay the same percentage amount, no matter what level of damage settlement is later agreed to with P. It's tougher if, for instance, D-1 has a limit—e.g., she's willing to pay 50% of the damage up to a $600,000 overall settlement, but at $300,000 out-of-pocket she's just about tapped out and wouldn't be willing to pay the same percentage at a higher settlement. This may call for D-1 and D-2 to agree on a schedule of percentage sharing that varies at different settlement levels. (By the way, even if D-1 and D-2 are able to resolve their split, they still have the problem of who will handle the negotiation with P—a question which may be especially significant when they're not on the same page as to how much they'd be willing to pay if P hangs tough.)

So there are problems, complete with lots of finger-pointing, but at least when you arrive at the magic numbers for the aggregate damage and the split, you're home. The even tougher case occurs when, in addition to resolving the dispute by a negotiated damage allocation, you also have to work out the terms of a forward-looking arrangement for at least two of the parties, in order to reach final settlement of the whole shebang.

There are numerous areas in the commercial world where multi-party disputes arise. Distressed company situations, for example, require resolution of the conflicting disputes between the various creditor groups and other players to achieve a consensual bankruptcy—avoiding a forced sale (or worse, padlocking the company and selling it for scrap)—a sector made more complicated in recent years by dueling crisis managers and hedge funds with interests in several camps. Complex construction projects with many stakeholders (architect, construction manager, consultant, general contractor, subcontractors, vendors/suppliers, insurers) are a prime source of multi-party disputes. Another obvious area is mass torts, with multiple plaintiffs and defendants creating many moving parts on the way to an overall settlement—one that not only avoids the litigation but also obviates the threat of some plaintiffs making separate deals with individual defendants.

The Case for Settlement

As set forth in Chapter 1, I'm a strong believer in the proposition that most commercial disputes should be settled rather than decided in court. This applies in spades in a multi-party dispute, especially one with some forward-looking deal aspects.

The omnipresent litigation—often taking place in separate suits in different jurisdictions—is incapable of generating an outcome that effectively apportions the pie, and it certainly can't cut that necessary prospective deal. Only a negotiated resolution can accomplish what's needed.

But this is something that's very difficult for multiple parties to achieve on their own, where their interests vary widely, the issues between any two often differ from those dividing other pairs or threesomes, and the pending multistate litigation could generate inconsistent results. Just getting everyone together in one place at one time may pose an awesome task for parties who frequently are hostile to each other and whose litigators— hired to protect their clients' postures in the various lawsuits— are unlikely to be spouting conciliatory verbiage.

I'm going to take you through a hypothetical multi-party dispute *cum* deal situation shortly. You'll be able to see why, with all of the moving parts, it's so difficult for the parties to resolve the whole mess on their own.

My experience in such matters—both in acting as mediator and representing a party—convinces me that, although it may take time and is definitely no sure thing, mediation offers the best hope for getting the parties to the finish line.

Getting the Mediation Started

Let's assume that the several parties to a dispute, having de-cided to try mediation, select me as the mediator. Here's what I think a mediator should be doing (or at least thinking about) before the actual in-person phase of the mediation begins, so as to maximize chances for a successful outcome.

The first big hurdle is scheduling a time and place for the mediation proper. This task alone, undertaken in conjunction with the lawyers for each party, is often challenging—trying to conform so many individual calendars. And it's crucial here for the mediator to try to schedule extra consecutive days, which will undoubtedly be needed to perform the complex task of getting multiple parties to agree upon a mutually satisfactory outcome. If everyone goes home before the job is completed, there's a risk of losing any ground that may have been gained.

A related point—previously discussed in Chapter 5—is the importance of each party having its decision-maker (usually a responsible business executive) present for the duration of the mediation. The mediator should make sure that all parties are fully committed on this score. It's so frustrating when the party representatives on the premises can't commit to anything. Mediation just doesn't work well unless the person who calls the shots (or at least recommends approval to a higher-up who is likely to abide by the recommendation) is on the scene.

In any mediation (but especially one with multiple parties), I try to get an early sense of whether each party is on board to resolve the dispute in this manner. As I observed in Chapter 5, I'm wary of getting into a situation—which can and does occur, particularly when the parties have been pushed to mediate by a judge or arbitrator—where one side prefers the impasse to remain unresolved, unless it can achieve in the mediation its adversary's unconditional surrender (which, of course, is well-nigh impossible). Through my conversations with the lawyers before the in-person process has begun, I try to satisfy myself that all the decision-makers are entering the mediation in good faith, and that they understand a successful outcome will require some compromise.

I'll level with you—I also try to ascertain whether one or more of the lawyers involved may have an interest in keeping alive the existing situation and pending litigation. Now, don't get me wrong. If a trial lawyer representing his client in the mediation has an honest and rational belief in the strength of his case—based on which he advises his client not to accept a negotiated result that's a lot worse than what he hopes to attain in court—I may (as mediator) disagree with his view of the merits, but I don't question his *bona fides*. What I'm concerned about here is the relatively rare case where the trial lawyer, irrespective of the merits, doesn't want to see his big case terminated prematurely.

Partly for this reason, and partly because I often sense that some new deal will have to be fashioned to resolve this imbroglio, I'm encouraged when I hear that a party's mediation team includes a transactional lawyer as well as the litigator. And if I don't hear that, I may suggest it—although always stating that it's for the second reason, never the first!

Because a multi-party mediation is so much more time-consuming than one with just two parties, the mediator should make a special effort to get as much done in advance of the mediation proper as possible, so as to maximize effective use of the time that everyone is together. In this vein, the mediator ought to ask the parties to make written submissions of their views on the merits of the dispute. The mediator needs to receive these sufficiently prior to the meeting to absorb the information, pose any pertinent questions (as I usually do), and request necessary supplements.

In my experience (as I've previously noted in Chapter 5), these initial submissions are as uniformly favorable to the submitting party as a trial brief. So I ask everyone to send copies to the other parties, in order that they all can see what's being argued. (I do tell the parties to feel free to share privately with me anything of a conciliatory nature they want to pass along. . . . fat chance.) I treat as confidential both the questions I pose in response to the submissions and the answers I receive—I don't want others drawing any inferences from what I ask a particular party, and I'd like to encourage (though I rarely receive) candor in the replies.

One further word on this confidentiality issue. In the mediation proper, the general rule is that what a party tells me in private—and especially a party's sentiments relative to the resolution of an issue—is confidential unless I'm expressly authorized to reveal it. But with regard to the allegations that one party is making against another (or the pugnacious replies to those allegations), I tell the parties I'm going to assume (unless specifically advised otherwise) that I'm free to relate these to others. After all, these charges are obviously intended to influence my thinking, so the other parties should be given an opportunity to respond.

For reasons I've gone into in more detail elsewhere, I think a mediator of tough commercial disputes (and a multi-party controversy is certainly that) needs to be activist and judgmental.

He or she has to bring reality to the parties' often exaggerated aspirations and intransigent postures—making them see the holes in their "winning" positions through impartial eyes, in order to justify the movement needed to bridge big gaps.

So when I'm the mediator, and assuming the parties are receptive to my playing such a role, I give my views on the merits of the issues involved, help the parties arrive at a substantive basis for settlement, and try to play an instrumental part in actually negotiating it. And I make sure to include in the mediation agreement the provision (discussed in Chapters 5 and 14) that if the mediation doesn't result in a mutual agreement, I will then recommend a specific overall resolution for all parties. Nothing short of all this, in my view, has a decent chance of success in a significant commercial dispute mediation involving multiple parties.

CHAPTER
22

THE CASINO CAPER

As in previous sections of *Anatomy of a Mediation*, I find it most instructive to provide analysis and advice against the backdrop of a specific situation. Take a few minutes to review the following fact pattern I've devised—The Casino Caper[26]— from the practice area I'm most familiar with, mergers and acquisitions. Mastering the facts—as any conscientious mediator or other dispute resolver must do in the real world—will help you grasp the negotiating points I'll be making down the road. And having a bird's-eye view of a mediator in action will give you the flavor of what's actually involved. Although the situation may seem complex at first, it really isn't—other than involving four parties whose interests are, shall we say, rather divergent.

This situation is entirely hypothetical—I have no actual model or precedent in mind. I confess to knowing very little about the hotel and casino businesses involved, so please excuse me if I ignore some of the fine points. You should assume that all of the companies involved are privately held, so there are no disclosure or securities regulatory issues involved.

The Facts

The central entity in The Casino Caper is a company that owns and operates hotels in the western United States—we'll call it "Hotels." A man named Herb Honcho owns all of Hotels' stock and is its chief executive officer.

Through a subsidiary, Hotels has a joint venture with a large casino owner and operator (let's name it "Craps"), under which Craps operates the casino in H-C, a Nevada hotel owned by Hotels. The joint venture runs for another ten years, and its terms are favorable to Hotels but have become unfavorable to Craps. In fact, Craps has asked several times to renegotiate the deal or, failing that, to be released from the joint venture.

A company in the entertainment business (we'll call it "Shows") wants to make a major move into the hotel business and is especially attracted to the idea of owning a casino hotel where its talent can perform. It focuses on Hotels, covets the H-C casino hotel, and after studying the situation, proposes an acquisition to Herb Honcho.

Honcho, who is 65, decides it's time for him to leave the rat race and get into socially redeeming activities. He considers the price that Shows has offered for Hotels to be a pretty good one. And so, without extensive negotiating (and not too much lawyering)—and without notifying Craps—Honcho enters into a short-form agreement with Shows for Herb to sell 100% of the stock of Hotels to Shows for $900 million cash. A clear proviso to the sale is that Shows will be willing to pay that $900 million only if it ends up with Hotels' favorable interest in the H-C casino joint venture.

On that score, however, there's a little problem. The H-C joint venture agreement is ambiguous as to whether a transfer of the stock ownership of Hotels can effect a transfer of its interest in the H-C joint venture without the consent of Craps, as would clearly be required if Hotels tried to transfer its interest in the joint venture directly. (I must pause here to note how many of the mediations I've been involved in over the years have featured ambiguous contract language at the very core of the dispute—and remember the situation in The Art Case, discussed in Chapters 13 and 14.)

When the Hotels-Shows deal is publicly announced—including reference to the H-C casino joint venture remaining in place—Craps sees this as an opportunity to get out of the unfavorable joint venture, or at least to better its terms. So it promptly brings a court action in Nevada (whose law controls the joint venture) against both Hotels and Shows.

The suit seeks a declaratory judgment that the Shows acquisition of Hotels, in the absence of consent from Craps as to transfer of control of H-C (which Craps makes clear will *not* be forthcoming), will terminate the joint venture. The joint venture agreement provides that if Hotels unilaterally terminates the joint venture (including an involuntary termination arising through an unpermitted transfer of its interest to which Craps doesn't consent), Craps is entitled to a substantial break-up fee from Hotels; and Craps demands payment of such fee in its complaint. Shows promptly challenges Nevada's jurisdiction over it—an issue as to which there are arguments on both sides.

The public announcement of the deal also sparks interest on another front. A large food company (we'll call it "Foods") has also been contemplating an entry into the hotel business. Now, hearing that Herb Honcho has put Hotels up for sale, Foods approaches Herb. He encourages Foods to top Shows' price, which it does, offering $1 billion for Hotels. In addition to price, the other major difference between the Foods offer and the Shows deal is that Foods (a Bible Belt stalwart) does *not* want to get into the casino business, so its offer is conditioned on *termination* of the H-C casino joint venture.

Of the two deals, Herb Honcho prefers the Foods offer. Not only is it $100 million higher than the Shows price, but it eliminates the problem he faces on the Shows deal (namely the Craps lawsuit to terminate the joint venture), since Craps would presumably consent to being let out of the joint venture in the Foods deal.

But wait, you say, isn't Herb already committed to Shows? Not so fast, says his lawyer—the Hotels-Shows short-form agreement fails to state clearly whether it's a binding contract or just an agreement in principle. So Honcho, taking the position that it was merely an agreement in principle (and without notifying Shows as to what he's about to do), proceeds to enter into a long-form binding agreement with Foods at the $1 billion price, conditioned on termination of the joint venture—and with Honcho indemnifying Foods against any claim by Shows. Honcho's lawyers then go into the Nevada court where Craps sued for a declaratory judgment and tell the judge that the suit is now moot, since its deal with Foods accomplishes what Craps is asking for—termination of the joint venture.

But when it learns of the Hotels-Foods deal, Shows is predictably furious over Honcho's perfidy. Shows brings an action in a Delaware court (where Hotels is incorporated and whose law controls the Honcho-Shows agreement), suing Honcho for breach of contract, suing Foods for inducing that breach of contract (as to which Foods challenges Delaware jurisdiction), and seeking specific performance of its agreement to buy Hotels. At the same time, Shows tells the Nevada court to wait a minute, that issue over the transfer of the joint venture without consent hasn't been mooted.

So now the parties have a real mess on their hands.

- Shows and Foods are vying to own Hotels.
- Shows is relying on a questionable short-form agreement, but Foods still has to worry about whether or not it's enforceable.
- In one state, Craps is suing Honcho and Shows, and in another state, Shows is suing Honcho and Foods—in each case with an uncertain outcome.
- Jurisdictional questions have been raised in both courts that will serve to delay any judicial decisions on the merits.
- Both Honcho and Craps (for different reasons) prefer Honcho's deal with Foods, but Shows still has the piece of paper that's arguably binding.

You can see, can't you, why this contretemps will be very difficult for the parties to resolve by themselves—especially since the various events and lawsuits have created bad feelings all around. As for the litigation in two different jurisdictions, it could drag on for a long time through appeals and such, might result in inconsistent verdicts, and is bound to make somebody unhappy with the ultimate decisions.

So wisdom prevails, and all four parties decide to see whether a four-way mediation can lead to a breakthrough. Let's assume I'm the mediator chosen by the parties for this task. All the preliminaries have taken place and now everyone is assembled in one place.

The Opening Rounds

As you've seen in prior sections of this book, my usual practice at the outset of a two-party mediation is to put everyone in a large room and let the parties and their counsel vent about the merits of their respective cases. (My reasons for this are spelled out in Chapter 7.) In a multi-party dispute, however, I suggest foregoing this: it takes up too much time, is too disruptive, and gets things off on the wrong foot. The parties have told the mediator where they stand in their written submissions. Now it's time (and time is a valuable commodity here) to strike a positive note in terms of reaching an overall accommodation. (I do, however, let each party put its best foot forward to me privately in our initial separate caucuses, so they can feel satisfied they've had the opportunity to do this in person.)

When I start the mediation, I bring all the parties together briefly in order to deliver a positive message, perhaps along these lines:

> "I've never seen a stronger case for working out a negotiated resolution. The litigation alternative is a multi-state mess, and no quick rulings are available. Even if you got some timely decisions, the judges wouldn't be able to structure the kind of deal that's necessary to meet the needs of all parties.
>
> "You're in a quagmire—the legal equivalent of the situation in chess called *zugzwang*, where the only moves a player can make will cost him pieces or have a damaging positional effect.
>
> "I'm hopeful, though, that with some help and prodding from me, you'll be able to work this out on your own, and everyone will walk away reasonably satisfied with the outcome. So, without further ado, let's get going. I'll be meeting with each of you separately in the following order. . . ."

In the early stages of the mediation, in addition to trying to ascertain the parties' underlying desires, I attempt to get a handle on the dynamics among members of the respective teams.

Let's say that each group contains a decision-making executive, a financial guru, an inside counsel, an outside litigator, and a deal lawyer (who may at times be the inside counsel). Sure, I know who the ultimate decision-maker is in theory, but I'm also looking to see who's the *de facto* leader of the pack. The more the dispute involves a financial decision, the greater chance the financial guru may be the key player; if litigation looms large, the litigator may take the lead; if the inside counsel has a lot of mediation experience, the executive in charge may defer to him or her. Once I've identified the leader, I'll gear my strategy to getting both that person and the anointed decision-maker behind a resolution.

Within any group, there are often some hardliners and some people of a more reasonable bent. Since a certain flexibility is needed to achieve a good outcome here, when the decision-maker (or group leader, if that's someone else) is a hardliner, then I know the mediation is in trouble before it even starts. But as I survey the participants in The Casino Caper, I'm pleased to note that, at least on the surface in our private conversations, everyone seems willing to listen and be reasonable. I'm beginning to think they might actually realize the mess they're in. . . .

CHAPTER 23

DEVISING A STRATEGY

In every mediation I preside over, there comes a point where I need to go off by myself and figure out what's feasible to effect a resolution of the situation. In the one-shot dollar dispute (as discussed in Chapter 9), this takes place after a lot else has gone on—so that I've been able to develop some significant information on which to base my thinking. In a deal-dispute mediation (as set forth in Chapter 18), this usually occurs at an earlier point—although not until the issues separating the parties have been thoroughly aired.

In multi-party proceedings such as The Casino Caper—where there's a variety of possible directions to take and outcomes to evaluate—I feel the need to go off by myself rather early in the session to analyze what form a resolution might take. I'm concerned that, without having a sense of direction, I might be guiding participants down an inferior path that will be difficult to pull back from later on. I want to know—at least tentatively—where I'm heading.

Discerning a Tentative Format for Resolution

In The Casino Caper, I can envision at least three plausible outcomes to this mess.

1.   *The parties return to their original pre-dispute situation and all litigation is dropped.* In other words, Hotels doesn't get sold under the existing agreements with either Shows or Foods—those agreements are terminated. The parties

can begin new rounds of negotiations if they wish—and if the Hotels properties are growing more valuable each day, that might not be so bad for Honcho (although worse for Shows and Foods). Craps will have to live with the unfavorable-to-Craps existing H-C joint venture for the time being.

I can see a big problem with this outcome right off the bat. Although the matter isn't free from doubt, I've reached my own conclusion that Shows' position as to the enforceability of the short-form agreement is a lot stronger than Honcho's argument that it's just an agreement in principle. Shows apparently believes this in spades and will undoubtedly demand some meaningful payment for giving up its rights under the Shows-Honcho agreement. That payment will presumably have to come from Honcho, since there's no way that Foods is likely to chip in. (Actually, Foods will probably seek something for itself from Honcho, especially through the indemnification provision in the Foods-Honcho deal.) Honcho is not going to be happy making a payment of any kind, especially since he can't be sure of his ability to rekindle negotiations for the sale of Hotels.

I also have a strong sense (which the parties undoubtedly share) that this back-to-square-one resolution doesn't really accomplish much and fails to take into account what has transpired in recent months. So I consider this strictly a fall-back position if the other possibilities don't eventuate.

2. *Foods gets to buy Hotels and all litigation is dropped.* Under this outcome:
   (a) Craps receives a benefit because the H-C casino joint venture (that's unfavorable to Craps but that Foods doesn't want) is terminated and no longer presents a problem.
   (b) Shows will have to get paid a substantial sum for going away without Hotels. The bill, however, can be shared by Honcho and Foods. So, assume that Honcho and Foods are still talking about a $1 billion valuation for Hotels, and that Shows needs to receive $100 million to walk. Half of this might come from Foods (so its total

cost is $50 million more than the $1 billion purchase price). The other half would be paid by Honcho out of the purchase price, so he ends up with $950 million—less than under the first Foods deal, but better than under the original Shows deal.

3. *Shows gets to buy Hotels and all litigation is dropped.* Here's what Shows has to do to get there:

   (a) It will have to pay a lot more than the $900 million it agreed to pay in the first deal. The excess would be divided up between Honcho (to get him to give up the richer Foods deal) and Foods (which must receive something significant to walk away from the situation).

   (b) At the same time (and this can only serve to diminish its eagerness to pay more to Honcho and Foods), Shows has to renegotiate the terms of the C-H casino joint venture to make it more favorable to Craps (and thus less favorable to Shows). That's what is needed in order to get Craps to drop its claim that Honcho's sale of Hotels without Craps' consent terminates the joint venture and triggers the break-up fee.

My initial impression is that No. 2—the sale to Foods—appears logical and is the preferable direction in which to steer the negotiations. I'm influenced here not only by the complications inherent in No. 3, but also for several affirmative reasons:

- Foods already has more money on the table than Shows, and for the purchase of fewer assets (since its deal excludes the H-C casino joint venture with Craps that's favorable to Hotels). Money is what it's going to take to incentivize Honcho and to pay off the losing bidder in either event.
- Foods will be able to get Honcho to chip in on paying off Shows—the motivation being that Shows has a good legal claim against Honcho for breach of contract.
- Since Foods doesn't want the casino, the lawsuit with

Craps is moot, allowing the latter to terminate the joint venture with Hotels that's unfavorable to Craps.

I'll proceed tentatively with that in mind (although not sharing my initial determination with the parties), while keeping my eyes and ears open to evidence that a different format might be preferable. As a mediator, you can't get fossilized—you never can tell how you might have to adjust your thinking.

Gaining Valuable Information

As I noted in Chapter 5, it's important for a mediator to be a good listener—an attribute that's especially vital in one of these multi-party cases like The Casino Caper. And this isn't just a passive exercise—it's also being alert to what's left unsaid, what's hovering between the lines. A good mediator stays alert to the signals and clues that abound in a negotiation.

It's time now for me to shift away from just listening to the parties vent and begin to make my own probes, in order to confirm that I'm headed down the right path. This, of course, requires confidentiality. As in the other mediations discussed in this book (and for many of the same reasons), I'm a strong advocate of the private caucus to accomplish this.

One technique I sometimes use is to ask each of the groups three questions: (a) what their favored outcome is (but on a realistic basis, recognizing that everyone has to give something up in order for a settlement to take place); (b) what their second favorite outcome is (again on a realistic basis); and finally, (c) what their least favorite outcome is. I avoid labeling their answer to this last question as an absolute no-no or other similar indication of inflexibility, since I may have to push things in that direction, and I don't want anyone to lose any more face than it has to.

Another thing I'm looking for in any dispute that has multiple issues (but of particular value when multiple parties are involved) is ranking the importance of the various issues to each party. Because the parties frequently have different views, it helps for me to know what's important to one (or a matter of relative indifference to another) in terms of overseeing the trading that will eventually have to take place. In this regard, I also take note of which issues carry an added emotional component for one of the parties (as issues often do) that goes beyond the dollars involved—the emotional issues, as we've seen, not always being the big ticket items. As in two-party mediations previously discussed, this means that I may be able to arrange a swap of one party's acquiescence on a small dollar issue that represents a real matter of principle for the other party, in exchange for the other's concession on a larger dollar issue that it doesn't care so much about.

In a multi-party dispute, I'm also looking for information that suggests to me some shared interests between two of the parties. These interests may lead to a coalition or alliance that I can use later to overcome some obstacles—although (as we'll see later) it also has the potential to hamper my efforts.

At any rate, my probing of each of the parties produces some interesting information that I need to factor into my determination of what's the best format for moving ahead.

In talking with Foods, for example, I learn several things of note:

- That Hotels is not the only hotel chain Foods considered buying before making its move, and that at least one other chain is still available, although at a somewhat higher price;
- That the $1 billion price tag Foods put on the deal is just about its limit, especially since under its offer, a key element of Hotels' value—the C-H casino joint venture—is specifically excluded;
- That the dollars Foods might receive for walking away could come in very handy in buying this other more expensive hotel chain; and
- That although its legal team puts up a brave front on the issue, Foods' top management is clearly bothered by Shows' claim against it for inducing a breach of contract—the kind of allegation that a Bible Belt company like Foods finds hard to stomach.

With Honcho, I find myself reading between the lines. Herb says it all comes down to how many dollars he can put in his pocket and not be harassed by lawsuits, and he claims not to care who ends up with Hotels (as between Foods and Shows). My sense, though, is that deep down he'd be sorry to see the H-C casino joint venture—which has formed a major part of his professional image—go out of business. As for the money, although he definitely wants to end up with more than the $900 million he was going to get originally from Shows, I think he realizes he'll have to take less than the $1 billion offered in the Foods deal.

With Craps, when I probe beneath the termination rhetoric and break-up fee bravado (which a mediator has to do), I find out something that should have been obvious to me from the start. Hey, dummy mediator, Craps is in the casino business! Notwithstanding its complaint in the Nevada lawsuit, Craps' first choice isn't getting out of the unfavorable H-C joint venture agreement—that's strictly second choice, even with the break-up fee. Its first choice—duh!—is to stay in the joint venture under revised terms more favorable to Craps. After all, Craps invested a lot of time and money in developing the H-C casino business—its management would be disgruntled to have to abandon ship.

But the biggest education I receive comes from the time spent probing Shows. What I find out is that Shows is genuinely determined to end up with Hotels, including the H-C casino. For Shows, there's no other company comparable to Hotels on the market—in effect, Shows doesn't have a second favorite outcome.

Moreover, Shows is convinced it has a binding contract to buy Hotels, is prepared to go to the mat in court to uphold its position, and gives short shrift to Craps' argument that the H-C casino joint venture isn't transferred by the transfer of control of Hotels. (And, I must say, I find myself generally in accord with Shows' views, especially as to the flimsy Craps argument.)

As a mediator, I'm always drawing inferences from what I detect under the surface in these private caucuses. I'm careful not to give these inferences too much weight—they are, after all, only suppositions—but they often can shed some useful light. The inference I drew here is that Shows' firmness on the "binding contract" issue is driven by its outside law firm, which isn't about to admit that the firm's short-form acquisition agreement didn't do the trick. (By the way, on occasion I run across the flip side of that situation—where the lawyer whose document is at issue does *not* want to face the embarrassment of a court decision holding it inadequate, and accordingly works hard to achieve a negotiated resolution of the dispute.)

At any rate, the conclusion I reach is that Shows isn't just posturing and that to induce Shows to go away would cost more bucks than the other parties could afford. There's one more piece of the puzzle I need, and that's Shows' finances. I probe this, and what I find is that, far from being tapped out, Shows has substantial excess funds available. These, I realize, could be used to up the ante for acquiring Hotels (with the H-C casino) and also to pay Foods for going away.

All of this leads to my "Aha!" moment—when I realize that the resolution format I originally considered the most promising (No. 2) is unlikely to be consummated, and the format I considered too complicated (No. 3) could actually take root.

Marketing the Revised Format

At this point, I go off by myself to figure out what such a deal would look like. That's important, but it's not enough. What's equally critical is how to get there. I ask myself—what's the most effective sequence for me to follow in the negotiations I'll be conducting with each of the parties? As a mediator in a multi-party dispute, you must have a game plan that enables you to steer negotiations toward a successful outcome.

Here's what I work out and then proceed to do. I start with Craps, which in my mind is the keystone to the whole resolution. I now know Craps is prepared to stay in the H-C joint venture under improved terms. What its people have to understand, though, is they can't push too hard to better those terms, or else Shows (which needs a valuable H-C casino to buttress its big investment in this project) won't be able to justify the ad-

ditional dollars needed to make this work. They hear me out, and while no one swears fealty, enough heads nod to suggest I've made my point.

I next approach the Shows team. This is my pitch to them (which I've paraphrased here, as I'll do in the subsequent pitches to the other parties recounted below).

> "I've got good news and bad news for you guys. The good news is that, in my opinion, the best way to resolve this is for you to 'win' by acquiring Hotels with an H-C casino deal in place. And on that score, I've satisfied myself that if the joint venture terms can be revised somewhat for Craps' benefit, Craps would stay on and relinquish any claim that it's entitled to terminate the joint venture and receive a break-up fee.
>
> "But here's the bad news, fellows. You're going to have to dig deep into your wallets to up the ante—both what you have to pay Honcho for Hotels and what you'll have to pay Foods to go away. And, let's face it, you won't have as favorable a deal on the H-C casino as you originally thought you were getting—although at least here, you won't have the specter of the Craps termination lawsuit.
>
> "Are you guys willing to go down this path? If you are, my next stop is to try to convince Foods to give up its claim to Hotels and go away for some bucks. If you're not, tell me now, and I'll start working on a plan whereby Foods wins and you end up taking that dollar walk."

Well, Shows replies, we want to buy Hotels, and we have the funds—but we don't know how much we'll be willing to pay until we see what the new H-C casino joint venture agreement is going to look like. It's a fair point, and I tell them I appreciate it—"so any numbers we discuss for you to pay Honcho and Foods are conditioned on your ability to work out a satisfactory forward-looking deal with Craps." The response from the Shows team is guarded but not unfavorable.

Then I go to the Foods group and tell them the bad news—that in order to achieve an overall resolution here, they won't be ending up with Hotels. Here's my pitch, which I believe to be realistic:

"Shows is just intransigent, feels strongly that its contract is binding, and is prepared to go to court to prove it. And by the way, fellows, as a matter of law, I think Shows' position is much the stronger one. As for you guys, well, Hotels isn't the only fish in the sea; and you'll be entitled, as the price for giving up your claim, to receive a walkaway payment from Shows and/or Honcho. I'll work hard on getting you something substantial—something that you'll find very helpful in reaching for that alternative hotel chain that's more expensive than this one."

Finally, I go to Honcho, who lets me know right off the bat that he's peeved I'm spending so much time with the others. I reply:

"That's because all I've got to work out for you are the dollars (plus, of course, ending the litigation), while the other groups have some more complicated paths to tread and decisions to make. Whichever way we go, Herb, you're going to end up with more than $900 million but less than $1 billion."

I tell him why that's so and give the reasons I've decided to go the route of Shows ending up with Hotels. Then I get down to business.

"But look, Herb, it's not only Shows that considers you bound under the original short-form agreement—it's me, too. [Here I explain why I come out this way] I'll try to get you as good a price as possible, but whatever you receive in excess of $900 million is gravy—found money, you might call it. That $1 billion Foods price is illusory—it needs to be reduced by the potential big cost of the indemnity you gave them. As a matter of fact, even the original $900 million you agreed to take from Shows isn't firm, because of the possibility that Craps might win its case to terminate the joint venture and claim the break-up fee—in which case, Shows is entitled to walk and would presumably do so."

And now I present the real kicker. It's blunt, but that's what a mediator has to do if any progress is to be made.

"Listen, Herb, here's the key fact you have to face. To keep Craps in the picture, the H-C joint venture terms will be getting worse from Shows' perspective than what it originally planned on. Therefore, I'm not going to be able to wrench a lot of extra money from Shows. So you have to be prepared to chip in to whatever it takes to pay off Foods."

Honcho looks glum but doesn't kick me out of the room.

Now I put Honcho and Foods into cold storage while I work on Shows and Craps, where the real action has to take place. This is especially true with the Shows team, by far my biggest task. I have to raise their sights—paying more to Honcho, paying a sizeable amount to Foods, and at the same time conceding better terms to Craps on the joint venture (which has the effect of making the Hotels acquisition less valuable to them). For this, I have to pull out all the stops—underscoring the negatives, but also reminding them of the positives.

"You guys may be overvaluing the effectiveness of your short-form agreement, which might be questionable practice to an unsophisticated jury—or in the hands of a judge who thinks a traditional long-form agreement is what's needed to bind companies on a major deal like this. And by the way, even if the short-form agreement is upheld, the Craps argument that it doesn't serve to transfer the joint venture isn't frivolous—so you may find you're not getting what you bargained for.

"Let's face it, fellows, you made a great bargain the first time around. The fact that Foods was willing to pay $100 million more than you—and not even get an interest in the money-making H-C casino joint venture—is irrefutable evidence that there's a lot more value here. So, bottom line, you can afford to pay up."

Shows' reply is predictable—we don't know how much we can pay until we know the terms of the revised joint venture with Craps. But I want to find out *now* how much they're willing to invest in this situation. What I do in cases like this— where there's an uncertainty affecting the final number—is to hypothesize things on a best-case basis. So here's what I say to them:

> "Look, I'll go to work on Craps, but meanwhile tell me how far you'd be prepared to go if (hypothetically) the terms of the Craps joint venture were to stay the same as they now are. Sure, I understand that this won't happen and that your ultimate number is contingent on how the joint venture terms actually work out—and I won't tell anyone else what your top number is—but how about it?"

At this point, there's a lot of hemming and hawing on Shows' part, and nothing crystallizes. But I've gotten enough of a response to feel I'm on the right track—albeit with some distance yet to travel.

In a situation like this, there's always a question (with no inevitable answer) of whether to discuss in aggregate terms the dollars in excess of $900 million that Shows will have to put up, or whether to negotiate separately the amounts that will go to each of Honcho and Foods. In this case, my preference is to split up the two. In part, my reason is psychological. Sure, the Shows people can add the two numbers together and moan loudly over the aggregate, but at least I'm not contributing to that malaise. The more compelling reason, however, is that it allows me to furnish better specific rationale to Shows for what's needed to incentivize those two other parties to sign on to the deal.

Now I go back to Craps with this pitch:

> "Forget all this lawsuit stuff about termination and break-up fee. Shows gives short shrift to your argument that the transfer of control of Hotels doesn't transfer the joint venture without your consent, and frankly, so do I.

"The fact is, you're a major player in the casino business. The best outcome for you is having Shows acquire Hotels, with you staying on in the H-C joint venture under improved terms.

"For that to happen, Shows has to come up in price to Honcho and also has to pay big bucks to make Foods go away. I'm hopeful of getting Shows to do that, but not if you try to renegotiate the joint venture so much as to make it unprofitable for Shows.

"So don't push it too far—no heroics please. Only seek improvement up to the level of equilibrium. And don't try to change everything—keep focused on a few key elements that make the terms unfavorable to you."

The Craps' executive nods but doesn't commit; once again, the nod is good enough for me.

So now I return to the Shows group and tell them I believe that Craps is amenable to making a reasonable deal—they'll only seek changes in a few areas that shouldn't restrict Shows' ability to make big profits. My implicit message to Shows should be clear: don't use this contract revision (which I'm likely to refer to as just a "tweaking") to shrink the amounts you're willing to pay Honcho and Foods.

Then I go to the Foods group, give them the lay of the land, and try to figure how much money will be needed for them to leave the field. Here, of course, I take the position (which I do believe) that Shows' short-form contract is binding, that Foods won't win in court trying to upset it, and that they face a very real problem in terms of the claim against them for inducing a breach of contract. "So, you better be reasonable."

Finally, I sit down with Honcho (who by now is really miffed at the lack of attention he's receiving), and here's what I tell him:

"You did a bad thing [breaching the contract with Shows], but nevertheless I'm going to get you something more than you would have received in that first Shows deal—albeit not as much as the illusory $1 billion Foods deal that was fraught with legal problems."

And then I work on getting an idea of what figure Honcho would be willing to take.

So there are four moving parts, disputes to resolve, and one going-forward deal (the revised terms of the joint venture) to help negotiate. How to proceed now will depend to some degree on the various positions the parties take, but I'm definitely on my way.

Some Reflections on Multi-Party Mediation

In a multi-party mediation, where the mediator is meeting separately with each of the parties, a real issue can arise as to what the people who aren't engaged with the mediator at that moment should be doing. They become restless the longer they're away from where "the action" is. How does the mediator keep them actively involved in the process?

I try to set up a regular rotation, where my time with any one group isn't excessive, and the others know I'll be meeting with them before too long. I also try to give each group an assignment as we part company—something to work on in the interim, so they can come back to the next session with pertinent new information or with a response to some suggestion or request I've previously made to them.

I usually discourage representatives of the parties from talking to each other outside the mediation room. I worry about a variety of things here: at one extreme, that they'll get angry at each other and depart the premises (or at least be tougher to deal with); at the other end of the spectrum, that one of them will concede a point I want to use as leverage for a swap later on; or that an alliance may form that sidetracks the mediation away from the direction I'm working hard to establish.

Take this last point, for example. What if Foods and Craps were to get together and sketch out a deal along these lines: Craps would agree to allow the Honcho-Foods acquisition agreement to transfer Hotels' interest in the H-C casino joint venture; and Foods would agree to let Craps buy out Hotels' interest in the joint venture right after the first closing. This would allow Foods to pay extra for Hotels because of the funds it will be receiving from Craps. This may not be a bad solution for three of the parties, but Shows is certainly not going to let it happen; and if this were to get off the ground, it could derail the entire mediation.

I make an exception to the no-fraternization rule if two of the parties (in this case, Shows and Craps) will have to do business together going forward, and I think their respective executives might need to get to know each other better. Assuming I consider the individuals reasonable enough to behave, I could encourage a get-together—perhaps warning them not to discuss the merits of the dispute but just to schmooze.

As noted earlier, a strong reason for why I like to operate in private caucus is to be able to tell a party which of its arguments are strong and which are not—going right to the merits. The party doesn't like the mediator's negative judgments, but it would be substantially more painful (and make the dispute harder to settle) if the negative judgments were conveyed with other parties present.

In this vein, a concern I expressed previously—but that's exacerbated with multiple parties—is the need to preserve the appearance (as well as the reality) of the mediator's neutrality. A party's team will listen to, and may well be influenced to move by, the mediator's negative judgments on an issue, but only so long as they're convinced the mediator is telling it like it is—not being influenced by bias against them or in favor of someone else. And believe me, in the emotional, frustrating context of a multi-party dispute, this kind of paranoia can find fertile ground.

There are various ways a mediator can (and should) attempt to combat this problem. She cannot, for instance, be peremptory—rather she must listen, acknowledge and discuss, at least at first. She can't be relentlessly negative on every aspect of a party's position; she has to balance this, at least partially, by speaking with approval of some aspect of the party's case.

As I noted earlier (but it's worth repeating here), I often go even further than this. I find some aspect of the matter that's obviously critical to the party's decision-makers—an aspect that, unless I'm able to get it for them (or a good approximation), they're unlikely to do the deal. It also has to be something that I suspect can be squeezed out of the other parties, at least if they receive something in exchange.

I then tell the first party that I want to try to get them their pet point—that they deserve it—but it won't be easy. So, I say, "Let's work together to develop some arguments I can make to the other parties on this point—arguments that will have a lot more force coming from the neutral mediator than from you as the partisan party."

I've previously pointed out (as one advantage of working in private caucus) the mediator's ability to adopt a party's constructive suggestion as the mediator's own—as if the mediator had thought it up—which makes it a lot easier to sell to the others. If it's presented as coming from a party, the others will immediately be suspicious as to what the offeror has up its sleeve. So I ask the people who make the suggestion if they have any objection to me presenting it as my idea—to avoid that reflexive negative reaction. Usually they're agreeable, and that's how I do it.

CHAPTER
24

REACHING A RESOLUTION

Let's assume I make progress in The Casino Caper toward getting everyone on the same page in terms of the format an ultimate resolution could take. I'm still a long way from home, though, in terms of both the actual dollars to be transferred and the revisions to the H-C casino joint venture agreement. So the question is, what to do next?

A Draft Agreement in Principle (with Holes)

I think it makes sense at this juncture for me to draft a simple agreement in principle that sets forth the basic format of the deal. On matters where there's no agreement (such as the dollars involved), I simply leave a blank (or say "[amount to be negotiated]"). With respect to the joint venture deal, the draft agreement in principle can simply refer to it as "to be revised in accordance with the terms set forth in Annex A," and then I leave Annex A blank. What I'm trying to accomplish here is to smoke out whether anyone has a problem with the basic format; if not, I can then press ahead on the numbers and the joint venture terms.

Let's say that everyone indicates a willingness to proceed with the format I've proposed. But each of the parties lets me know in no uncertain terms that it's not going to be any picnic to arrive at mutually agreeable terms.

- The Foods team, for instance, lectures me that it will take a blockbuster of a dollar figure to make them go away—

especially, they say, "because the merits of the lawsuit as to who's entitled to buy Hotels are definitely with us."

- Honcho argues that he doesn't want to sell for a lot less than the $1 billion Foods was willing to pay him—particularly since Shows is now going to get the valuable casino it wanted so much.
- The Craps people tell me that the H-C casino joint venture agreement has to be substantially improved in a number of significant respects to make it worthwhile for them to stay on—otherwise, "we're outta here," and "pay us our break-up fee."
- And Shows, while admitting it can pay more than its original $900 million price, warns me that its total outlay "won't be that much more"—adding that "Honcho's not going to do a lot better than in the original deal, and we're not about to make Foods rich. And, by the way, the more Craps squeezes us on the joint venture terms, the less we'll have available to take care of the other two guys."

In other words, I've got my work cut out for me. Hey, no one said this would be easy.

The Forward-Looking Deal Aspects

One question I have to deal with right away is whether Shows and Craps should be negotiating (through me) the deal aspects of the forward-looking H-C casino joint venture *concurrently* with the negotiations that are taking place among Honcho, Shows and Foods on resolving the dispute. Under some other scenarios, I could see deferring the bargaining on the deal until the dispute negotiations have been successfully concluded, or at least until the parties are close to agreement. That's not the case, however, in The Casino Caper. Here the deal negotiations need to proceed concurrently, because Shows has to be satisfied with the revised joint venture terms in order to be willing to cough up the extra dollars required to take care of Hotels and Foods.

A good rule to keep in mind in conducting a multi-party mediation is that not all the parties have to be involved in every aspect of the resolution. If an issue can be isolated as raising only two-party concerns, it can be negotiated (with the mediator's help) just between them—the others not being invited to participate.

So, in terms of the forward-looking deal aspect of The Casino Caper, I consider that strictly a two-party negotiation (with my assistance) between Craps and Shows. Although Honcho and Foods have an obvious interest in seeing this negotiation succeed (because the overall four-way resolution depends on it), I don't permit them to take part in the joint venture bargaining, whether through me or otherwise. The specific terms of that deal are none of their business, and I don't feel any need to keep them updated on what's happening there (other than noting that "we're making progress").

You'll recall that my own favored technique in a dollar dispute is to get away from traditional bargaining—carrying offers and counters back and forth—and engage in simultaneous private negotiations between myself and each of the parties in separate caucuses. That's what I do here on the various dollar negotiations. With regard to the forward-looking deal aspect, however, I do shuttle back and forth on specific issues, telling each party where the other stands (having received permission to do so) and urging them to close the several gaps. As in the deal-dispute mediating of Part IV, my experience has been that this approach—playing each party off against each other directly—is better suited to trying to resolve multiple future business issues on which the parties clash.

The further question is whether to bring them together in the same room and let them negotiate directly with each other. There's no historic bad blood between Shows and Craps, so my frequent fear that they won't be civil towards each other isn't dispositive here. A strong argument can be made for bringing them together if the issues to be negotiated are highly technical ones outside my area of knowledge, and I'm leery about being able to convey the parties' positions on matters I don't really understand.

Nevertheless, in most instances I prefer to keep the negotiating parties separate and deal with each in private caucus. As a mediator, it's not enough for me just to carry their messages back and forth; I feel the need to help shape the proposals transmitted, to boost the chances of constructive movement toward an eventual agreement. The fact is, I'm still negotiating with each party—telling them when I think a position they take is overreaching, urging them to move in a certain direction, trying to extract from them a variety of concessions. I can "call 'em as I see 'em" in private—and believe me, I do—but, for reasons stated earlier, I'm reticent to do this in public.

So, for instance, I spend a lot of time here with the Craps group to restrain them from trying to cut too sweet a deal with Shows, since that will discourage Shows from adequately funding Foods' departure from the scene. I try to educate myself on what's significant in a casino joint venture. I make the Craps team show me precedents from deals they have with other hotels (or from the deals other casino companies have made) and insist they hew to those terms, rather than trying to better them. I tell them that Shows is relying on me to opine that the revised terms Craps is seeking are reasonable, as to which I need to be persuaded—to feel confident that they're not attempting to exploit the situation unreasonably. And when Craps isn't able to achieve as much as it seeks in a particular area, I point out that what they're getting is still a lot better than the status quo (if no deal were to take place) and certainly better than being out on their ear (if Honcho were to sell to Foods).

Much of the advice I might offer to lawyers who represent adversaries in a multi-party mediation consists of suggestions equally applicable to two-party mediations, which I'll discuss in Part V.

The Denouement

Let's assume I make significant progress with each of the parties, but as the end of the two-day scheduled mediation draws near (and people are preparing to leave to catch planes), gaps still remain on all four fronts. Assume also that progress has slowed to a crawl, the bargaining arteries have hardened all around, and tempers are beginning to flare. Here's where things stand at this point:

- Shows has come up from its initial offer of $900 million to $930 million as the price for buying Hotels, resisting my efforts to move higher with the argument that any additional moneys they put into the hopper are needed to pay Foods for dropping its claim. Honcho has come down to $970 million from his initial asking price of $1 billion (the amount he was originally slated to get from Foods). So, some ground has been made up, but a $40 million gap remains.
- After a lot of angst, Shows has come up (from its original $25 million offer) to offering Foods $50 million to go away. Foods has reduced its ask to $75 million from the $100 million it originally sought. So, there's still a $25 million gap.
- Shows and Craps, with my assistance, have negotiated numerous points in a revised H-C casino joint venture deal and managed to reach tentative agreement on all of them except one important expense-sharing provision. If this provision were to come out Craps' way, it would be very costly tax-wise for Shows. If it came out Shows' way, it wouldn't be so bad tax-wise for Craps. No one's budging, and there's no obvious middle ground.

At this point, I call all the parties together, and here's what I say to them:

"In my judgment, we're unlikely to make much more progress today and time is running out. So you have a decision to make (and you can each caucus separately on this before replying to me). Do you want to set a date down the road to resume the mediation, at which time we can try to close the gaps that so far have resisted closure? Or do you want me to invoke the provision in the mediation agreement under which I recommend a specific resolution of all outstanding issues?"

This is a decision on which people can obviously differ, so each party holds a private caucus to deliberate on its response. If one or more parties are unwilling to resume the mediation at a later date, then it's over—and that triggers my role. Let's assume this is what happens here—all of them are discouraged with the recent lack of progress, have wearied of the effort, remain pessimistic about a future breakthrough, and want to get on with their lives. So it's up to me to propose a resolution—something that has to be accepted by all four parties or else they go back to war.

Depending on the circumstances, I could make my recommendation that same day (after a short break to collect my thoughts) or defer it to a later date if I need time to work out some more intricate arrangement and accompanying rationale. (The deferral here may be less desirable, but since I'll be presenting it to each of the parties separately, at least they won't need to come together in one place at that later date.) For our purposes, let's assume that I feel comfortable making the recommendation to each of the parties while everyone is still assembled at the mediation location.

My Proposed Resolution

As I go off to ponder the terms to recommend, the main concept that runs through my mind is that of feasibility—what's attainable under the circumstances. As I've advised everyone from the outset, I'm not making a value judgment as to where the resolution *should* take place or what is *fair* under the circumstances. I have to come up with a resolution that has a chance of being accepted by all parties—finding that precise juncture at which each of them would rather shake hands than return to court.

My recommendation is going to require movement by all parties, some more than others. Where, I ponder, is flexibility most likely to come from? The relative positive and negative leverage factors affecting the various parties is crucial in determining this.

If everyone knew where everyone else stood at this point, I'd probably feel a lot of pressure to "split the difference" between their several positions. But (other than on the joint venture agreement) each one knows only where it stands, not its adversaries. So I can adopt an approach more consistent with the rationale I'll be using to persuade them to accept my resolution.

I never lose sight of the fact that what I'm proposing is nothing more than a proposal. It's not like an arbitrator's award that the parties have to accept—they're free to reject my recommendation. So the rationale I offer each party (which may differ, although the resolution itself is uniform) has to be convincing enough to generate a positive response.

Turning now from the general to the specific, I obviously have to loosen up Shows' pocketbook, which is crucial to the dollars involved. The best means of accomplishing this is to have Shows prevail on that tax-sensitive expense-sharing provision in the joint venture with Craps, thus freeing Shows up to pay more to both Honcho and Foods. And I'm hopeful that this "victory" for Shows (coupled with its prior major victory in ending up as the acquirer of Hotels) will make it easier psychologically for the Shows people to accept the dollar stretch that's going to be required from them.

What's my risk with Craps if I award that provision in the H-C casino joint venture agreement to Shows? Frankly, I don't think it's very much. In pitching my resolution, here's what I'm going to point out to Craps:

"This mediation has been very beneficial to you. It's responsible for keeping you as the operator of the H-C casino, and it has provided you with a number of improvements in the joint venture terms. Look how much better this result is for you guys than if the mediation were to fail and you'd have to go back to operating under the existing agreement or fighting about termination in court. And by the way, the tax result of that expense-sharing provision isn't so terrible from your perspective. But here's the bottom line—having this provision come out in Shows' favor is the only way I can get them to pay enough to satisfy Honcho and Foods."

Consistent with this, when I tell Shows how much it has to move up on the payments to Honcho and Foods, I'm able to say, "Hey, I gave you what you wanted from Craps—now you have to be willing to pay more to these other guys."

My proposed resolution is for Shows to pay $940 million to

Honcho for Hotels ($10 million more than Shows' last bid, $30 million less than Honcho's last ask), and to pay $60 million to Foods to go away ($10 million more than Shows' last offer, $15 million less than Foods' last ask). The total out-of-pocket for Shows—not just coincidentally—will be $1 billion. Here's how I put the news to Shows:

> "You have to spend in the aggregate at least as much as Foods was willing to pay for Hotels without the valuable H-C casino—that's an indication of market value that simply can't be ignored. Obviously, all of this increase does not have to go to Honcho, and I've made it clear to him from the outset not to expect anything like that.
>
> "I could have divided the extra $100 million equally between Honcho and Foods, but I think Foods needs to come away with something more than $50 million—given its view as to the uncertain judicial outcome on your short-form agreement. And, although it's a lot less than the one billion smackers that have been dancing around in Honcho's head since Foods arrived on the scene, I'm hopeful that Honcho will be influenced by the arguments I've made to him and will accept the $940 million price."

Next I go to Honcho, and here's what I say:

> "You're getting $940 million—a lot more than the $900 million you were originally willing to take; and in that deal, it was even questionable whether the transfer of the H-C casino joint venture was permissible. The Foods $1 billion price has always been subject to you indemnifying them against the very strong claim that Shows has against Foods for inducing breach of contract—that indemnity could have ended up costing you a lot."

As for Foods, well, remember the point I made previously about how important it is for the mediator to be a good listener? I forgot to mention that in nosing about earlier, I learned that $60 million would serve nicely as the extra dollars needed to fund that other hotel company acquisition they'd been looking at. So I remind them of this and then say, "And look, guys, that's exactly what I'm recommending you receive—as well as getting you out of a nasty lawsuit that you walked into with your eyes wide open."

That's my proposed resolution and a little bit of my pitch. I also give each party a forceful speech (along the lines I discussed in Chapter 1) about why it's preferable to settle rather than litigate. In addition, I'm very much aware—although I may not refer to it explicitly—that my judgment as to the ultimate resolution provides neutral cover for the responsible executives of the corporate parties, making it less likely that they'll be second-guessed by higher-ups, boards of directors and shareholders.

The parties let me know they'll consider the proposal and get back to me in an hour. So, what do you think? Will everyone accept it? Because if even one of them doesn't, they're back at war.

I'll tell you one thing—they better accept it, because I'm plumb tuckered!

So that's what the mediation of a multi-party dispute *cum* deal is really like. It's not brain surgery or rocket science, that's for sure, but it does call for a certain degree of energy, analysis and persuasion. If it works—no sure thing—it gets the parties to the finish line with an overall compromise resolution each of them can live with. That's something the courts can't accomplish and the warring parties have a very hard time doing on their own. So, until someone comes up with something better, I consider this the way to go.

PART

REPRESENTING
A PARTY IN MEDIATION

Up to this point, my primary focus has been on the role of the mediator. Now, in Part V, I'll be viewing the process from the standpoint of the lawyers who represent clients in a mediated dispute. In all candor, though, since my role in mediations in recent years has been almost exclusively through serving as the mediator, much of the advice I'm offering counsel here represents a mediator's-eye view—what I think works best for the lawyer (and thus for the lawyer's client) in mediations generally, but especially in one of mine!

I've divided the topic into three somewhat overlapping segments. In Chapter 25, I contend that negotiating skill should be a mediation lawyer's prime attribute. This chapter also contains sections on selecting the mediator and on why transactional lawyers—who often shun active participation in dispute resolution—ought to become more involved in mediations, which have aspects that are right up their alley. The focus of Chapter 26 is on the relationship between the lawyer and his/her mediation client.

Chapter 27 is about the lawyer's dealings with the mediator (and, by extension, with the adversary).

I've put a spotlight on the lawyers in a few previous sections—for example, some thoughts about litigators in Chapter 2, my views regarding the mediator's proposed resolution in Chapter 14, and the significant role lawyers play in a deal-dispute mediation in Chapter 19.

CHAPTER 25

NEGOTIATING—THE MEDIATION LAWYER'S KEY ATTRIBUTE

The most important thing for a lawyer participating in a mediation to understand is that the process is basically a negotiation, not an adjudication. What I've observed as a mediator, though, is that while lawyers may pay lip service to this tenet, many of them don't practice it with any flair or enthusiasm.

The Importance of Negotiating Skills

As a lawyer, your role in any negotiation to resolve a difficult dispute (irrespective of mediation) can be thought of as two-fold. First, it's to present your client's position energetically and persuasively, but without crossing over into unreality. Second, it's to be agile and constructive (and sometimes even creative) in coming off that position to obtain for your client a good (if not stupendous) outcome—one that the other party (whose lawyer has also presented an energetic and persuasive opposing position) will be willing to accept. In a *mediation* (which, as I say, is really just a special kind of negotiation), most of the lawyers I observe in action are excellent at the first of these roles (although I'll take the Fifth on the unreality factor). A number of them are something less than excellent at the second.

Part of the reason for this disparity, I think, is that the mediation process is so different from the regular activities in which these lawyers engage. As a litigator, for example, you're used to crossing swords directly with your adversary in pursuit of victory in the lawsuit. But when you find yourself in a mediation where the parties are in separate rooms after their initial exchange, your further dealings with the other side take place through a neutral intermediary—a neither-fish-nor-fowl process that may make you uneasy and often operating at less than your sure-footed best.

Your dealings with the neutral are also *sui generis*. Unlike appearances before a judge or arbitrator where you go all out to "sell" your case, here you need to reach an accommodation with the mediator. The objective is less the victory you're used to seeking and more the achieving of a reasonable compromise. And, in contrast to most direct dispute negotiations, here the client is constantly on the scene, often being directly engaged by the mediator—which makes you justifiably nervous about what might slip through your client's lips.

By the way, it's not just litigators who have trouble here. Transactional lawyers (about whom I'll have more to say below) are used to bargaining directly in deals. Not only may they feel uncomfortable negotiating a dispute, but operating through an intermediary isn't something they're accustomed to doing. I can well recall the first mediation I participated in representing a party—it definitely took a while to adjust to the new circumstances.

And yet, I have to say—notwithstanding my prior emphasis on the key role of the mediator—that effective negotiating by the lawyers involved can do much to make the mediation succeed. On a personal note, of all the mediations in which I've participated (acting as the mediator in over 90% of them), I'm proudest of the central role I played as counsel in helping negotiate the settlement of a thorny multi-party dispute, with my client ultimately paying only a fraction of the huge amount of dollars at risk in court if the case hadn't settled.

Most of the litigators who become involved in mediations will already be skilled in the effective presentation of their case. So, to my mind, the most important skill for them to develop and bring to the mediation process is the ability to negotiate. This holds true whether the mediator acts primarily as a conduit to encourage the parties to make proposals that the mediator passes through from one party to the other, or where (as in my case) the lawyer is essentially negotiating with the mediator. I'll have more to say on that subject in Chapter 27.

Being a good negotiator calls for a variety of attributes: acting in a constructive fashion, adopting a problem-solving attitude, thinking creatively, being a good listener, and so on. I don't think this is the place to delve deeply into such a basic skill. If you're interested in exploring the subject further, I can recommend my book, *Smart Negotiating* [27] (certain aspects of which are summarized in Chapter 26).

If the dispute contains some aspects that aren't solvable by just moving money around, then what's requisite is a sense of how to do a deal—especially if forward-looking elements are involved. That's not the same as compromising a one-shot dollar dispute, and not all litigators are comfortable playing that role. If you're not, then by all means add someone to your team who will be.

A Note to Deal Lawyers

Here's something I don't understand.[28]

At the risk of oversimplification, the world of business lawyers is divided between those who negotiate deals (consensual agreements) and those who litigate disputes. But there's a third category of lawyering that falls in between these two areas—lawyers who resolve commercial disputes through negotiation.

It's a vital category, and what I don't understand is why the lawyers who do the deals have in large part ceded this territory to the litigators who handle the lawsuits. This needn't be the case.

To me, as an ex-deal lawyer, it makes no sense. Deal lawyers share certain professional traits: we relish our client relationships, we thrive on the role of white knight riding to the client's rescue, and we pride ourselves on our negotiating prowess and ability to strike advantageous compromises on tough transactional issues. We're self-styled problem-solvers, and Lord knows, these disputes are big problems! So why have we largely abandoned the field of negotiated dispute resolution to the litigators—who often don't have a pre-existing client relation-

ship, who have far less training in negotiating than in litigating, whose bargaining skills aren't honed on a daily basis, and who spend the bulk of their time in a win-lose universe that isn't conducive to generating compromise outcomes?

As Oscar Hammerstein's King of Siam was wont to say, "It's a puzzlement."

When a controversy arises and isn't quickly resolved, the litigator takes charge of the potential or actual lawsuit. And even if settlement talks get underway, it's the litigator whose presence supplies the necessary threat of going back to the fray should the negotiations prove unavailing. But in terms of those settlement negotiations, I believe the deal lawyer ought to play a very active role (not just as a backup in the office) alongside his or her litigator colleague. The optimal line-up I envision consists of the litigator and the deal lawyer, working side-by-side as a team.

As a deal lawyer, you may ask, why should we bother? You should because, in many cases, it's *your* client who's involved in the altercation. The client came to you with her dispute. You brought in the litigator to handle the lawsuit. But then too often, many of you excuse yourselves and move on to the next deal. You're busy—too busy to stay involved in the messy aftermath of the last one.

Big mistake! You should never be too busy to help a good client achieve the best practical result in a troublesome situation. You know your client—you know how she thinks, you can sense what's important to her, and you speak her language. And that decent result is often best realized through a settlement, as to which your input may prove quite constructive.

It almost goes without saying that inside corporate counsel should stay actively involved in monitoring significant company disputes, regardless of whether an outside law firm is handling the potential litigation. There are so many corporate considerations to take into account in approaching any dispute that it's evident the company's lawyers—and not just those with a litigation background—ought to play a crucial role in handling settlement discussions. In addition, their knowledge of the individuals involved and the corporate imperatives make them ideal intermediaries between the litigators and management.

303

Let me make a confession. The view I'm expressing here—urging deal lawyers to become involved in dispute resolution—is not the way I (and most other deal lawyers I encountered across the table) felt back in the days when I was doing M&A transactions.

We spent lots of time negotiating agreements that generated rights and liabilities, creating the potential for indemnification claims in situations where the company being acquired was privately owned or the subsidiary/division of a public company. But even though we knew these provisions could lead to post-closing disputes, there was little discussion of what would happen if a squabble actually arose. To be sure, the boilerplate contained a choice of law provision and perhaps a designated court for possible litigation, and arbitration was sometimes specified for dispute resolution. But there was rarely anything about what could be done to head off litigation or arbitration in the event a dispute arose. With all the effort given to defining rights and responsibilities—eliminating uncertainty and ambiguity—you would think we would have paid more heed to how to resolve any altercation that managed to slip through the net.[29]

Was it because back then we were living in a less litigious world than today? I don't think so, and the prevalent takeover wars of the day certainly spawned all kinds of litigation. Was it because we were more concerned with the conditions to closing—and in the old days, spent a lot of time on such arcane matters as registration rights and legal opinions? Not likely. Could it have been because, deep down, we knew how difficult it was to resolve a real fracas, and we didn't want to contemplate the fall from grace of being saddled with responsibility for a messy lawsuit?

Maybe, but bottom line, I think there were two main reasons, which I have to assume still play a role today. First of all, when you're under pressure to get a deal done, no one is anxious to raise the additional issue of how to resolve a potential lawsuit—especially when it relates to something that hasn't yet occurred and on which everyone is hard at work to prevent from happening. Second, there's a dose of the timeworn "not my problem" syndrome at work here—the deal lawyer figuring that any dispute cropping up later on will be turned over to the litigator, so it's the other person's worry.

But that's just where deal lawyers go wrong—*it is* their problem, and they shouldn't duck it.

As I said previously, to my mind the best line-up to handle any dispute that arises is a litigator and a deal lawyer, operating as a team. The lawsuit is clearly the litigator's turf. But settling the lawsuit—resolving the commercial dispute—is a chore on which we deal lawyers, paired with the litigators, can be very helpful.

One real plus the deal lawyer brings to the table is familiarity with the territory. The deal lawyer knows what the clauses in the disputed agreement are supposed to mean, how such language was intended to be interpreted, and the way the original negotiations affect the dispute.

I should insert a caveat here. It's something of a two-edged sword when the deal lawyer who is engaged in trying to resolve the dispute is the same lawyer who handled the original transaction that's the subject of the controversy. On the plus side, there's a familiarity with the details of the agreement and the course of the negotiations. The minus is the risk that the deal lawyer's advice today is not totally disinterested if there's some question about his conduct in the original deal—for example, if the agreement contains an ambiguous provision the meaning of which is now being debated, or the lawyer omitted to include some disclosure that's now under attack in a shareholder suit. In such a case, it may be preferable to bring another transactional lawyer onto the settlement team. And, of course, if the client has in mind a potential claim against the lawyer or the deal lawyer's law firm, a different firm should represent the client in handling the dispute.

In addition to the deal lawyer's presumed negotiating skill, there are frequently tax, accounting, or valuation aspects to the dispute that she may be better qualified to handle than the litigator, who is less likely to come into contact with these issues on a regular basis. Also, in those situations where the parties to the dispute have a continuing relationship and the best means of resolving the problem is to strike a new deal, the transactional lawyer is the person to handle it.

Since a mediation is basically a negotiation, I think an astute deal lawyer who negotiates for a living may have a lot to offer (alongside the litigator) in a mediated dispute arising out of, say, a corporate acquisition. The deal lawyer has a real grasp of how an acquisition agreement is supposed to work, an understanding of complex business-type issues as well as tax and accounting considerations, a positive problem-solving mentality, and a feel for developing a mutually acceptable compromise.

Having the deal lawyer in the picture may also be in the litigator's best interest. It frees the litigator to play his aggressive role with the other side to the hilt. Conversely the litigator's looming presence allows the deal lawyer to be constructive in trying to negotiate a settlement without conveying weakness.

That first phone call to suggest talks, for instance, or a call to propose mediation, is much easier for the deal lawyer to make— she can even announce that the call is being made against the advice of her litigating partner. The implication is that the litigator is waiting impatiently for the negotiations and/or mediation to fail so he can get back to the job of stomping on the adversary in court. The dynamic duo keeps the other side off balance, because it can't predict which of them will prevail in the councils of the duo's client.

If, in private caucus, an actual difference in viewpoint exists between the litigator and deal lawyer, this can actually be helpful to the client in deciding whether to fight or settle. Neither the litigator nor the deal lawyer should be committed to litigating or settling at any cost. Rather, they each ought to realize that the scales can tilt either way as the bargaining proceeds. When the negotiations stall, after being advised by both lawyers, it's the client's call on which course of action to take.

Choosing a Mediator

I'll begin this section by quoting one of the contributors to the AAA *Handbook on Mediation*[30]

"There are, of course, many factors that may affect the success or failure of a mediation. [listing various ones]. . . . However, none of these factors has the importance of selecting a capable mediator, one who has the experience and ability to bring the parties to the point where they can negotiate a settlement. Having participated in a good mediation and a bad mediation within months of each other, I can assure you that the key difference between a mediated settlement and a failed mediation may be the choice of mediator."

An important role for a party's lawyer is participating in the selection of a capable mediator. Much has been written about how you go about finding a good mediator, so I'll limit myself to commenting briefly on two aspects of the subject.

First, if I were representing a client and participating in the selection of a mediator, I wouldn't be satisfied with what's on a candidate's resume, or how good his or her reputation is, or what other people have reported about prior experiences. I'd want to personally interview each candidate before making any recommendation to the client. My purpose would be to make an assessment—and hopefully, the answers to the questions I'd ask would provide helpful input here—as to whether this man or woman is the right mediator for the particular dispute.

So, for instance, let's say the mediator candidate is an eminent practitioner of the facilitative mode, and you analyze this dispute as being one where that approach stands a reasonable chance of success—then this person is indeed a prime candidate. But if it's a dispute where the other side has dug in to a position that really isn't tenable under applicable law, then you might well feel that facilitation won't be enough here—you need an evaluative-type mediator to dispel your adversary's unreality. (Of course, this can also work the other way—if you realize your own case is hopeless on the merits, you might well shun a mediator who is itching to present you with his or her analysis!)

There's another aspect to this that the interview can help determine—whether the candidate's personality and approach to the process is such that the two of you "speak the same language." For instance, you don't want a stickler for detail if you're more of a broad-brush type, and vice-versa.

My second thought is that once you've selected the mediator, you should get involved with him/her in designing the process that the mediation will follow. If, for instance, you'd prefer that the bulk of the mediation take place in private caucus, make sure that's the basic path the mediator will take. If you don't want your client subjected to an inquisition by the mediator, get that point across early.

Find out how this mediator handles confidentiality. Does the mediator feel free to relay to the other side any information you tell her in private unless you specifically tell her not to; or does the mediator require a request from you to pass on what you've said? Does the mediator transmit to the other side proposals you've made, or are these just for the mediator's ears? And so on. Try to get as comfortable as you can with the manner in which the mediation is going to take place.

CHAPTER
26

THE LAWYER-CLIENT RELATIONSHIP

In this chapter, I want to focus on a few aspects of the relationship between the lawyer and his or her client in a mediation. (Chapter 27 covers the lawyer's interaction with the mediator and, through the mediator, with the other side.) For these purposes, let's assume that your client has not previously participated in a mediation, so it's a new ballgame.

The Decision to Mediate

The first—and perhaps most important—lawyer-client issue is the decision of whether or not to mediate. (I'm assuming here that participation in the mediation is totally voluntary—not due to a judge or arbitrator's direction or pursuant to a contractual clause requiring the parties to mediate their disputes before suing, as discussed in Chapter 5.) It's a decision on which you, the lawyer, play a significant role as the professional offering expert advice; but in the final analysis, this is the client's decision to make—you shouldn't make it for him. Still, if you favor the use of mediation in a particular case, there's nothing wrong with the client realizing that this is your preference—as long as you make it clear that it's the kind of decision on which the client doesn't have to follow your advice and can come to a contrary conclusion.

In posing the issue for the client, don't get mired in the minutiae of the process—focus on the big picture. Here's the nub of how I might put the question to a client (Jones) who is being sued by Smith for, say, $10 million, in a case where I believe the merits lie primarily with Smith.

- If we litigate and win, you pay Smith nothing—your only out-of-pocket expenses are my fees and other litigation expenses.
- If we litigate and lose, you pay Smith $10 million, and you also have my fees and the other litigation expenses.
- The outcome of litigation is always uncertain, but my take on this one is that although we have some reasonable arguments, Smith has the better case in court—let's say a two-thirds chance of winning.
- So in court, although you could end up paying Smith nothing, it's more likely that you'll have to pay him $10 million (which, you've told me, would be a real problem for your company).
- Mediation is basically a negotiation assisted by the mediator. For it to succeed, both sides have to agree on the resolution. Smith obviously thinks a lot of his case, so he won't agree to drop it for small change.
- If in the mediation we (and the mediator) were able to get Smith to agree to take, say, $5 or $6 million (which, although not chump change, is an amount you've indicated your company could handle without big dislocations), then mediation would make sense on a risk/reward basis—and you'd also be saving my trial fee and the other litigation expenses.
- If Smith holds out for, say, $8 or $9 million in the mediation, then—again on a risk/reward basis—you'd be justified in refusing to settle and letting it go to litigation; and you haven't really lost anything except the expenses of the mediation (including my fee), which are a lot less than the expenses of litigation.
- So, what do you think?

How about if I were Smith's lawyer in the same dispute? Assume I also favor mediation and am in the same ballpark regarding the merits as my counterpart—here's how I might put the issue to my client.

- If we litigate and win, Jones pays you $10 million, from which you have to deduct my fee and other expenses of litigation.
- If we litigate and lose, Jones pays you nothing, which is not a good result to contemplate—and you'd still have my fees and other expenses of litigation.
- I've been taking the position with Jones that our case is a certain winner in court, but the outcome of litigation is always uncertain; realistically, I think we have around a two-thirds chance of winning.
- If Jones agrees to participate in this mediation, he will probably have decided to pay you a significant sum to settle the case. How much, we won't know until we (and the mediator) test him.
- But if Jones would agree to pay, say, $7 or $7.5 million to settle this, the mediation resolution would make sense for you on a risk/reward basis—and you'd also be saving my fee for the lawsuit and other litigation expenses.
- If it turns out in mediation that Jones is only willing to come up to, say, $5 million, then—again on a risk/reward basis—you'd be justified in turning him down and letting it go to litigation; and you haven't really lost anything except the expenses of the mediation (including my fee), which are a lot less than the expenses of litigation.
- So, what do you think?

Now, I'm sure some lawyer-readers will be going "tut-tut—come on, Jim, you tilted it a little toward mediation." And so I did—although without misstating the facts—precisely because both of the lawyers considered the decision to mediate to be a wise one. (If you were to ask me how to present the issue to the client in a case where you favored litigation to mediation, I'd give you a short answer—go read someone else's book!)

Sometimes a client may say to you that he's heard people interpret a party's willingness to mediate as a sign of weakness, and this is holding him back from agreeing to the process. I don't see it that way at all—rather, I think of it as a validation

311

of strength. My rationale runs this way: our case is so good that we want the opportunity to persuade a mediator of this; once he agrees with our conclusion, the mediator will then be able to demonstrate to the other side how futile it would be for them to pursue litigation.

By the way, the flip side of this is that if you have a weak case, you should really think twice about whether to go to mediation—because once the mediator realizes it, you'll be in a very tough position.

Now, of course, part of the exercise will be acquainting your client with how mediation works—the joint session, the caucuses, the mediator's approach, and so on. You'll point to some of the advantages of mediation—no motions, little discovery, privacy, speed (compared to litigation), and, where applicable, the possible preservation of business relationships. You should also mention what might be viewed as disadvantages—the possibility of no resolution, some free discovery for the other side, his peek at your litigation strategy, etc.

Above all, you have to make sure that your client understands that the mediation is a negotiation, not an adjudication—and that this calls for a willingness to compromise. If the client is unwilling to do so, then my advice is to pass up the mediation—it won't work. There's no such thing as unconditional surrender in mediation.

Preparing Your Client for the Negotiating to Come

It's important that you and your client be on the same page regarding the negotiating that will occur in the mediation. If you have a client who insists on taking the lead here, you can offer suggestions as you go along; but unless he's clearly off-base, there's not much you can do about it—after all, he's paying the freight. But if the client defers to you, then you're well-advised to have a game plan to guide your movements—subject, of course, to the need to react to unexpected developments.

At this point, negotiators of the *Getting to Yes*[31] stripe would be talking about BATNA's and such; hard-nosed positional bargainers would be counseling that any concessions should be small and infrequent; proponents of the "decision tree" would be touting its merits; and so on. My approach to negotiating is contained in my book, *Smart Negotiating*.[32] While the book is primarily aimed at negotiating deals, much of it applies to disputes; and a good deal of that is applicable to negotiating in a mediation. So, if a client were looking for my negotiating advice, here's some of what I'd respond with.

I'm a firm believer in having a game plan—a logical approach to conducting and concluding the negotiation. It contains four steps: assessing your client's realistic expectations (*What does he want?*); determining an appropriate starting point (*Where do we start?*); devising a constructive concession pattern (*When do we move?*); and arranging the ultimate compromise (*How do we close?*).

The first crucial step in my approach to any deal negotiation is to help the client develop—before the negotiations begin—realistic expectations with respect to price and other key issues. Too many people enter into negotiations without determining in advance the outcome they want to achieve. But without a realistic expectation, you don't know where to start the bidding, you'll have trouble figuring out what steps to take along the way, and—most important of all—you won't know where to stop!

To my mind—although I'm sure many litigators who prefer a toe-in-the-water approach would disagree—I consider this step equally requisite in negotiating the resolution of a dispute, whether directly or through a mediation. As a negotiator on behalf of a client, I feel the need to have this information in order to conduct the negotiations intelligently.

I see a client's realistic expectation as being a good outcome of the negotiations—an outcome that the client would be agreeable to pay or receive and that the adversary could well accept. But to be of any use, it has to reflect a hard-headed determination—not some pipe dream or wish list. If I'm the lawyer, I would say to the client that it's neither the best outcome you might get if your adversary caves in, nor the worst you may be forced to pay or take if he hangs tough and you're anxious to resolve the dispute. On the one hand, you shouldn't count on an outcome that represents a real bargain (although we're certainly open to the possibility). At the same time, your realistic expectation isn't a "bottom line"—you can't tell at the outset of a negotiation how far you may be willing to go at the close of the day.

I must say to the reader, however, if not to the client, that in my experience, lurking beneath the surface of most realistic outcomes I hear, is some less favorable outcome—I call it the "stretch"—that the client may be willing to accept, if necessary, to resolve the dispute without litigation.

Here's the way I go about helping the client develop a realistic expectation for a satisfactory outcome. We start by determining his *aspiration.* In a deal, this is composed primarily of objective value (discounted cash flows, comparables, etc.) In a dispute, it's based on the lawyer's evaluation of the client's chances in the litigation that's the alternative to a negotiated settlement. What is the court likely to decide, what are the odds of it occurring, how long will it take, and what are the costs of litigation?

Then we have to temper the aspiration with *feasibility.* In a deal, this is an amalgam of what the guy on the other side likely has in mind for an outcome (not the outrageous positions he takes) and the relative leverage of the parties (regarding such factors as necessity, desire, competition, and time). In a dispute, you have to include other leverage factors, including the location of the money. In a dispute mediation, in addition to these factors, you have to add in an assessment of how helpful (or harmful) you think the mediator will be to your cause.

The resulting realistic expectation is your initial beacon to guide your negotiating moves as you go along. But it has to be reassessed along the way, as new information becomes available and leverage factors change. (How, for instance, are things going with that mediator?) Just make sure that revisions to your realistic expectation are based on actual developments, as distinguished from changes based on emotional factors (false jubilation, frustration, etc.)

In Chapter 27, I'll be making a strong point of the need, when dealing with the mediator in a multi-issue dispute, for the lawyer to differentiate between issues in terms of the fervor brought to their assertion. In that same vein, when I used to represent a party in a complex dispute with multiple dollar issues,

I would work with my client to develop what might be termed a "compromise matrix." We took each issue individually and assigned it two rankings—the first based on the amount of dollars it involved, and the second based on the relative strength of our side's arguments in favor of our position.

We would try to hold pretty firm on the issues with big dollars (for obvious reasons) and strong arguments (as to which there was less need to compromise, assuming we could persuade the mediator to concur in our assessments). On the other hand, we could be very flexible on the issues with small dollars, especially those on which our arguments were weaker. On big dollar issues with weak arguments, we would work hard for an even split, if possible. On medium dollar issues with strong arguments, we would aim for, say, 75% of what was at stake.

So we gave the most ground on issues that tended to hurt us less in the pocketbook and where we had less ammunition to support our position. Conversely, we remained stronger on the issues where more was at stake and we could stand tall. And for each issue, we devised a logical compromise that we ultimately were prepared to make—after going through some intermediate intervals and seeing some signs of reciprocation from the other side.

It makes a lot of sense to be prepared in advance as to where you want to take a stand and where you're willing to yield. The mediator will appreciate getting some indication about this from you at a relatively early stage in the proceedings.

So, now at least you have your goal. And, by the way, when a corporate party is involved, the authority given to the designated executive participating in the mediation should reflect that goal—rather than being limited to some useless pipe dream number that you have no chance of obtaining in the mediation.

Some Thoughts on the Negotiating Process

The next questions are: how should you start out, and what steps should you take to get to that goal? In a deal, I have a clear image of this process, which is spelled out in *Smart Negotiating*. In a directly negotiated dispute, much of that would be applicable, although with some variations. But in a mediation, it's a different ballgame, because so much of the negotiating depends on the mediator's approach—and we mediators each have our own way of going about things.

Take the question of what should be your first offer to compromise the dispute. It will presumably come in response to the mediator suggesting you put a proposal on the table. You should be ready for this—not have to spend a lot of time coming up with it. Promptness conveys to the mediator that you know why you're here; fussing around in search of an initial number suggests you may not be so dedicated to the process.

The real question is how far you should go. Now, I'm not naïve, and as a mediator I don't have exalted expectations as to what a party's first offer might be. But even this street-smart mediator is constantly amazed at the paucity of the proposals so many people start out with. It's like throwing me a bone that has no meat on it. (A plaintiff asking $10 million, offers to take $9.7 million; the defendant puts a measly $350,000 on the table.) As a mediator, I often find myself spending a lot of time pressing a party to move from an absurd initial position to one that's simply unrealistic!

If that piddling first proposal were intended to send the other side a message (hey, we think our case is rock solid), then I could understand it—even though I don't consider it constructive. (It's not constructive because not only doesn't the other side treat it as serious but they're infuriated by the disrespect they feel it shows.) But in my approach to mediation, the other side isn't even going to hear the offer. So, I figure, it must be designed to influence me. But not only doesn't it accomplish that, it just raises my hackles in a way that disserves your client's interests. (I'll talk more in Chapter 27 about your dealings with the mediator.)

How about in the more usual situation, where the mediator will deliver your first offer to the other side? In *Smart Negotiating*[33], I rejected both the approach of some who start with a truly outrageous opening offer and others who display overly modest ambitions, and had this to say:

"[My] general approach to the opening proposal lies well between the extremes of outrage and undue moderation. I advise making a first offer that is sufficiently reasonable to be viewed constructively by the other side and thus to evoke a positive response. On the other hand, it should give you enough room to move deliberately to your expectation without being forced to stretch."

The precise amount of room obviously depends on a variety of factors (such as leverage), but also on the rationale you're able to bring to bear. Without it, your number lacks backbone. To my mind, you need at least a plausible rationale to put something on the table—it's the litmus test of a defensible position.

I realize I may be in the minority here, but this would still be my advice to the client in a mediated dispute. Here's the way I'd make a proposal to the other side. (And if I didn't trust the mediator to get across to my adversary what I'm trying to say, I'd write it out for the mediator to use.)

Let's say I represent the defendant against a $10 million claim that I feel could go either way on the merits. Our realistic settlement expectation is in the vicinity of $5 million. Here are my words:

> "We think we have much the better case on the merits here, and are tempted to offer you just your legal fees and other expenses to date to go away. But we're in a mediation, the goal of which is to reach an accommodation; and we recognize that such an offer wouldn't advance the ball and would probably just result in you proposing a number close to your claim. So we want to start off with a serious proposal to settle our differences, and we're hopeful that you'll reciprocate in kind.
>
> "Here's our rationale for the offer we're making. [Explain rationale of how we arrived at the number]. . . . And so our offer is $2.7 million."

My hope, of course, is that the other side does view this constructively and responds with a number, say, in the 7's (with their rationale). At that point, I'm still a long way from home, but off to a good start, and hopefully some momentum will develop.

If the other side doesn't reciprocate and comes back at the

$9.5 million level, well, there's no sense bidding against myself. At that point, I'd try to enlist the mediator's assistance to lecture the other side on its failure to be constructive—and only if the mediator is successful in generating a more realistic response from my adversary would I then resume moving toward my client's realistic expectation.

If the other side goes first and offers a constructive proposal, I urge you to be constructive in your response. If, on the other hand, the other side's first offer is absurd, I'm sure there will be a great temptation to respond in kind. My thought would be, however, to disparage the other number, say something like "let's be grown-ups about this, if we want to get anywhere," and come back with something constructive (including rationale). This is the time to find out if you've got an adversary who's serious or who just wants to play games.

Once a serious negotiation gets going, you're in what bargaining theorists term the "concession" process. It's an unfortunate term, because it sounds like you're giving something up, which is how many people approach it—viewing each step as a tense, grudging struggle. I've always told my clients to avoid that attitude—the only real concession you make is when you're forced to stretch beyond your realistic expectation. Everything else is just part of the negotiating dance. That territory between what you start out asking and your realistic expectation is not your terrain—it's more of a no-man's land. So, no matter how you paint the pain you're suffering to the other side, don't fall in love with any of these intermediate positions you take along the way.

I have a lot more thoughts on this process in Chapter 9 of *Smart Negotiating*, but let's move on now to a few thoughts on the final compromise. It's the subject of Chapter 10 in that book, with material about timing the compromise, the possibility of bluffing, "splitting the difference," reducing principles to dollars, compromising among issues, the package deal, enlarging the pie, and so on. I've covered some of these aspects in prior chapters. Here, though, I just want to stress two points that can occur toward the end of a long, drawn-out negotiation—one when things are going well, and the other, not so well.

When you can settle the case with an outcome that's at least as favorable as your client's realistic expectation, you've done well indeed; and although there may be a real temptation to keep pressing the other side for slightly better terms, a smart negotiator has to know when to stop the music and grab a chair. The opportunity to make the deal that exists now may be gone in a few hours. When the risk of losing the deal altogether doesn't justify the possible incremental advantage of prolonging the process, that's the time to come to terms. (Just make sure that you don't agree to a deal unless you're satisfied it covers all the points you consider significant.)

The other side of the coin is that it's not always possible to do as well in the end as your realistic expectation, and the only compromise that will swing the deal will require your client to stretch beyond the safety net of his expectation. You've satisfied yourself that the other side isn't bluffing—the mediator has made that clear.

When that happens, I like to isolate the decision to be made from the emotions the client is feeling as a result of the frustration that has accompanied his journey thus far. (In the old days, I used to take him out of the smoke-filled room we'd been negotiating in and walk him around the block.) I phrase the issue for him simply: if the deal was good enough to do at the level of your realistic expectation, does it still make sense at this (say, 5%) stretch? Another way to phrase it is, if you stick on your terms and the mediation fails, will you regret not having paid (or accepted) the stretched terms available?

Then I tell the client that if his answer is yes in either case, he should go back in the room and shake hands on a deal, however reluctantly. If not, well, it's back to war.

THE LAWYER'S DEALINGS
WITH THE MEDIATOR

Turning now to the lawyer's dealings with the mediator, the obvious threshold question is what kind of mediator is presiding. An approach that may work with a facilitative mediator might not fare so well with an evaluative neutral, and vice versa. Even among the evaluative ones, tactics that make sense with a mediator whose *modus operandi* is to convey compromise proposals between the parties might not be well-tuned to a mediator like myself who (at least in dollar disputes) doesn't pass proposals along. And so on.

I'd be uncomfortable advising you on how to deal with a purely facilitative mediator and will limit my remarks to your dealings with a mediator who is evaluative—whose views on the merits and as to how the bargaining should proceed are central to the process. In fact, most of my advice is geared to the subject I know best—how to deal with a guy like me!

For a lawyer participating in a mediation with an evaluative mediator, the most salient fact to remember is that you're in a negotiation. You're negotiating, on behalf of your client, with two different people—the party (and his counsel) on the other side and the mediator in the middle. Don't assume for a moment that your relationship with the mediator is anything other than that, because—unless you've hired one who follows a very narrow facilitative path—the mediator is definitely bargaining with you and your client. It's not an adversarial negotiation (as it would be if you were negotiating directly with the lawyer on the other side of the dispute), but one that's more in the nature of two business lawyers charged by their clients with accomplishing an amicable arm's-length deal.

To be effective here, you have to develop special tactics suitable to the indirect bargaining format of mediation. Here's an example that you might use with an evaluative mediator who transmits provisions between the parties. It's what I term a "conditional offer" to the mediator—a useful tactic when you want to show the mediator that your client is willing to be flexible, but don't want to put a specific number or formulation on the table with the other side.

Say that the parties' present positions on an issue are far apart—the other side is at A and you are at Z—and you think that if the spread were reduced to B and Y, then some real progress could be made. But you don't want to go to Y first. Rather, you want to encourage the mediator to push the other side into the vicinity of B.

So you say to the mediator, "We are willing to move to Y, but only after the other side has come to B—and you are not authorized to mention our willingness to go to Y to the other side." Sometimes, you might go further and indicate that the mediator is not even authorized to make the suggestion himself to the other side (as in, "Maybe if you would move to B, I could get your adversary to buy into Y"), at least until the other side has shown a clear disposition to move to B.

How *Not* to Do It

Let's say you're representing the claimant in a one-shot $10 million dispute. (The points I'm about to make here are equally applicable when you're representing the defendant.) It's presided over by an evaluative mediator like me, whose technique (after a joint opening session) is to keep you and your adversary separated—not only physically but also by restricting direct proposals between the parties. Your client does want to settle the dispute, provided favorable terms can be obtained.

So, what's the best of all worlds for you? How about this:

1. You're able to persuade the mediator your case is bulletproof;

2. The mediator conveys this to the other side, as representing the mediator's own view of the merits; and

3. The other side is so cowed it collapses and agrees to settle for a number very close to your going-in position.

Hey, that would be great stuff for you and your client. And so you may not be surprised to learn that a number of lawyers I deal with seem dedicated to following precisely that approach. The problem, though, is that this gilt-edged scenario rarely happens. And lawyers who put all their eggs in this one basket end up not providing the best service their clients are entitled to receive.

Here's the thing. If the individual sitting in my seat were a judge or arbitrator, this approach would make a lot of sense. When the neutral is going to hand down a judgment binding the parties, you're justified in going at him with all guns blazing. But a mediator—even an evaluative one—is not a judge or an arbitrator. The mediator can't find facts, doesn't enforce the law, and won't deliver a binding ruling on anything. All the mediator can do is assist the parties in reaching their own agreement on a compromise resolution. To make headway with that kind of a neutral, the lawyer has to employ a much more nuanced approach.

That "best of all worlds" scenario doesn't work here because:

1. You won't be able to persuade the mediator that the merits lie entirely with your client. In the great bulk of cases that come my way, at least a few bona fide arguments run in the other direction—and we all know that predicting the outcome of litigation is an imperfect science.

2. But even if I (as the mediator) were completely sold on your view of the case, I wouldn't admit that to you, if I harbor any hope of moving you off your position in any meaningful way—which is just what I'll need to do in order to provide the other side with an outcome that tempts them to settle.

3. And by the way, what's likely to happen if the mediator were to tell the other side their chances in court were

slim indeed and they ought to agree to a resolution very close to your side's position? They'd say, "Thanks, but no thanks—we might as well take our chances in court. We can't do much worse, and you never can tell. . . ."

I'm sure some of you are thinking, "Well, Jim, that might be true in the preponderance of cases, but maybe I'll hit it on the nose in *this* one. And anyway, what's my downside if I give it a try and it doesn't work out?"

To which I reply that there *is* a downside. I'm not just talking here about irritating a mediator like me—I mean forfeiting an opportunity to have a more decisive impact on the ultimate outcome.

Look, there's nothing wrong starting out with the underlying premise of that best-of-all-worlds approach. I've always said that, as a lawyer for a party dealing with a mediator, you have two key objectives: getting the mediator disposed toward your view of the dispute, and persuading the mediator to communicate that opinion to the other side under the mediator's imprimatur. In my view, that's what it takes for mediation to have a real impact. (It's analogous, in a deal context, to convincing the other side's lawyer as to the merits of the approach you're taking, so the lawyer can advise his client it's acceptable.) Your adversary is unlikely to move a lot unless the mediator leans heavily on him—dishing up some uncomfortable reality, acquainting him with the perils of his case.

And so, when I'm the mediator, I listen to each of the parties trying to persuade me of the merits of their respective positions; I read their arguments in the parties' written submissions; I hear their points during the mediation's initial joint sessions; and I can even tolerate some of that when each side is making its initial private pitch to me.

But that's when we part company. Once the discussion in the private sessions has progressed from a party's initial pitch and the mediator's information-gathering to the mediator's attempt to find some basis for reconciling two widely disparate views, the atmosphere should change. At that point, the biggest mistake lawyers make is to reiterate each of those overblown theories and demands with the same degree of certitude— seemingly carried away by their own rhetoric.

By the way, if you haven't already read my mediator's pep talk in Appendix D, this would be a good time to do so. It contains the very words I use with the parties and their counsel in urging them to shift from their adjudicative approach to the more constructive attitude needed for the mediation to succeed.

The Better Way

A good lawyer should know that, once her side gets down to business with the mediator in private caucus, she has to start differentiating between issues—preserving her firepower to take strong but reasonable positions on those issues as to which she thinks the mediator can be persuaded. (In this regard, note my suggestion in Chapter 26 about using a "compromise matrix.") The mediator appreciates this rational approach and responds to it, and the mediator can then work together with her team to sharpen the "reality" message that the mediator delivers to the other side.

There's an apt dealmaking analogy to this point. In negotiating a transaction, a good deal lawyer knows what she has to do to achieve credibility. If she wants the other side to be persuaded that the position she's taking on a certain key issue is rock solid and not a bluff, she has to show how meaningful the point is to her side—since the common perception is that people don't become immovable over lightweight issues. The lawyer realizes, however, that she will not be able to achieve "sticking" credibility by taking a no-compromise "this is it" position on multiple issues—that would just demean the meaningful aspect of the precious few. Here's the way I put it in *Smart Negotiating*:[34]

> "Just as in art, where negative space defines form, or in music, where silence outlines sound, so in negotiations, *you gain credence for your inflexibility on a few choice issues by your willingness to give ground on the rest."*

So, what's a better way for you to deal with a mediator like me? I'll tell you the secret.

Once the discussion has turned from arguing the merits to

how to resolve the dispute, it's time to put aside the bluster and work with the mediator toward achieving a good (albeit, not overwhelming) outcome for your side. If you've followed my advice in Chapter 26, you will have helped your client work out a realistic expectation for a reasonably favorable mediated outcome of the dispute. That should be your point of reference, and the tactics you adopt ought to further your goal of ultimately arriving at that place.

But don't try to go there all at once. After all, this mediation is a negotiation, and you'll need to engage in a *process* that gets you there—there's no instant gratification. So, my advice is that you privately designate some intermediary landing points for your side.

Go back now to where you're representing a claimant who's seeking $10 million in a one-shot dollar dispute. Assume this is composed of several damage elements of different amounts, on some of which your merits are better than on others. The advice you gave your client as to a litigated outcome of the dispute was that although it could go either way, you like your side's chances better than the other guy's. So your client has set his realistic expectation at (a perhaps too hopeful) $7 million. That's the ultimate number you'd like the mediator to sell to the other side.

Your reading of the other side's lawyer and client is that, beneath their bluster, they realize it could go either way in court, and they'd be satisfied to sign onto a $5 million compromise. But to get them to pay $7 million will be tough—and for that, you need the mediator's help.

Before talking numbers, let me say once again that I'm a great believer in attaching rationale to the negotiating proposals you make—and that's true not only in a deal, but also in a dispute, a mediated dispute, or a mediated deal-dispute. Unless the other side's leverage is overwhelming, you increase your chances of success the more you can show how and why you arrived at your proposal. You want to force your adversary to try to take issue with your rationale—disputes over rationale being a lot more constructive than arguments over numbers.

I'm not talking here about, "Okay, we'll knock 15% off our

demand"—that's just a percentage, not a rationale. I'm talking about, "Here's the way we analyze the various issues. [Present the analysis]. . . and so that comes out to roughly 15% less than what we're seeking, and therefore that's what we're prepared to reduce our demand by."

So, in this case, I recommend you work out an elaborate rationale for a $7 million compromise settlement, based on an evaluation of the potential outcome of several of the sub-issues. But I also suggest you construct some rationale for at least two stops on the way to that $7 million number, which you'll trot out for the mediator at the appropriate time.

By the way, keep in mind that it's good negotiating practice for the absolute size of the concessions you make to progressively *decrease*. The message you want to send (which is undercut by increasing the size of your concessions or even by keeping them level) is, "I'm willing to give some ground here, but my tolerance is running out, and I'm getting down to real bedrock."

So, a typical (but not invariable) sequence here would be to offer to settle for $8.5 million (which is $1.5 million less than your $10 million damage claim); then go down to $7.5 million ($1 million less than your prior $8.5 million number); and then come to rest at $7 million ($0.5 million less than the prior $7.5 million proposal). You should strive for the rationale supporting the $7 million proposal to be convincing. As for your rationale for the $7.5 million offer, it doesn't have to convince but will hopefully be persuasive. The rationale for your initial $8.5 million proposal won't convince or persuade, but it should at least be plausible. To repeat once more, if you can't construct at least plausible rationale for a proposed number, then don't make the proposal—plausibility being the litmus test of a defensible posture.

One reason rationale is so important in a mediation is that it provides the mediator with ammunition in trying to sell an outcome to the other side. It's hard for a mediator to tell a party he should increase (or decrease) his position by a certain percentage without a reason; it becomes easier if the mediator can point to something analytical that justifies such a move.

Help!

There's a broader point that I'd like to make here. By now, you can see that the lawyers who bother me the most are the ones whose every effort is directed at vigorously defending their turf. To my way of thinking, they're not only not helping the mediation process—they're hindering it.

But I also have a pet peeve with another type of less aggressive lawyer. Whenever I encounter one of them, I'm reminded of the old story about a guy who goes to the dentist with a toothache. "Where does it hurt?" asks the dentist to the patient in the chair. "Figure it out yourself," replies the patient—"after all, you're the dentist!"

I sometimes feel like that dentist. As the mediation gets down to the stage of searching for a compromise, the lawyers I have in mind sit in their respective rooms, rummaging with their BlackBerries, waiting for something to happen. The sense I get from them is, "Hey, Jim, you're the mediator—you resolve the dispute."

That's not the way it should be. We mediators need all the active help we can get to do our jobs effectively. And the only sources for that help are the parties to the dispute, as represented by their lawyers.

So, don't just sit there and wait for something to happen. Put your analytical and negotiating skills to work in trying to help solve what's so often a knotty problem. Use those hours when the mediator is talking to the other side in productive fashion—coming up with new initiatives that might pique the mediator's interest or influence the adversary. Ask the mediator what kind of information or analysis he or she needs that you might be able to supply.

Keep this thought in mind. A lawyer who actively assists the mediator in furthering the compromise process is likely to have a lot more impact on the final result than one who just sits on his hands and leaves things up to the mediator.

Here's another consideration. In trying to get the mediator favorably disposed toward your side of the case, don't underestimate the importance of the mediator having a positive frame of mind toward you on a personal level. Mediators, after all, are human beings, and they operate with a lot of flexibility.

While a mediator strives to be even-handed in any event, it stands to reason that he's going to be more responsive to someone who rubs him the right way than the wrong way.

Now, this does not mean you have to fawn or prostrate yourself (which, in fact, is just about the worst style you could adopt); and you should be prepared to take a tough line with the mediator when that's called for. On the other hand, lawyers who are obnoxious—sarcastic, snickering, accusing the mediator of bias—or who make arguments that are clearly outrageous, do themselves and their clients no favor with the mediator. Your client is much better served if you prove yourself to be trustworthy, businesslike, and constructive—traits that the mediator will certainly appreciate.

Handling Negative and Positive Leverage

Let's say the claimant in one of my mediations tells me in confidence that he needs to resolve the matter as soon as possible—and latch onto whatever money is coming his way—because he's in dire personal financial straits. I immediately assess this need as exerting negative leverage on the claimant. It could well translate into his acceptance of a resolution that's not the best he might achieve if he were willing to hold out and risk a delayed outcome (or even no resolution at all).

Now, even if the claimant's lawyer didn't instruct me to shield my knowledge of this from the other side (as he certainly should), that's what I'd do. I don't want the defendant to be aware of this pressure on the claimant or I'll never get anything accomplished. But as an evaluative mediator, I'd find it difficult not to factor this need into my assessment of where a deal might be struck.

Does that shock you? It shouldn't. I'm not a judge sitting in a courtroom or an arbitrator, for whom a leverage factor like this ought to be irrelevant in terms of ruling on the merits. I'm a mediator trying to help the parties reach a consensual deal, and the presence of negative leverage is one of the facts of life. Certainly, no one is ever bashful about trumpeting the existence of positive leverage in his favor (for example, the possession of the money at issue). In the real world, there's no such thing as a clean slate or a completely level playing field. The personal circumstances of the parties (including, but not limited to, their financial well-being) are factors to take into consideration.

Okay, I know what you must be thinking just about now. If the mediator is going to use a party's frank disclosure of negative leverage to his disadvantage—as one factor in persuading the party to cede more than he otherwise might in terms of the ultimate resolution—wouldn't this discourage the party from confiding in the mediator? Might it even erode the element of trust so vital to the process? These are fair questions, which I'll try to address.

First, let me dismiss the trust issue. If the mediator were to tell the defendant about the claimant's dire financial straits, that would certainly impair trust; but assuming no such breach of confidentiality occurs, I don't consider the issue to be one of trust. Rather, it concerns what's appropriate in conducting a negotiation, because (as I've said many times before) that's just what a mediation is; and much of the bargaining is going on between a party and the mediator.

So, if I were representing a party in a mediation, I'd advise him to be truthful with the mediator on all factual matters relating to the dispute; and (assuming he trusts the mediator not to tell the other side) he can also confide matters of intention, motivation, desire, and the like. The mediator will appreciate this information and may even be put off by a party who holds a lot of it back. I'd add, however, that with regard to matters constituting negative leverage, it's not always wise to tell the mediator everything. There's a fine line here—one that an astute negotiator should be able to ascertain—between what you reveal to the mediator and what you hold back.

In this case of confessing dire financial straits, my advice as counsel to the claimant would ordinarily be not to disclose this to an evaluative mediator, even if I were convinced the mediator would keep it to herself. Why not? Because the mediator can't help but factor it into her determination of where she thinks a resolution might be reached—and it's unlikely to be helpful to the claimant's cause.

I can think of two exceptions to this advice. The first occurs in a case where the mediator really needs to know this fact in order to pursue an appropriate resolution. So, for instance, if the beleaguered claimant has to emerge from the mediation with cash to pay debts, it wouldn't make sense for the mediator (ignorant of this need) to be promoting a resolution under which the needy party ends up with illiquid securities that don't serve his purpose.

The second exception comes into play when the knowledge is important for the mediator to know in terms of the mediation process itself. If, for example, the mediation were dragging on endlessly and your client had to have things resolved by a certain date to take care of pressing debts, it may be prudent to tell the mediator this in order to get her to step up the pace. Even if you decide to do this, though, you shouldn't give the mediator the impression that your client is desperate or lacks alternatives. In fact, you might want to tell the mediator precisely what course you intend to pursue if the mediation isn't resolved promptly, so that she can see you're not totally without resources—and thus that your client wouldn't be tempted to accept an inferior deal.

Here's a different issue. Say that you represent the claimant on a legal issue that forms one segment of a larger mediation. In your opinion, your client has a weak case on this issue and should ultimately be willing to accept even a modest amount in settlement of it, if that's the best he can do. Should you take the mediator into your confidence and admit your weakness on the merits?

I don't recommend you doing that, even if you're sure the mediator won't pass along the admission to the other side. I think you should take a more balanced position on the merits of the issue and then show your client's willingness to be "constructive" on the dollars involved, *notwithstanding* the arguable merits. (Notice, I said "balanced" here—i.e., "It could go either way." Stay away from being falsely positive, which will not ring true with a savvy mediator and can only hurt your case.) When a mediator knows you're very dubious about the merits of your case, she reasons that you'll ultimately back down rather than try it. If you want any help from the mediator in achieving more than nominal damages, you want her to infer that, absent an adequate settlement, you'd be willing to take your chances in court.

So much for repelling negative leverage. The parties to a mediation should also be alert to the importance of utilizing positive leverage, where it exists. Let's try this out in a specific situation—the business divorce of Part III.

Assume that, in addition to their main business, the two partners (Mike and Robert) also jointly own an asset outside the business—a small shopping center. While divorce discussions are going on, they receive a favorable offer to buy the shopping center from a third party. Sale of this asset requires the consent of both partners.

Mike, who is the more recalcitrant of the two in terms of seeing the split-up resolved, very much wants to sell the shopping center at the good price offered. Because he doesn't want to let it slip away, he favors making the sale right now, even though the split-up hasn't yet been resolved. Robert, on the other hand, very much wants to see the *entire* situation resolved. Although he considers the shopping center offer to be favorable, he and his lawyer are also aware of two important things: how much Mike wants the asset to be sold, and how difficult it has been to get Mike's agreement on the split-up.

So, Robert's lawyer advises him to tell the mediator (and through him, Mike) that Robert's consent to selling the shopping center is conditional on everything else in the divorce being settled. This is an entirely proper negotiating position for Robert to take. The leverage he possesses, through the need for his consent to the asset sale, would be dissipated if he were simply to give the consent up front without other matters having been resolved. Put another way, if Robert doesn't play it this way, he's unlikely to get out of the divorce mediation what would otherwise be coming to him, and the split-up might not even occur.

The broader point for counsel to remember is that the mediator is constantly assessing the feasibility of particular settlements. You have to make the mediator believe that pushing your client beyond a certain point just isn't feasible. (In doing so, you need to be credible—if not, we mediators can see through you.) If you succeed in this, then it will cause the mediator to work harder on the party in the other room.

So, in the example, if (as the mediator) I'm convinced that Robert really means it, I'll make it clear to Mike that he needs to reach total agreement on everything before Robert will consent to the sale of the shopping center. This will have some added weight coming from me. Mike might not like this, but that's what leverage is all about.

*   *   *

Well, that's enough advice to give you lawyers in dealing with a mediator like me. Just remember, I'll be looking for your help the next time we meet to resolve a dispute.

Wrapping Up

I've just finished re-reading *Anatomy of a Mediation*. As invariably happens when you analyze your own activities in depth, you not only reveal fresh perspectives on the activity but also uncover insights about yourself. These comprise my final reflections on the subject.

One thing that writing this book has confirmed for me is how different serving as a mediator is from being an M&A lawyer (as I was in my prior incarnation)—and it's not just due to the contrast between making deals and resolving disputes.

An M&A lawyer (and this applies to other fields of transactional law) is always in the middle of a large-scale happening. In my practice, I had associates to help me get things done and partners available for advice on tax, real estate, and a dozen other specialties. There were clients and investment bankers to consult and keep abreast of developments. We had contract forms to mark up, articles and memos to read, court decisions to peruse. I was very much part of a larger whole.

That has not been true of my post-retirement life as a mediator. Let me tell you straight, this is one lonely gig.

It's not just because of the jousting that takes place between the solo mediator and the multi-person team representing the party. I actually relish that part of it. When I was negotiating for a living and listened to others worry about our side not fielding as many representatives as the other side, I invariably considered us to be better off with *fewer* members of our team. To me, it meant there was less chance that one of my colleagues would say something I didn't want him to. I could control things better with fewer voices—perhaps even with just one.

No, for me the loneliness in mediation occurs *in between* the sessions, when I'm trying to assimilate what I've just learned and work out my strategy for how best to approach the other side. That's when I'd like to have a few teammates to bounce tactics off, get some fresh ideas, hear feedback about whether I'm heading in the right direction. But sadly, there's no one to talk to. As a result, it requires a lot of self-confidence to be satisfied with the direction being taken.

I'm sure there are mediators who talk to other mediators, compare notes, attend conferences, and sit on mediation committees. I don't. As contrasted with the M&A world—where everyone and his brother bends your ear with detailed recitations of their exploits—no mediator has ever bothered to tell me how he or she goes about it. Other than the relatively few times years ago when I represented a party, I've never really witnessed other mediators in action. I've read very little of help on the subject. Whatever I know, I picked up on my own.

So, in deciding to do this book, I was well aware of my limitations. I wasn't qualified to write a tome that purported to reflect what's going on throughout the mediation universe. Rather, this had to be a very personal book—the way I see things and how I go about it, reflecting my dealmaking background. And so, *Anatomy* unashamedly concentrates on my own style of mediating.

But if this were just a catalogue of cases I've handled (with the names removed), it might be considered merely a *sui generis* ego trip. That's not what I had in mind. Rather, my hope is that what I've been discussing here will be helpful to someone who's called upon to conduct or participate in a mediation. (Thus the takeaways that precede or follow many of the situations I've set up in the cases.) This is not brain surgery—it's quite replicable. And since I've been reasonably successful doing it my way, I harbor the hope that others might find it instructive.

I should note that this is similar to the approach I've taken in my other books—*Anatomy of a Merger*[35] guided readers on how to do an acquisition; *Lawyering*[36] informed young lawyers how to practice their craft; *Smart Negotiating*[37] told people how to negotiate in the real world—all based on how I went about those activities. That's the way my mind works. I think of it as the view from the trenches—not from a think tank or law library. It's not a matter of "this *should* work"—instead, it's "this *did* work" for me in similar circumstances.

Anatomy is written from a mediator's-eye vantage point—that's the only perspective I know well. I'm sure a lawyer who regularly represents parties in mediations would have a much different (and undoubtedly valuable) point of view. But even when I focus on the lawyers (as in Part V), I'm observing them from a mediator's perspective—which (I'll bet) is *not* the way they see themselves.

As you've undoubtedly noticed, the bulk of my observations flow from extended hypothetical situations that I use to illustrate the pertinent points. I've long believed that any advice provided is more meaningful when the reader can observe it in context. Thus the journeys here through The Put Case (a one-shot dollar dispute with relatively realistic parties); The Art Case (a one-shot dollar dispute with an unrealistic party); The Split-Up Case (featuring deal-dispute mediating); and The Casino Caper (involving a multi-party mediation).

But there's another reason I focused on these situations—as a way to hammer home the point that what's crucial here is the *process*. Things don't just happen in a mediation; there's no instant gratification. The momentum needed to steer the parties toward a resolution has to be generated by the mediator. So I've tried to lead you through the heart of the process as a mediator tour guide might—that's why I call it, *Anatomy of a Mediation*.

By now you know that pervading everything I do as a mediator is my determination to take an activist, judgmental role. I'm unabashedly evaluative in terms of the dichotomy of styles that exists in the mediation community. A facilitative mediator who's able to foster a deal between the parties without telling them where he or she stands—hey, I'm in awe of that. How do they ever do it? Every so often I hold back on telling the parties where I come out, in hopes of encouraging some voluntary movement on their part. When I do, what do I get? Zilch!

Here's how I look at it—my view of human nature, you might

say, based on personal experience. The more a party thinks his chances in court on a key issue approach 100% in his favor, the more reluctant he'll be to move very much in order to settle. And if he doesn't move, no settlement is going to occur. When a party has a strong (albeit, not unassailable) position, and the mediator says nothing to dissuade him from that, I figure the party will extrapolate that the mediator basically agrees the issue will come out his way—which just reinforces his reluctance to bargain.

So, I feel the need to tell that party his position isn't bullet-proof—he has real risk here. "Hey, buddy, come on into the real world. I'm neutral, I'm calling it as I see it, and I'm telling you that a judge can come out the other way on this." How else can I get this bird off his high perch?

In my view, the biggest impediment to a party making a meaningful move in response to my urging is the timeworn lament, "I ain't moving if the other guy isn't." All that focus on the other guy strikes me as so unhelpful—especially since (in the usual case) the other guy's piddling moves do nothing to encourage constructive movement from the lamentor.

So, in a dollar dispute, I do something that (while it seems so sensible to me) appears to strike some parties and their counsel as a radical deviation from the norm: I don't tell either side what the other is up to. Sure, I'm conscious of how it bothers people not to know—but believe me, it's better this way. I won't reiterate here my rationale for this (see "In a Nutshell" and Chapters 4 and 10), but what it comes down to (as I tell each side) is: Concentrate on your own case; ignore the other guy; negotiate on an amicable basis with me, not him; decide what's a good number for you to pay or receive to settle this dispute.

As I've reiterated *ad nauseum*, the toughest case to mediate is a pure one-shot dollar dispute—more or less money for each side, nothing else to play with. The great bulk of what I find myself mediating (and, I have a hunch, for most other commercial mediators, too) falls into that category.

Hey, it's a real bonus for a mediator when the controversy has a lot of moving parts to juggle, to swap, to be creative about. That's what I did for a living in M&A for three decades. And deal-dispute mediating (as in Part III) has lots of that stuff, including the negotiation of forward-looking agreements. But most of the time I don't have that luxury. It's all about dollars being divvied up between tight-fisted adversaries.

What you always have to remember—and what's often so frustrating about mediation—is that it may *not* work. Don't let the satisfaction of guiding a few deals to fruition—which can be exhilarating to the mediator (if not to the parties)—give rise to hubris. This is no walk in the park. As a mediator, you can evaluate, cajole, plead, offer solid rationale, whatever—but no one has to listen. And sometimes, they don't want to listen— often for reasons unrelated to the merits of the dispute (e.g., a public company defendant who's unwilling to pay a relatively modest amount to settle because of the consequent hit to its reported earnings).

More often than not, though, things work out, as in The Put Case. Other times, as in The Art Case, the parties move a lit- tle and then stop—still far apart and not budging. (If the gap were smaller, I'd keep negotiating in hopes of closing it.) That's when I have to revert to the mediator's proposed resolution, discussed in Chapters 5 and 14. I think of it as my doomsday weapon—the last clear chance to achieve a resolution.

But there's no magic nostrum here. Given the big gap and the hardening of the bargaining arteries, it's a real challenge to discover the precise number or formulation that satisfies both sides—and to generate rationale that each side will buy into. Finding the right groove is the toughest of all mediation tasks— for which you not only need good judgment and a handy calcu- lator, but also a healthy dose of self-confidence.

Most of the time what I propose and pitch earnestly to the parties is accepted by both sides. No matter how unyielding they've been up to then, my proposal forces them to finally face up to either agreeing or going to court—and the latter is rarely a desirable choice.

But regretfully, there are times when one side rejects my pro- posal, which makes me unhappy but powerless to force accep- tance, no matter how persuasive a case I make for settlement. I had a case recently where I laid great stress on the fact that the number I recommended the defendant pay to settle was less than the legal fees the defendant would incur if he tried the case and resultant appeal and ended up *winning*! In other words, not only did he have a real risk of losing in court and having to shell out a lot of bucks, but he'd be better off taking my resolution even if he emerged victorious in the courts. Can you guess what he did? He rejected my proposal! Can you believe it? That's what we're up against.

By the way, I can't remember a time when *both* parties rejected my resolution. Actually, if both parties were to reject, I might feel better about it than having just one party reject—it simply would mean that no outcome existed where the parties could voluntarily come together. So, I'd be disappointed but cognizant that this case needs to be litigated.

But when one party accepts and the other rejects, I can't help but contemplate the possibility that if my number had been closer to the rejecting party's desired outcome, he might have accepted it—and the accepting party might have been willing to buy into a number less favorable to him than the one I used. But now, because this is the end of the line, I'll never know. . . .

So, if you aspire to being a mediator, you not only have to be prepared for the tremendous challenge it presents, but also for the fact that it doesn't always work out. Oh, I guess some mediators might say, well, I tried, and I'm getting paid anyway—but not me. I still feel rotten if I can't get the parties all the way home.

As I'm writing these words, I'm also preparing for the one-shot dollar dispute I'm going to be mediating tomorrow. I've talked to the lawyers, read their submissions, asked them questions, received responses, planned my approach, and now we'll be ready to go at 9 a.m.

And the two sides—each well-represented—are so far apart you wouldn't believe it.

- They have disputes over the facts;
- They have disputes as to the applicable law;
- They have disputes about the language in the agreement;
- They have disputes regarding the valuation of damages.

Up to now, no one has given an inch in any of these areas.

Before going to mediation, they tried negotiating their differences and got absolutely nowhere—no one even put a tentative compromise proposal on the table.

The parties could very well decide to litigate this case. There are enough dollars at stake to justify the big legal fees it would churn up. And the outcome is sufficiently uncertain that it's not just wishful thinking for each side to believe it could prevail in court. They both have first-rate counsel, who are undoubtedly itching to try the case. And on top of all that, the two sides really don't like each other—past grievances, a touch of paranoia, etc.

The cases that make it to me are the tough ones—the disputes that are readily amenable to settlement get resolved without the need for a neutral. In one day, I'm expected to bring these warring parties to a handshake that settles the matter. And I have no help, no support system—no one to bounce off ideas about strategy and tactics, or to compare evaluations of the merits.

How am I going to move each of those parties in dramatically opposite directions all the way to a compromise? I'll be damned if I know. It's frightening—but it's also exhilarating, and I'm hooked on the challenge.   .

Well, I gotta get going. So long for now—see you all *out of court*.

APPENDICES

Appendix A
The Mediation
Morning Line

Ihave a theory about why some mediations fail—an overly simplistic view, perhaps, but one that I've developed through years of personal experience.

Obviously, there are numerous possible reasons for failure. Here, for instance, is a summary compilation by one commentator[38] as to a variety of causes:

- The participants' lack of understanding of the mediation process (as distinct from what's involved in litigation and arbitration).
- A communication failure between lawyer and client (creating unrealistic expectations).
- The absence of the key decision-maker.
- A wrong client representative in the room.
- A case that's not suitable for mediation.
- The mediation occurring before the parties have adequate information to make a reasonable settlement evaluation.
- A failure to identify or understand the other side's feelings, motivations, perspectives and perceptions.
- Mutual hostility so prevalent as to keep the parties from communicating effectively.
- A lack of patience and perseverance.
- A mediator who is either unskilled or inappropriate for the case.

I agree that any of these factors can derail a mediation, and

I've encountered each such obstacle in my time. But most of them don't occur in my typical mediation; and so, for purposes of this exercise, here's what I'm going to assume:

- The participants do understand the process (notwithstanding the vibe they often emit of being involved in an adjudication rather than in settlement discussions).
- The key decision-makers are is in the room (or at least readily accessible), and the parties are well-represented.
- The case is one that's suitable for mediation.
- Mutual hostilities may indeed exist, but they don't prevent effective communication (as long as the mediator helps to promote constructive interchange).
- There may be some itchiness, but the adversaries I'm exposed to do persevere.
- The mediator is reasonably competent.

The point about adequacy of information can't be easily dismissed. When the mediation is taking place before the litigation has gotten going, parties are often reluctant to agree upon a resolution that's a good distance from their desired outcome, without having first seen what might emerge from discovery of the other side. As a mediator, I often get involved in identifying what information may well be essential to settlement and then urging the parties to exchange it in the mediation. For this exercise, let's assume I've been successful in that regard.

The listed factor involving a failure to identify and understand the other side's feelings, motivation, perspectives and perceptions is a little trickier. My observation is that this is often an accurate description of how the parties start out in the mediation—showing little interest in the other side, other than to complain bitterly about their actions and words. But I see this as a vital role for the mediator to play—opening the eyes of each side to the other's motivations, perceptions, etc.; and I'll assume for purpose of the exercise that this has been adequately handled.

So, putting these various factors aside, here's what I consider the two most significant determinants of whether the mediation of a commercial controversy—particularly, although not exclusively, a one-shot dollar dispute—will prove successful or fail:

- The attitudes of the parties regarding the desirability of reaching a settlement; and
- The degrees of reality the parties exhibit.

I've referred (in Chapter 5 and elsewhere) to a party's degree of desire to see the dispute settled by means of the mediation, versus pursuing the alternative course of litigation or arbitration. (I include here, as a prime font of indifference, the participation of an intransigent lawyer single-mindedly seeking total victory.) This is especially problematic when the parties aren't engaged in the mediation on a totally voluntary basis, but rather have been directed there by a judge or arbitrator, or are participating as the result of a previous contractual requirement to mediate before litigating.

As we've seen in Chapter 9 and various other sections of this book, there can be wide variances between the parties—especially in a one-shot dollar dispute—in terms of how realistic they are about aiming for the kind of compromise settlement the mediation has a chance of producing. In the compilation above, the blame for unrealistic expectations was laid on a communication failure between lawyer and client. That's one possible reason, but what's even worse is when *both* lawyer and client are unrealistic, lending mutual support to each other's misreading of the situation.

It's clear to me that a mediation has the best chance of succeeding when both parties are committed to the process and both are realistic about the possible outcome. Conversely, the slimmest possibility of success occurs when each of the parties is indifferent as to whether a settlement will be achieved (they're just as willing to litigate), and both are unrealistic regarding the potential terms on which a settlement could eventually occur. The in-between cases involve splits on the realistic/unrealistic and committed/indifferent scales. And, of course, there can be a wide range in the degrees of reality and commitment displayed, which serves to muddle the impact of these factors on success or failure.

In the world of horse racing, there's something called "The

Morning Line," which refers to the pre-race betting odds that appear in racing programs and other publications. It represents the predictions of various handicappers (provided as much as 48 hours prior to post-time) as to what the public will ultimately bet on each horse. Because of the anticipatory timing, certain items (like late workouts) can't be taken into account.

So, to provide a visual context to my two-factor analysis, I've taken a page from the Daily Racing Form and prepared a chart that I call "The Mediation Morning Line." It contains my advance assessment of the percentage odds (expressed as a range) of being able to reach a settlement in each of nine possible situations, as discussed following the chart.

Now, I'm the first to admit that this chart does only rough justice to the subject matter. The percentages reflect situations where the views of parties are at the extremes of the ranges; in more nuanced cases, with parties who are relatively realistic or who prefer-settlement-to-litigation-but-not-by-that-much, different evaluations would be appropriate. And, like racing's early bird version, there are factors that my Mediation Morning Line doesn't take into account—such as the possibility of one of those other deal-killers (referred to above) rearing its ugly head. So, please don't hold me to any of the numbers or ranges used. But I thought that portraying things in this manageable format will give you some idea of what we mediators are up against.

The Mediation Morning Line

As far as box I (upper left corner) goes, if I'm presiding over a mediation with two parties who want to settle, and both of them are realistic about the potential outcome, and yet I can't sponsor a resolution of the dispute, then I should probably get out of the business! I'm giving it an 85%–90% chance of success, because it's always possible that one of those other impediments listed above might arise, but I'll take this situation any time. This doesn't mean that reaching a satisfactory conclusion will be easy—it almost never is—but the problems that exist can and should be overcome. (In each of the other eight situations, the task becomes progressively more difficult.)

	Both Parties Want to Settle	One Party Wants to Settle; the Other is Indifferent	Both Parties are Indifferent to Settling
Both Parties are Realistic	I 85%–90%	II 70%–80%	III 50%
One Party is Realistic; the Other is Unrealistic	IV 60%–70%	V 35%–45%	VI 20%–25%
Both Parties are Unrealistic	VII 30%–40%	VIII 15%–20%	IX 10%–15%

On the other hand, in a box IX situation (lower right corner), where both parties are indifferent about settling, and each harbors unrealistic expectations that occupy opposite ends of the spectrum, I consider the chances of reaching a negotiated resolution to be between slim and none. I'll give it 10%–15%, because miracles do happen from time to time. But let me level with you—if I knew this was the situation before accepting the role of mediator, I'd turn down the assignment. (The problem, of course, is that everyone tells the mediator they're dedicated to the process—it's rare to hear, "I'd prefer litigation"—and all concerned subscribe to being realistic, without noting that their idea of a realistic outcome is the other side's unconditional surrender.)

In a box II situation (top row, middle), with two realistic parties but one of them indifferent to settling, I'm reasonably optimistic that a resolution can be achieved. It may well depend on my being able to persuade the indifferent party of the advantages a realistic settlement enjoys over the uncertainties, time, expense and angst of litigation—but that's the kind of challenge I enjoy. So I rate our chances of success here at 70%–80%.

A box IV situation (middle row, left), with both parties interested in settlement but one of them unrealistic, should also wind up being successfully concluded. But this is tougher than the case in box II—it's more difficult to bring around an unrealistic party than an indifferent one—so I'm only giving it a 60%–70% chance of being resolved.

The other five situations are, to put it candidly, a bad lot. If I had to choose among them, I'd take box III (upper right corner), where although each party is realistic, both are indifferent to settling. I like the idea of working with two realistic parties, but their extreme indifference is sufficiently troublesome that I only give this a 50-50 chance of working out.

In box VII (lower left corner), both parties want to settle but neither of them is realistic about the outcome. I applaud their attitude, but the mutual unreality (again, at the extreme) is a real downer. It's hard enough to persuade one unrealistic party to come around—convincing two becomes geometrically more difficult. I'll be generous and give this a 30%–40% chance of success based on attitude, but at best it could take months to pull off.

I see little chance of arriving at a settlement in either box VI (middle row, right) where both parties are indifferent to settling and one of them is unrealistic, or in box VIII (bottom row, center) where both are unrealistic and one is indifferent to settling. It's a little better than the even bleaker prospect in box IX, but not that much—so I'll give them 20%–25% and 15%–20% odds of success, respectively (indifference being a little easier to overcome than unreality).

In box V (middle row, center), one of the parties is realistic, the other not; and one of the parties is interested in settling, the other indifferent. If it's the same party who is both unrealistic and indifferent to settling, getting him to a viable compromise will be difficult indeed, but not impossible. The other conceivable situation seems unlikely to me—where the unrealistic party is interested in settling and the realistic party is indifferent—but I'd prefer that chore, working on each of them in different ways. I rate the odds of success here at 35%–45%, with the higher end limited to the second situation.

So, for what it's worth, that's my Mediation Morning Line. What use, if any, I'll make of it (or you can make of it) in future mediations, I'm not yet sure—I'll let you know in the sequel!

I'm pleased to note that, in my experience, more of the people whose disputes I mediate want to settle than those who are

indifferent, which is definitely a good starting point. In terms of reality, though, the parties and their lawyers that I encounter are all over the place. Still, I see that as the mediator's primary (and toughest) task—to bring a sense of reality to the proceedings.

And while the mediator is preaching a sense of reality to the parties, he or she should also possess that trait. I realize it's important for a mediator to be optimistic, but that has to be tempered by an awareness of what a neutral without decisional power is up against. And it's for just such a purpose that I've proffered The Mediation Morning Line.

APPENDIX B
DIFFERENT STROKES

A COMPARISON BETWEEN MEDIATING GLOBAL CONFLICTS AND COMMERCIAL DISPUTES[39]

There are mediations—and then there are mediations. . . .
I mediate business disputes of a commercial nature. One company, convinced that it has been wronged by another company (a view seldom shared by its adversary), is suing or commencing arbitration to rectify the offense. Although feelings can run high, usually just dollars are at stake.

If mediation is invoked, the mediator's task is to help the parties reach an agreement somewhere in between their hardball initial positions—an outcome satisfactory enough to both sides that it's preferable to taking their chances in court or before an arbitrator.

A different kind of mediation—discussed at length in *Statecraft*[40], an excellent book by Dennis Ross—is what he calls "mediation in a world of local conflict."

In this arena, the United States—through the good offices of such skilled practitioners of the trade as George Mitchell, the late Richard Holbrooke and Ross—attempts to help reconcile differences and conflicts between other feuding parties. (Examples are Mitchell's work in Northern Ireland, Holbrooke's in the Balkans, and Ross's in the Middle East.) Although our national interests aren't directly engaged, we often have an important stake in trying to prevent conflict between others; and much like diplomacy, according to Ross, it's not always what you positively achieve—it's also what you can prevent, limit, contain or defuse.

As you might expect, this sort of proceeding (let's call it

"grievance mediation") is very tough on the mediators. The United States, as Ross points out, is never strictly neutral (as we commercial mediators hold ourselves out to be), although that's not requisite if American influence can be used to help meet the needs of each party. The mediators are frequently subject to criticism from both sides as they try to get them to face reality and adjust their behavior to what's required for a deal. It requires passion, the determination to succeed, and a thick skin.

The chapter in *Statecraft* I found most interesting is where Ross sets forth his "Eleven Rules for Mediation"—guidelines for aspiring grievance mediators to keep in mind. I found his perceptive maxims not only absorbing in their own right, but useful for comparison to the commercial mediation techniques I've employed and written about.

In some cases, his guidelines are mirror images of my own; in others, they're quite different; and in a number of them, it's a mixed bag—some aspects similar, some not.

I think commercial mediators will find it instructive in evaluating their practice to spend some quality time in the dicier environment that Ross and his colleagues inhabit. So let me take you through the eleven *Statecraft* rules, juxtaposing my own commentary on how I think each applies (or doesn't) to the commercial mediation landscape.

Rule 1. *Identify Shared Objectives*

For Ross, a mediator's first task is to determine (and expand, where possible) the scope of the shared objectives between the parties. In cases where the mediator initiates the process, the only possible shared objective may be a negative one—ending bloodshed and suffering—but even that can provide a basis on which to begin discussions.

In the commercial world, by contrast, the parties typically share the specific objective of settling the case, so the mediator doesn't have to engage in much scope determination or attempted expansion.

But Ross then goes on to point out something that is definitely analogous to what we do. Grievance mediation, he says, only works if conflict is feared and not desired. Where one or both of the parties thinks that further conflict serves their objectives more than negotiation (as was the case in the early stages of the Balkan conflict), efforts at mediation falter.

I take pride in having been successful in mediating the resolution of many commercial disputes where both sides have wanted to settle but needed outside assistance to find the dollar amount or formula that worked. I haven't been as successful, however, when one (or both) of the parties is sitting in the room only because of a court-ordered or contractual requirement to mediate, with a mindset that prolonging further conflict or seeking a judicial verdict better serves its purposes.

As the saying goes, it takes two to tango; and since the mediator (unlike a judge or arbitrator) has no power to impose his or her will on the parties, attempts to resolve differences in these cases often end up in frustration and failure.

And so, with due regard to the "identify shared objectives" dictum in *Statecraft*, I make it a point early in discussions with the parties' attorneys to try to ascertain—sometimes through direct questioning, at other times by indirection and inference—how committed the parties are to the goal of reaching a settlement, assuming mutually satisfactory terms can be worked out.

Rule 2. *Assess What Can Be Negotiated And Frame The Talks*

Ross sees the need to hold parallel discussions with each side to create a framework for discussions—boundaries within which to negotiate—that both sides see as useful. The search is for which of their differences lend themselves more to compromise than others—something that the parties themselves don't always know going in.

In my world, there's a lot less framing of the talks to worry about. The parties using my services know how an agreement will look, and they're certainly aware of what topics to discuss—they've been wrangling about them for months (albeit futilely) and provide me with legal briefs justifying their positions on the major points at issue.

But here again, Ross makes a further point that hits home. The parties to a grievance mediation need to feel that the discussions could lead somewhere. So he tries to build up their hopes that certain agreements are possible, and to alter for the better each side's perception of the other side's intentions.

My parties need some of that also, which is one reason why my usual technique is to get away from traditional bargaining—carrying offers and counters back and forth between them—and instead engage in simultaneous private negotiations between myself and each of the parties in separate caucus to find a common resolution area, but without either side knowing (until the end) exactly where its adversary stands. It's my belief that the often outrageous demands and frequently paltry proposals each side makes along the way, if communicated to the other side, would only add fuel to the adversarial fire, buttressing the typical initial perception that "no deal is possible with this crazy guy on the other side."

Still, there's a delicate balance to strike here. On the one hand, you can't paint a false Pollyanna-tainted picture of the other side's obdurate behavior; yet you don't want to allow feelings of futility to permeate the proceedings. The sense I try to instill privately with each of the parties (if not in these exact words) is that, "We can get there, provided your side moves appropriately, and if I'm successful in loosening up those tough guys in the other room. . . ."

Rule 3. *Sensitize Each Side To The Other's Concerns And Grievances*

In the deeply rooted grievances that Ross and his colleagues deal with (described by one participant as "your grand-pappy did it to my grand-pappy"), each side sees itself as a victim of the other side—with history shaping their views and blinding them to the hurts and grievances of the other side.

The mediator's job is to get these self-absorbed parties away from the "blame game" and onto an awareness of what's driving their adversary—the psychological, political and practical problems that the other side faces.

This is tough going, because each side is much more intent on having the mediator understand its own needs—and cares a lot less about the other. As a result, the mediator often takes the blame, sometimes even accused of "being the other side's lawyer."

Ross understands this and points out that a good mediator first has to show how well he understands the grievances, concerns and needs of the party he's talking to before he has any chance of getting them to focus on the other guy.

In my realm, while happily I seldom encounter grand-pappy problems, the self-absorption of the combatants is often all too evident. I know that before I can point out the adversary's practical and psychological problems, I need to show each side that I understand its own concerns and needs—but without implying I'm overly sympathetic, or else I won't be able to move them off that perch later on.

Still, just as happens to Ross and his colleagues, this chore can make the mediator appear insufficiently balanced; and from time to time, I've been queried as to whom I'm working for. But hey, that's life. As I've written about in more detail elsewhere, my experience is that facilitative mediation doesn't work in the complex commercial disputes I mediate, where one (or often both) of the parties is unrealistic in overestimating the strength of its case, or in anticipating the other side's unconditional surrender, or is misreading the situation in some other respect. These parties need an activist, judgmental mediator, providing a splash of reality to undermine these exaggerated aspirations. And for mediators like myself who fulfill this role, the carping about even-handedness simply comes with the territory.

Rule 4. *Think Outside The Box When Forging Critical Compromises*

When inevitable stalemates occur in the negotiations, Ross sees the need to come up with new ideas—not just splitting the difference, but some third way that shapes and redefines the issues at stake. It's an attempt to meet the needs of both sides, furnishing something that matters to each of them.

This need is usually less crucial in the one-shot dollar disputes I frequently mediate—you're much more focused on finding the magic number or formula that gets both sides reasonably comfortable.

I know that many commentators swear by such outside-the-box thinking techniques as "enlarging the pie," but I've never found this especially helpful in bridging the typical huge dollar gaps I'm faced with at the outset. It can, however, play a role toward the end of the day in overcoming small but pesky differences remaining between a pair of fossilized combatants.

A measure of creativity plays a larger role in two other situations that I've been involved in and written about. One is what I call "deal-dispute mediating," applicable to such situations as a business breakup between partners, where not only do past disputed issues have to be resolved but there's also a need to strike some new forward-looking deals. The other is mediating one of those knotty disputes involving multiple parties, especially when some facet of the resolution calls for negotiating a prospective arrangement.

Rule 5. *Make Sure The Parties Demonstrate Their Seriousness*

In the Ross arena, an advantage the mediator possesses is that neither side wants to be seen as the one responsible for a breakdown of the mediation process. As the proceedings move along, the mediator can insist on mutual seriousness, lest the United States declare publicly that this party was serious while that party was not.

So, as the process nears a close, each side has an interest in proving to the mediator that it's doing all it can to reach agreement—both to avoid being blamed for a stalemate and to keep the onus on the other side to make the next move.

In a commercial dispute, by contrast, no one seems too daunted by the risk of going back to court if the process ends without a resolution. I don't find this too surprising, given the ambivalence I often detect—especially among litigators—about settling without a trial. And since the mediation is not a public process but rather one that's under tight confidentiality wraps, neither side worries too much about being seen as the cause of the breakdown.

I do, however, have a substitute for this particular mediator's lever. As discussed elsewhere, I try to get the parties to agree in advance that if the mediation doesn't otherwise result in an agreement, I'll then recommend to both a specific overall resolution (not subject to further negotiation). Although each side is free to reject my recommendation, my hope is that they'll be influenced by the fear of being second-guessed if they don't take it and then end up a lot worse off at trial—to say nothing of the neutral cover my number or formula provides to executives responsible for opting to settle.

In this section, Ross also describes an interesting technique he uses—although, he warns, not prematurely—of asking each side to explain what it thinks the other side can accept. He has received some useful input here from parties who recognized this as a way to reveal something sensitive about what they might actually be able to accept, but without having to say anything about themselves.

I realize I haven't done enough of this kind of thing; and in appropriate cases, I intend to incorporate it into my process in the future.

Rule 6. *Get Each Side To Adjust To Reality*

According to Ross, conflict resolution is about meeting "needs," not "wants." Neither side can achieve everything it wants, but it should be able to achieve its most crucial needs.

Getting people to give up what they want—to reconcile to reality and adjust their expectations—isn't easy but is absolutely necessary to successful mediation; you have to make them realize that some of it won't be attainable if there's to be an agreement.

Here's an area where I'm on the same wavelength as Ross. As I indicated previously, it's the mediator playing the role of agent-of-reality that moves the parties together—although I have to concede that my task, unhampered by the mythologies pervading the mindsets of the grievance parties, is a lot less strenuous than his.

Rule 7. *Set Aside Each Side's Principles And Focus On Practicalities*

As Ross puts it, a basic rule of thumb for mediators is that "one side's principle is the other side's impossibility." Principles drive each side to its most rigid position, and no one wants to be seen as conceding on those principles. So, in order to solve problems and reduce differences, a mediator has to avoid a debate over principles and strive for practical arrangements.

This holds true in spades in commercial mediation and negotiating generally. Although combatants frequently refer to seemingly sacred principles, my experience is that these are seldom strongly held. Cut through them and boil the issue down to dollars (or their practical equivalent), which can then be moved around—perhaps with a face-saver to satisfy hardnosed or insecure bargainers.

Rule 8. *Make Agreements Where You Can*

Ross advises mediators to nail down small agreements when they're available, thereby creating new baselines from which to proceed (or to go back to, if talks are temporarily derailed).

In deeply rooted grievance conflicts, reaching any understanding at all represents the crossing of a threshold, with positive psychological effects on both sides. His one caveat here is to avoid finalizing a small agreement that will enable one side (having so agreed) to then make impossible additional demands on the other side.

In other words, Ross is saying, never lose sight of the big picture.

In my prime, I was a deal lawyer handling M&A transactions, which lent themselves to making daily progress through agreements on a variety of small issues. When I crossed over to the more frustrating task of resolving disputes, with a single mutually agreeable dollar figure as the usual goal, I found it very tough to measure intermediate progress—everything was keyed to the big breakthrough.

Still, I recognize the applicability of the Ross dictum in handling multi-issue conflicts, or where the claimed damages contain a number of separable items. In these cases, I do try in private caucus to get the parties on the same page in as many respects as possible.

Sometimes, though, I keep these meetings of the minds to myself, since they may be needed at a later time to provide a degree of momentum to an otherwise artery-hardening process—perhaps merely noting to A that "I think I'll be able to sell B on this one at the appropriate time."

Rule 9. *Act Swiftly To Contain Crises*

In the Ross bailiwick, there's always the threat of external events—acts of terrorism, for example—causing crises that must be dealt with, in order that the mediation process not unravel.

When these crises occur, he says, you can't sit there passively and let them play out; rather, urgent intervention is often required to give everyone pause and get back to business.

Thankfully, outside crises of this type aren't endemic to my business. But one of my long-term prime tenets is that a smart negotiator has to know when to stop the music and grab a chair. The opportunity that exists to make a deal today may be gone tomorrow. People change their minds, new factors may intervene, newspaper headlines proclaim doom and gloom, the market can plunge.

You may achieve a little more by prolonging the process, but so often the possible incremental advantage doesn't justify the risk of losing the deal altogether. And, as paydirt nears, I get this message across to the parties in the strongest possible terms.

Rule 10. *Use Anger As A Tool—But Use It Rarely*

Ross believes that a mediator has to give parties both barrels when they act outrageously or go back on their word or challenge the mediator's word.

He wants to let them know he's out of patience—that they've provoked him beyond his endurance level. In his mind, genuine anger is the credible way to show them they're going to have to pay a price.

Nevertheless, he notes, if you use anger too often, it's devalued. So his advice is to pick the right moments, saving your ire for when it can have the greatest impact—such as when an agreement is within reach, and both sides have to realize that there can't be any more games or they may lose both the mediator and the deal.

I empathize with Ross on this one. Sure, a commercial mediator has to operate for the most part on an even keel. You shouldn't get overtly angry just because you're frustrated by a party's consistent lack of movement, although you can certainly convey disappointment and impatience (and, if truth be known, I've gone a little further than that on occasion).

It's a different story, though, when someone reneges on a concession previously made, or suffers a convenient loss of memory, or purposely misquotes you. In those cases, I feel that a brief but convincing display of controlled indignation is needed to signal him he's heading down a dangerous path.

Rule 11. *Put Your Drafts On The Table*

When a draft agreement in principle or similar document needs to be introduced into the proceedings to encourage progress, Ross believes it should emanate from the mediator. When this is done by a party, he's invested in the draft and will be reluctant to back away. Moreover, it represents his framing of the problem, since each side wants to define the terrain so as to play on favorable ground.

As a result, this often causes a reflexively negative response from the other side. It's much preferable to have the mediator be the one who frames the issues—who shapes, channels and narrows the bounds of discussion.

I agree totally with Ross here. The mediator has to pick the appropriate time to put any kind of draft on the table and then prepare it himself. So, for instance, in disputes requiring complex solutions, at the point where everyone is in tacit accord as to how to proceed (although not yet on the number), I find it often helpful to draft an unadorned document that sets forth the basic format of the deal.

The idea, of course, is to smoke out whether either side has a problem going forward on that basis. In the space for the dollars, I simply put "[amount to be negotiated]," with comparable caveats for other terms yet to be determined.

* * *

So those are the eleven Ross guidelines and my reactions. I hope you found this as helpful a comparison as I did; and I encourage readers to go through the same exercise, perhaps reaching different judgments.

All I can say in conclusion is that whenever we commercial mediators feel a little frustrated in our work, we ought to pause for a moment and envision Dennis Ross, in a room permeated by ancient myths, dealing with a couple of Arafat wannabees, plus some terrorists in the wings—and be thankful for the dollars-and-cents "problems" in front of us. . . .

APPENDIX C
ON THE NATIONAL SCENE

I don't consider myself especially political, but I find myself appalled at the state of American politics today. Obviously, I'm not alone in this regard. As Tom Friedman put it in the New York Times:[41]

"We're a country in a state of incremental decline and losing its competitive edge, because our politics has become just another form of sports entertainment . . . and our main law-making institutions [are] divided by toxic partisanship to the point of paralysis."

Another Times op-ed piece after the 2010 mid-term election written by Charles M. Blow[42], stated it this way:

"We now stand in the twilight of American Moderation. We have retreated to our respective political corners and armed ourselves in an ideological standoff over the very meaning of America, having diametrically opposed interpretations of its past and visions for its future. Talking across the table has been reduced to yelling across the chasm."

Let me be clear here. I'm not dismayed that differences of opinion exist over specific issues—that's to be expected, and is actually a sign of good health in the populace at large. And although it pains me, I'm not surprised that so many individuals spout their loud, polarizing views on these issues—people have always done that, and it's what I hear weekly in my mediations.

No, what appalls me is that so few effective people are stepping up to the plate to try to broker honorable compromises on these issues, in order that the country can move ahead. While our historical record as a nation in this regard is by no means flawless, by and large, we've been able to do this in the past—even when the issues at stake were far more grave than the ones that divide us now.

I was an American History major in college, and that field remains one of my prime interests. The past episode that best illustrates my point is the memorable Compromise of 1850. It featured the man known to his contemporaries as "The Great Compromiser"—Henry Clay, the Whig senator from Kentucky. I've recently read a book on the subject. *At the Edge of the Precipice*[43] by Robert V. Remini, which I recommend highly. Here's a blueprint for what needs to happen today.

The drama began in 1849. Zachary Taylor had just assumed the presidency. The issue before the nation was whether slavery would be introduced in the new areas we got from Mexico following the Mexican-American War—principally California and New Mexico. The battle lines between the North (for whom Daniel Webster was a principal spokesman) and the South (led by John Calhoun) were sharply drawn and chock full of invective. The southern states were holding a convention in Nashville to decide on what unified action to take—up to and including secession—if the South didn't obtain equal rights to the acquired territory. According to Calhoun, the South needed "justice, simple justice," and could offer no compromises—"no concession or surrender." The nation, in the author's words, "verged on a sectional crisis of catastrophic proportions—headed toward disunion and possible civil war."

Hey, folks, we're not talking here about a health plan or tax cuts for the wealthy—this was big stuff in a very complicated situation. And then, coming out of retirement and wading head first into this morass, was Henry Clay, who recognized immediately that a complex compromise had to be struck. He devised the plan—an omnibus bill with a lot of moving parts and something for everyone. He worked the Senate floor and cloakroom tirelessly. He even persuaded Daniel Webster—who disagreed with some of the bill's features, but recognized its importance—to give a memorable and influential speech in its favor. And when the omnibus bill faltered, dispiriting the elderly Clay, Stephen Douglas stepped up to lead the fight for enactment of each of the separate parts.

It was messy, sure, but that's the way good compromises often are. It split the northern and southern Whigs and the party didn't survive. It was denounced by those who focused solely on the provisions that were negative to their cases—so what else is new? It also took a little ghoulish luck—the sudden death of Zachary Taylor, who had a different approach to this issue and might well have vetoed the bills, and his replacement by Vice-President Millard Fillmore, a Clay ally who eagerly signed them into law.

But one way or another—because enough people realized how important it was, and their leaders provided the impetus—it got done, and the nation avoided the catastrophe for the moment. The Compromise gave the North ten years to build enough strength to enable it to defeat the South when war finally broke out, and a decade to find a leader who could save the Union—Abraham Lincoln.

But the author had more on his mind than simply recounting the absorbing tale of what happened 160 years ago. He puts it so well that I won't paraphrase, but quote him directly:

"I also seek to show the importance of compromise in resolving problems of great magnitude in the history of the country. It has proven time and time again that little of lasting importance can be accomplished without a willingness on the part of all involved to seek to accommodate one another's needs and demands. This point is especially important today when the nation faces myriad problems, both foreign and domestic, that defy easy solution, and that will, in all likelihood, require both major political parties to agree to compromise their differences. With severe economic problems that threaten to pitch the nation into a deep recession; with other domestic issues, such as health care, energy, immigration, and social concerns such as abortion and gay marriage; with wars in the Middle East that verge on escalation throughout the region; and with terrorism rampant around the globe, compromise on the part of this nation's political leaders, and the leaders of the other countries, becomes all the more necessary."

I agree wholeheartedly with Mr. Remini, and am working hard to foster accommodation in my own commercial sphere. I just hope that those who are responsible for the well-being of our nation will, like Henry Clay, rise to the occasion once again—overcoming all that toxic partisanship with a healthy dose of American Moderation.

APPENDIX D
MY MEDIATOR'S PEP TALK
TO THE PARTIES

In every one-shot dollar dispute mediation I handle, there's a particular moment, occurring early in the sit-down session, that I now realize is a critical juncture. For too long, though, I've been letting the moment pass without much comment. Of late, however, I've decided to begin marking the occasion.

The moment arrives at the point where the parties have concluded making their initial "winning" presentations in the opening joint session (discussed in Chapter 7). What lies ahead, at least in my mediations, will be many hours spent in separate caucuses with the mediator, as he or she tries to discern whether there's some way to bridge the huge gap that exists between the initial positions the parties have taken.

The attitude to be adopted and the approach needed from the parties and their counsel during those next hours should differ greatly from their attitude and approach up to this point —but sadly, too often this doesn't happen. And so, in order to remind all participants of the reason why we're here, I've started giving them what I'll dub a "mediator's pep talk"—before sending them off to their separate conference rooms.

Here's a scrubbed version of my pep talk, eliminating the usual specific references to the facts or issues of the case being mediated. For more detail as to my views on this subject, please refer to the material under "How *Not* To Do It," "The Better Way," and "Help!" in Chapter 27.

My advice to you mediators—faced with two parties squaring off on seemingly irreconcilable sides of a one-shot dollar dispute—is to do something of this sort at this point, consistent with your individual style, personality and methodology. (The pep talk may or may not be appropriate for other kinds of disputes, depending on the circumstances.) I haven't been making this speech for long enough to report any measurable positive effect, but it certainly can't hurt. Moreover, it serves as a useful point of reference later on—when a party or its counsel is behaving in a way contrary to the spirit of the pep talk—to remind them of what I'm looking for from both sides.

Jim's Pep Talk

Thank you both for your presentations. Each team will now be going back to its separate conference room for the balance of the mediation. What I'm about to say is important—something I want you to keep in mind as we move forward.

This thing that we're involved in today is a mediation.

Up to this point, an outsider viewing the situation would hardly have guessed that. Rather, what's occurred so far has had all the trappings of an adjudication proceeding.

Both in your written submissions and your presentations today:

- *Each side has argued for maximum treatment in its favor, without any recognition that some of the points it makes aren't as strong as others.*
- *Each side has totally disparaged every single element of the other side's case, without the slightest indication that any of its adversary's assertions might carry some weight.*
- *Each side has emphasized language in the agreement at issue that it contends supports its posture, and has either dismissed or studiously ignored other language in the agreement that the other side contends favors their case.*
- *Each side has plucked from the leading relevant authorities elements that buttress its position and has been quick to distinguish any element that supports its adversary's position.*

I could go on, but I think you get my drift. In short, up to this point, other than some generalized statements by each side in favor of mediation as a process, I haven't gotten a single specific inkling as to a possible meeting of the minds.

That's disappointing, to be sure, but in all fairness I must concede to you that, in my experience as a mediator, the great majority of disputants in one-shot dollar disputes of this kind have done just about the same thing. You're in good—uh, make that "bad"—company.

Now, however, you've each had your say—you've unfurled your big guns, predicted your ultimate vindication in court, marginalized your adversary. We've come now to the juncture where things have to go in a different direction.

Up to this point, you've been busy moving away *from each other—now, you have to move* toward *each other, if there's going to be any chance of resolving your dispute.*

No one gets everything he wants in the mediation of a one-shot dollar dispute like this. "Compromise" may be a dirty word for some politicos and op-ed pundits, but I'm a great advocate of compromise—and it's the name of the game *here.*

To compromise a dollar dispute never comes easy, and it sometimes doesn't come at all—especially when the parties (or one of them) have unrealistic expectations regarding the outcome.

Compromise doesn't work unless you negotiate. A mediation, after all, is just a fancy kind of negotiation. The two of you have been unable to directly negotiate a resolution of your dispute. My role here is to see whether, with my assistance, a settlement can possibly be reached.

I'm going to make the process less painful for you by conducting these negotiations with each side myself, rather than fostering any additional pyrotechnics arising from your direct dealings with each other. You'll each be speaking with me confidentially—so you don't have to worry that any conciliatory words you choose to utter or constructive postures you find yourself espousing will get back to the other side to your detriment.

But I can't do this alone. Both of you have to actively join with me in a search to find a negotiated outcome that's reasonably satisfactory for each side.

What I don't *need from you going forward is a reiteration of the same maximum positions you've already taken, expressed with the same degree of absolute certitude. I've been, if anything, over-exposed to all that, both in your written submissions and what I've heard in this room today. It's not necessary to keep reminding me as to where you'd like to come out in a perfect world.*

Rather, what I want you to do is get down to business with me—and by that I mean my *business, which is settling disputes. I'd like to see you:*

- *Develop some realistic expectations as to what can be achieved through the process;*
- *Differentiate among issues as to the strength of your side's position;*
- *Recognize the viability of some points your adversary is asserting; and*
- *Come up with fresh initiatives and persuasive rationale that point the way to constructive intermediate steps in the direction of compromise.*

If we work together in that vein, I'm confident that real progress can be made toward resolution of your dispute.

The ultimate settlement, if we achieve it, won't be a victory *for either of you, in the sense of what you might achieve if you went to court and* prevailed. *But it also won't be a* loss, *as you might incur if you went to court and were* defeated.

I urge you strongly to eschew the uncertainty of litigating this dispute—to say nothing of the expenses, time, and angst that are hallmarks of litigation. Don't outsource *the decision on how this matter comes out to a third party judge, whom you may think you can influence but you certainly can't control. Help* me *help* you *to fashion your own outcome—a compromise you can live with—and then, having put this behind you, get on with the more fruitful aspects of your business.*

Okay, let's go at it.

ENDNOTES

[1] J. Freund, *Anatomy of a Merger: Strategies and Techniques for Negotiating Corporate Acquisitions* (Law Journal Press, 1975) [hereinafter, *Anatomy of a Merger*]. It was because of the parallel with the title of that book (and the application of its dealmaker attitude to the world of resolving disputes) that I named this book *Anatomy of a Mediation*. I have since become aware of a book entitled "The Anatomy of Mediation: What Makes It Work" by Sam Kagel and Kathy Kelly (The Bureau of National Affairs, 1989), which is a case study of a collective bargaining agreement; and a panel discussion led by mediator Stephen Hochman that used "Anatomy of a Mediation" as its title. I have a hunch others have also previously utilized this phrase or variants on it, and more will probably do so down the road.

[2] R. Fisher and W. Ury, *Getting to Yes: Negotiating Agreement Without Giving In* (Houghton Mifflin, 1982) [hereinafter, *Getting to Yes*].

[3] *Anatomy of a Merger* at 2.

[4] J. Freund, *Smart Negotiating: How to Make Good Deals in the Real World* (Simon & Schuster, 1992), at 29 [hereinafter, *Smart Negotiating*].

[5] D. Ross, *Statecraft: And How to Restore America's Standing in the World* (Farrar, Straus and Giroux, 2007).

[6] *Getting to Yes, Ibid.*

[7] *Smart Negotiating, Ibid.*

[8] *Getting to Yes, Ibid.*

[9] *Smart Negotiating, Ibid.*

[10] B. Picker, *Mediation Practice Guide: A Handbook for Resolving Business*

Disputes (American Bar Association, 1998), at 36–37.

[11]Lewis Carroll, *Through the Looking Glass* (Macmillan, 1871) at 136 (International Pocket Library edition).

[12]For a good discussion of the differing styles evaluative mediators use, see D. Geronemus and M. Shaw, "Mediation in the Public and Private Sectors: Similarities and Differences," chapter 35 of *Alternative Dispute Resolution in the Employment Arena* (Kluwer Law International, 2004).

[13]This was the subject of my first article about mediation, co-authored with Marguerite Millhauser: *ADR: A Conversation*, The National Law Journal, Feb. 27, 1989. At the time, I was a deal lawyer who had been recently introduced to the resolution of disputes through mediation; Ms. Millhauser was a prominent mediator; the article contained an extended dialogue between us (including some amusing banter) on the virtues of mediation. The main message we conveyed to transactional lawyers was clear: make sure to include a clause in the acquisition (or other business) agreement, obligating the parties, in the event of a dispute, to mediate before litigating. Sample clauses to use were included. Re-reading the article recently, I'm convinced that this was good advice back then and remains so today. Meanwhile, my good friend and co-author of the article (now Miriam Millhauser Castle), although no longer active in the field, retains all her good sense and valuable insights into the process, and kindly offered me helpful editorial assistance on this book, for which I'm quite grateful.

[14]*Getting to Yes, Ibid.*

[15]Much of the material in The Put Case was originally contained in my article entitled *The Neutral Negotiator—Why and How Mediation Can Work to Resolve Dollar Disputes*, published by Prentice Hall Law & Business in 1994. It was awarded the 1994 First Prize for Professional Articles by CPR Institute for Dispute Resolution. In view of the then current popularity of 12-step programs to cure a variety of ailments, I divided my approach to the malady of a dollar dispute into a dozen segments and dubbed it "The 12-Step Mediation Program for Dollar Disputes." That was then, this is now, and I've learned through hard experience that things don't

always fit so neatly into a prescribed pattern—so although you'll be introduced to various steps along the way in the current treatment, they won't be numbered.

[16]*Smart Negotiating, Ibid.*

[17]J. Freund, *Lawyering: A Realistic Approach to Legal Practice* (Law Journal Seminars Press, 1979)[hereinafter, *Lawyering*] at 299–307.

[18]*Smart Negotiating, Ibid.* at 139–140.

[19]*Getting to Yes, Ibid.*

[20]Some mediators ask the parties privately about their "bottom lines." I don't subscribe to this, and good arguments for refraining from doing so are contained in a useful book, J. A. Little, *Making Money Talk: How to Mediate Insured Claims and Other Monetary Disputes* (American Arbitration Association, 2007), at 188–189. Little's five reasons can be summarized as: (1) People resent being asked for this private information; (2) The mediator wouldn't get truthful information from the party in any event; (3) The number will change over time; (4) It only reinforces old positions and may require "losing face" later on; and (5) Why discourage everyone with the resulting inevitable gap between the parties' numbers?

[21]*Getting to Yes, Ibid.*

[22]*Smart Negotiating, Ibid.* at 157–160.

[23]Much of the material in The Split-Up Case was originally contained in my article entitled *Anatomy of a Split-Up: Mediating the Business Divorce*, 52 The Business Lawyer 479 (1997).

[24]*Smart Negotiating, Ibid.* at 125–126.

[25]*Smart Negotiating, Ibid.* at 98–112.

[26]Much of the material in The Casino Caper was originally contained in my article entitled *Three's A Crowd: How to Resolve a Knotty Multi-Party Dispute through Mediation*, 64 The Business Lawyer 359 (2009).

[27]*Smart Negotiating, Ibid.* For a helpful article regarding various styles of negotiating, see C. Craver, "Negotiation Styles: The Impact on Bargaining Transactions," *Handbook on Mediation* (American Bar Association, 2010), at 401–410.

[28]Much of the material in this section was contained in my article entitled *Calling All Deal Lawyers: Try Your Hand at Resolving Disputes*, 62 The Business Lawyer 37 (2006).

[29]The *Calling All Deal Lawyers* article (note 28) contains a section entitled "Early Steps to Prevent a Dispute from Ending Up in Litigation." It includes a recommendation to build a compulsory mediation provision into the agreement. The parties will then have to give mediation a shot (albeit they're not bound to settle the case) before heading off to the judge.

[30]Robert S. Peckar, American Arbitration Association Handbook on Mediation, Second Edition, 2010, pp. 237–238.

[31]*Getting to Yes, Ibid.*

[32]"Decision trees" are discussed, e.g., in the article by M. C. Aaron and D. P. Hoffer, "Decision Analysis as a Method of Evaluating the Trial Alternative," appearing as Chapter 11 in D. Golann, *Mediating Legal Disputes: Effective Strategies for Lawyers and Mediators* (Little Brown, 1956).

[33] *Smart Negotiating, Ibid.*, p. 119.

[34]*Smart Negotiating, Ibid.*, p. 70.

[35] *Anatomy of a Merger, Ibid.*

[36]*Lawyering, Ibid.*

[37] *Smart Negotiating, Ibid.*

[38]B. Picker, *Mediation Practice Guide*, pp. 22–23.

[39] This appendix (in slightly altered form) first appeared as an article I wrote for *Alternatives to the High Cost of Litigation*, Vol. 28, No. 9 (October 2010).

[40]*See* footnote 5.

[41]*The New York Times*, September 29, 2010.

[42] *The New York Times*, November 6, 2010.

[43] R. Remini, *At the Edge of the Precipice—Henry Clay and the Compromise That Saved the Union* (Basic Books, 2010).